Addison-Wesley's Review for the
AP* Computer Science Exam in Java™

Surfaz Khan

Second Edition

Addison-Wesley's Review for the
AP* Computer Science Exam in Java™

AP*JAVA

Second Edition

Susan Horwitz
University of Wisconsin

Leigh Ann Sudol
Fox Lane High School

PEARSON

Addison
Wesley

Boston San Francisco New York
London Toronto Sydney Tokyo Singapore Madrid
Mexico City Munich Paris Cape Town Hong Kong Montreal

Publisher	Greg Tobin
Executive Editor	Michael Hirsch
Editorial Assistant	Lindsey Triebel
Senior Production Supervisor	Marilyn Lloyd
Cover Designer	Joyce Cosentino Wells
Prepress and Manufacturing	Carol Melville
Text Design	Paul C. Anagnostopoulos
Production Coordination	Windfall Software
Composition	Windfall Software, using ZzTEX
Illustrations	LM Graphics
Proofreader	Jennifer McClain
Printer	Bradford & Bigelow

* AP and Advanced Placement Program are registered trademarks of The College Board, which was not involved in the production of, and does not endorse, this product.

Many of the designations used by manufacturers and sellers to distinguish their products are claimed as trademarks. Where those designations appear in this book, and Addison-Wesley was aware of a trademark claim, the designations have been printed in initial caps or all caps.

The programs and applications presented in this book have been included for their instructional value. They have been tested with care, but are not guaranteed for any particular purpose. The publisher does not offer any warranties or representations, nor does it accept any liabilities with respect to the programs or applications.

Library of Congress Cataloging-in-Publication Data

Horwitz, Susan (Susan B.), 1955–
    Addison-Wesley's review for the AP* computer science exam in Java /
Susan Horwitz, Leigh Ann Sudol.
    p.   cm.
    Includes index.
    ISBN 0-321-39572-7
    1. Computer science—Examinations, questions, etc.   2. Java (Computer
program language)   3. Advanced placement programs (Education)   I. Sudol,
Leigh Ann.   II. Title.
    QA76.28.H68 2007
    005.13′3—dc22   2005031895

0-321-39572-7
2 3 4 5 6 7 8 9 10—BB—09 08 07 06

Contents

Topical Review Contents

Addison-Wesley's Review for the
AP* Computer Science Exam in Java™

Second Edition

Introduction

This book provides a review of the material that is tested on the College Board's Advanced Placement Computer Science A and AB Examinations. It consists of the following two sections:

The first section provides topical review. This section has nine chapters, covering the main topics that are tested on the AP Computer Science Examinations. Each chapter includes practice multiple-choice questions (and answers) for the material covered in that chapter.

The second section includes some hints on taking the AP Computer Science exams, followed by six complete practice exams (three A exams and three AB exams) with no duplicate questions. Immediately following each exam are the answers to the multiple-choice questions, solutions for the free-response questions, and grading guides for the free-response questions.

AP Computer Science

The Advanced Placement Program offers two computer science exams: Computer Science A and Computer Science AB; the A course is a subset of the AB course. Both courses emphasize computer science concepts (for example, abstraction, algorithms, and data structures) rather than details of language syntax. The AB course involves more in-depth study than the A course; for example, linked lists and trees are included in the AB course, but not in the A course.

Starting in the spring of 2004, both the A and the AB courses will use a subset of the Java language, and all parts of the exams that require reading or writing actual code will use Java.

Complete course descriptions for AP Computer Science A and AB can be obtained from the College Board at (800) 323-7155 or via the AP Computer Science Web site. To help you access the most up-to-date information, Addison-Wesley maintains a Web site at *http://www.aw.com/APjava* with links to course descriptions and other useful information about the AP CS curriculum, case studies, and exams.

The AP Computer Science Examinations

The exams are written by a committee of computer science faculty from universities and high schools, and they are designed to determine how well a student has mastered the key concepts in the A or the AB course. Each exam is three hours long and consists of two sections. Section 1 (one hour and fifteen minutes) includes forty multiple-choice questions. Section 2 (one hour and forty-five minutes) includes four or five free-response questions. The free-response questions usually involve writing Java code to solve specified problems. They may also involve higher-level programming tasks such as the design and analysis of a data structure or algorithm, or identifying errors in faulty code.

Both the multiple-choice and the free-response sections include some questions based on the current year's case study (see Chapter 9). The multiple-choice and free-response sections of the exams are given equal weight in determining the final exam grade. Final exam grades consist of a number between one and five with the following intended interpretation:

5. Extremely well qualified
4. Well qualified
3. Qualified
2. Possibly qualified
1. No recommendation

Many universities give credit and/or advanced placement for a grade of three or higher.

To compensate for guessing, one-quarter of a point is subtracted for each wrong answer on the multiple-choice questions (whereas omitted questions neither add to nor subtract from the total). Students who get an acceptable score on the free-response questions need to answer about 50 to 60 percent of the multiple-choice questions correctly to get a final grade of three.

Within the free-response section, each question is given equal weight. The free-response questions are graded by a group of college and high-school computer science teachers called readers, under the supervision of a college professor (the chief faculty consultant) who has had extensive previous experience as a reader. Considerable effort is expended to ensure that the grading is consistent and fair. A detailed grading guide is prepared for each question by the chief faculty consultant and is used by all readers of that question. Questionable cases are resolved by the most experienced readers and the chief faculty consultant. Students' names and schools are removed from the questions when they are graded, and the readers cannot see the scores that were given for previous questions. To maximize consistency, each of a student's free-response questions is graded by a different reader, and each reader's work is carefully monitored.

---

* AP and Advanced Placement Program are registered trademarks of The College Board, which was not involved in the production of, and does not endorse, this product.

TOPICAL REVIEW

1

Basic Language Features

1.1 Expressions: Types and Operators

Every expression in a Java program has a type. In Java, there are two kinds of types: *primitive types* and *objects*. The AP Computer Science subset includes the following primitive types:

```
int     double    boolean
```

Strings and arrays are two special kinds of objects that are included in the AP CS subset; they are discussed later in this chapter and in Chapter 2. Other objects are instances of classes, which are also discussed in Chapter 2.

Associated with each type is a set of operators that can be applied to expressions with that type. The AP CS subset includes the *arithmetic*, *assignment*, *increment*, *decrement*, *equality*, *relational*, and *logical* operators described below.

Arithmetic Operators

The arithmetic operators are as follows:

addition	+
subtraction	−
multiplication	*
division	/
modulus (remainder)	%

All of the arithmetic operators can be applied to expressions of type `int` or `double`. The addition operator can also be used to perform string concatenation: if at least one of its operands is a `String`, then the result is the concatenation of that `String` with the `String` representation of the other operand. For example:

Concatenation Expression	Value of the Expression
`"book" + "worm"`	`"bookworm"`
`"version" + 3`	`"version3"`
`.5 + "baked"`	`".5baked"`

Integer division (when both the numerator and the denominator are integers) results in truncation, not rounding. For example, 2/3 is zero, not one; −2/3 is also zero, not minus one. If you want to round a double variable x to the *nearest* integer (instead of truncating it), you can use:

```
(int)(x + .5)
```

when x is positive, and

```
(int)(x - .5)
```

when x is negative.

Casting can be used to convert an int to a double (or vice versa). For example:

Expression	Value of the Expression
(int)3.6	3
(double)3	3.0
(double)2/3	.667
(int)2.0/3	0

Assignment Operators

The assignment operators are as follows:

plain assignment	=
add-then-assign	+=
subtract-then-assign	−=
multiply-then-assign	*=
divide-then-assign	/=
modulus-then-assign	%=

The types of the left- and right-hand sides of an assignment must be compatible, and the left-hand side must be an *l-value*. (An *l-value* is an expression that has a corresponding memory location. For example, a variable is an *l*-value; the name of a type or a method is not an *l*-value, nor is a literal like 10 or "abc".)

The last five assignment operators listed above are called *compound assignments*; a compound assignment of the form

```
a op= b
```

is equivalent to

```
a = a op b
```

---

* AP and Advanced Placement Program are registered trademarks of The College Board, which was not involved in the production of, and does not endorse, this product.

For example:

Compound Assignment	Equivalent Noncompound Assignment
a += 2	a = a + 2
a -= b	a = a - b
a *= 5.5	a = a * 5.5

Assignments are expressions, not statements; the value of an assignment expression is the value of its right-hand side. This means that assignments can be "chained." For example, the following is perfectly legal:

```
int j, k, n;
j = k = n = 0;  // all three variables are set to zero
```

Increment/Decrement Operators

The increment/decrement operators are as follows:

increment	++
decrement	--

The increment operator adds one to its operand; the decrement operator subtracts one from its operand. For example:

Using Increment/Decrement Operator	Equivalent Assignment Expression
a++	a += 1
a--	a -= 1

Equality, Relational, and Logical Operators

The equality, relational, and logical operators are as follows:

equal to	==
not equal to	!=
less than	<
less than or equal to	<=
greater than	>
greater than or equal to	>=
logical NOT	!
logical AND	&&
logical OR	||

The equality and relational operators must be applied to expressions with compatible types. The logical operators must be applied to expressions with type boolean. An expression involving the equality, relational, or logical operators evaluates to either true or false (so the type of the whole expression is boolean). Expressions involving the logical AND and OR operators are guaranteed to be evaluated from left to right, and evaluation stops as soon as the final value is known. This is called *short-circuit evaluation*. For example, when the expression

```
(5 > 0) || isPrime(54321)
```

is evaluated, the method `isPrime` is not called. The subexpression

```
(5 > 0)
```

is evaluated first, and it evaluates to `true`. Since logical OR applied to `true` and any other expression always evaluates to `true`, there is no need to evaluate the other expression. Similarly, since logical AND applied to `false` and any other expression always evaluates to `false`, the method `isPrime` is not called when the following expression is evaluated:

```
(5 < 0) && isPrime(54321)
```

It will be helpful for students to be familiar with *deMorgan's laws*:

```
! ( x && y ) == !x || !y
! (x || y ) == !x && !y
```

Students should also be familiar with the use of *truth tables*. For example, a truth table can be used to determine which of the following three boolean expressions are equivalent:

```
!(a || b)
(!a) || (!b)
(!a) && (!b)
```

The truth table has one column for each variable and one column for each expression. A row is filled in as follows: First, each variable is given a value (*true* or *false*). Then each expression is evaluated assuming those values for the variables, and the value of the whole expression is filled in. A different combination of values for the variables is used in each row (and the number of rows is the number of possible combinations).

The truth table for the three expressions given above is:

a	b	!(a || b)	(!a) || (!b)	(!a) && (!b)
true	*true*	*false*	*false*	*false*
true	*false*	*false*	*true*	*false*
false	*true*	*false*	*true*	*false*
false	*false*	*true*	*true*	*true*

Two expressions are equivalent if their entries match in every row. So using the truth table given above, we can see that `!(a || b)` and `(!a) && (!b)` are equivalent to each other, but not to `(!a) || (!b)`.

e **Questions**

llowing expressions?

cribes the circumstances under which the expression

rue

true

nd b is true

ment:

```
(2/x == 0)) System.out.println("success");
                            ("failure");
```

Which of the following statements about this code segment is true?

A. There will be an error when the code is compiled because the first && operator is applied to a non-`boolean` expression.

B. There will be an error when the code is compiled because a `boolean` variable (`y`) and an `int` variable (`x`) appear in the same `if`-statement condition.

C. There will be an error when the code is executed because of an attempt to divide by zero.

D. The code will compile and execute without error; the output will be "success."

E. The code will compile and execute without error; the output will be "failure."

4. Assume that the following definitions have been made, and that variable x has been initialized.

    ```
    int x;
    boolean result;
    ```

    Consider the following three code segments:

Segment I	Segment II	Segment III

`result = (x%2 == 0);`	`if (x%2 == 0) {`
	`    result = true;`
	`}`
	`else {`
	`    result = false;`
	`}`
		`if (((x * 2) / 2) == x) {`
		`    result = true;`
		`}`
		`else {`
		`    result = false;`
		`}`

    Which of these code segments sets `result` to `true` if x is even, and to `false` if x is odd?

    A. I only

    B. II only

    C. III only

    D. I and II

    E. I and III

5. Consider the following code segment:

    ```
    if (y < 0) {
        x = -x;
        y = -y;
    }
    z = 0;
    while (y > 0) {
        z += x;
        y--;
    }
    ```

    Assume that x, y, and z are `int` variables, and that x and y have been initialized. Which of the following best describes what this code segment does?

    A. Sets z to be the sum x+y

    B. Sets z to be the product x*y

    C. Sets z to be the absolute value of x

    D. Sets z to be the value of x^y

    E. Sets z to be the value of y^x

Answers to Multiple-Choice Questions

1. B
2. E
3. E
4. D
5. B

1.2 Control Statements

The AP Computer Science subset of Java includes the following control statements:

```
if   if-else   while   for   return
```

If and If-Else

The two kinds of `if` statements choose which statement to execute next depending on the value of a boolean expression. Here are the forms of the two statements:

```
if (expression) statement
```

```
if (expression) statement else statement
```

If you want more than one statement in the `true` or the `false` branch of an `if`, you must enclose the statements in curly braces. In general, it is a good idea to use curly braces and indentation to make the structure of your code clear, especially if you have nested `if` statements. For example:

Good Programming Style

```
if (x < 0) {
   System.out.println( "negative x" );
   x = -x;
   if (y < 0) {
      System.out.println( "negative y, too!" );
      y = -y;
   }
   else {
      System.out.println( "nonnegative y" );
   }
}
```

Bad Programming Style

```
if (x < 0) {
System.out.println( "negative x" );
   x = -x;
```

```
if (y < 0)
{ System.out.println( "negative y, too!" );
y = -y; }
else
System.out.println( "nonnegative y" );
}
```

Note that the "good" style shown above is only one of many good possibilities. For example, some programmers prefer to put curly braces on separate lines. They would write the code above like this:

Good Programming Style

```
if (x < 0)
{
    System.out.println( "negative x" );
    x = -x;
    if (y < 0)
    {
        System.out.println( "negative y, too!" );
        y = -y;
    }
    else
    {
        System.out.println( "nonnegative y" );
    }
}
```

While and For

The `while` and `for` statements provide two different kinds of loops or iteration (a way to repeat a list of statements until some condition is satisfied). Here are the forms of the two statements:

```
while ( expression ) statement
```

```
for ( init-expression; test-expression; update-expression ) statement
```

As with the `if` statement, curly braces must be used to include more than one statement in the body of a loop. For example:

```
while (x > 0) {
    sum += x;
    x--;
}
```

A `for-loop`:

```
for ( init-expression; test-expression; update-expression ) statement
```

is equivalent to:

```
init-expression;
while ( test-expression ) {
   statement;
   update-expression;
}
```

In other words, the *init-expression* of a `for-loop` is evaluated only once, before the first iteration of the loop; the loop keeps executing as long as the *test-expression* evaluates to `true`; and the *update-expression* is executed at the end of each iteration of the loop.

Although they can be any expressions, standard practice is to make the *init-expression* be an assignment that initializes a loop-index variable to its initial value, and to make the *update-expression* be an assignment that changes the value of the loop-index variable. The *test-expression* is usually a test to see whether the loop-index variable has reached some upper (or lower) bound. For example:

```
for (k=0; k<10; k++) ...
```

It is important to understand that a loop may execute zero times; this happens for a `while-loop` when its condition is `false` the first time it is evaluated, and for a `for-loop` when its *test-expression* is `false` the first time it is evaluated.

Return

The `return` statement is usually used to return a value from a non-void method. For example, the following method reads numbers until a negative number is read, and it returns the sum of the (nonnegative) numbers. (Assume that method `readInt` reads one integer value.)

```
public int sumInts( ) {
   int k, sum = 0;
   k = readInt( );
   while ( k >= 0 ) {
      sum += k;
      k = readInt( );
   }
   return sum;
}
```

A `return` can also be used to return from a method before the end of the method has been reached. For example, here is another version of method `sumInts`. This version uses a `return` statement to exit both the loop and method `sumInts` as soon as a negative number is read.

```
public int sumInts( ) {
   int k, sum = 0;
   while ( true ) {
      k = readInt( );
      if (k < 0) return sum;
      sum += k;
   }
}
```

Practice Multiple-Choice Questions

1. Assume that x is an initialized `int` variable. The code segment

   ```
   if (x > 5) x *= 2;
   if (x > 10) x = 0;
   ```

   is equivalent to which of the following code segments?

   A. x = 0;

   B. if (x > 5) x = 0;

   C. if (x > 5) x *= 2;

   D. if (x > 5) x = 0;
      else x *= 2;

   E. if (x > 5) x *= 2;
      else if (x > 10) x = 0;

2. Consider the following code segment:

   ```
   for (int k=0; k<10; k++) {
       for (int j=0; j<5; j++) System.out.print("*");
   }
   ```

   How many stars are output when this code segment is executed?

   A. 5

   B. 10

   C. 15

   D. 50

   E. 500

3. Consider the following two code segments:

Segment 1

```
int x = 0;
while (y > 0) {
  y--;
  x++;
}
System.out.println("x = " + x);
```

Segment 2

```
int x;
for (x=0; y>0; y--) {
  x++;
}
System.out.println("x = " + x);
```

Assume that y is an initialized int variable. Under which of the following conditions will the output of the two code segments be different?

A. The output will never be different.

B. The output will always be different.

C. The output will be different if and only if y is zero just before the code segment executes.

D. The output will be different if and only if y is greater than zero just before the code segment executes.

E. The output will be different if and only if y is less than zero just before the code segment executes.

4. The two code segments shown below are both intended to return true if variable A (an array of ints) contains the value val, and otherwise to return false.

Version 1

```
for (int k=0; k<A.length; k++) {
  if (A[k] == val) return true;
}
return false;
```

Version 2

```
boolean tmp = false;
for (int k=0; k<A.length; k++) {
  if (A[k] == val) tmp = true;
}
return tmp;
```

Which of the following statements about the two versions is true?

A. Only version 1 will work as intended.

B. Only version 2 will work as intended.

C. Both versions will work as intended; version 1 will sometimes be more efficient than version 2.

D. Both versions will work as intended; version 2 will sometimes be more efficient than version 1.

E. Both versions will work as intended; the two versions will always be equally efficient.

5.   Consider the following two methods:

```
public static void printStuff( int x ) {
    int y = 1;
    while (y < x) {
        System.out.print(y + " ");
        y *= 2;
        if (y == x/2) return;
    }
}


public static void mystery( ) {
    int x = 8;
    while (x > 0) {
        printStuff(x);
        x /= 2;
    }
    System.out.println("x=" + x);
}
```

What will be the output when method `mystery` is called?

A. 1 2 1 1 1 x=0

B. 1 2 1 1 x=0

C. 1 2 2 x=0

D. 1 2 4 x=8

E. 1 2 x=8

Answers to Multiple-Choice Questions

1. B
2. D
3. A
4. C
5. B

1.3 Strings and Arrays

For the AP Computer Science course, you need to know about two special kinds of objects: *strings* and *arrays*. Computer Science A students only need to know about one-dimensional arrays, whereas AB students also need to know about two-dimensional arrays.

There is an important difference between variables that have primitive types (`int`, `boolean`, or `double`) and variables that are objects. In both cases, each variable has an associated location in the computer memory. However, for a primitive type, the integer, boolean, or double value is stored directly in that location, whereas for objects the location contains a pointer to another chunk of memory where the object is stored. The chunk of memory where the object is stored is allocated using new. For a String, the allocation usually includes the sequence of characters in the string; if not, an *empty* string (one with no characters) is created. For an array, the allocation includes the size of the array. For example:

Code	Runtime Representation

```
int k = 5;
String s = new String("hello");
String mt = new String();
int[] A = new int[3];
```

```
k: 5
s: ──▶ "hello!"
mt: ──▶ ""
A: ──▶ 0 0 0
```

A String can also be initialized using a string literal:

```
String s = "hello";
```

and an array can be created and initialized using a sequence of values inside curly braces; for example,

```
int[] A = {10, 20, 30};
```

creates a one-dimensional array of length three, with the values 10, 20, and 30 in A[0], A[1], and A[2], respectively.

The fact that array variables really contain pointers means that it is possible for an assignment to an element of one array to change a value in another array. For example, consider the following code:

```
int[] A = new int[3];
int[] B;
A[0] = 2;
B = A;
B[0] = 5;
System.out.println(A[0]);
```

In this code, A[0] is set to 2 (and there are no other assignments to A[0]). However, the assignment B = A sets variable B to point to the same chunk of memory as variable A. This means that the assignment to B[0] also causes the value of A[0] to change. Therefore, the value printed is 5, not 2. A picture of how each line of code changes the runtime representation is shown on the next page.

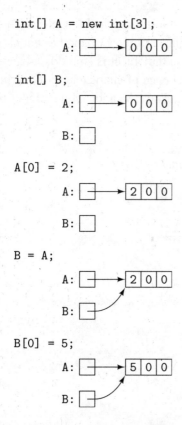

```
int[] A = new int[3];
```

```
int[] B;
```

```
A[0] = 2;
```

```
B = A;
```

```
B[0] = 5;
```

Unlike arrays, `Strings` are *immutable*. To understand what that means, remember that a `String` variable `S` has an associated memory location that contains a pointer to a chunk of memory that in turn contains characters. If you assign to `S`, you change the pointer to point to a different chunk of memory; you do not change the characters in the original chunk of memory. Here are some pictures to illustrate these ideas:

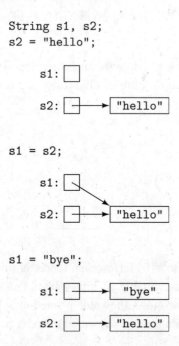

```
String s1, s2;
s2 = "hello";
```

```
s1 = s2;
```

```
s1 = "bye";
```

```
s2 = s1;
```

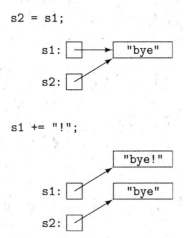

```
s1 += "!";
```

Note that after executing s1 = "bye", the value of variable s2 is still "hello"; assigning to s1 made it point to a new sequence of characters rather than changing the characters in the chunk of memory to which it (and s2) pointed. Even using string concatenation (the + operator) to change s1 simply makes it point to a new chunk of memory that contains the concatenated string; the old chunk of memory (containing "bye") is not affected.

Every array has a field named length that contains the current length of the array. For example, when the following code is executed, the values 3 and 10 will be printed.

```
int[] A = new int[3];
System.out.println(A.length);
A = new int[10];
System.out.println(A.length);
```

Every String has a method named length that returns the current length of the string. For example, when the following code is executed, the values 0, 3, and 1 will be printed.

```
String S = new String();
System.out.println(S.length());
S = "abc";
System.out.println(S.length());
S = new String("?");
System.out.println(S.length());
```

Because Strings and arrays are objects, they inherit the methods defined for the Object class (see Section 8.1.4). For AP Computer Science, you need to know about the equals and toString methods. (AB students also need to know about the hashCode method, which is discussed in Chapter 6.)

The equals method is what you should use to determine whether two Strings are the same. For example, assume that s1 and s2 are String variables. Then the expression s1.equals(s2) (and the expression s2.equals(s1)) will evaluate to true whenever s1 and s2 contain the same sequences of characters.

A comparison of two `Strings` using the `==` operator only evaluates to `true` when the two `Strings` contain pointers to the same chunk of memory. Here's an example to illustrate the difference between using the `equals` method and using `==`:

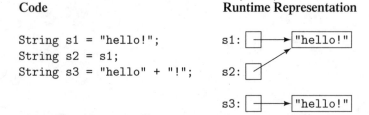

Code	Runtime Representation

`String s1 = "hello!";`
`String s2 = s1;`
`String s3 = "hello" + "!";`	

Given these definitions of `s1`, `s2`, and `s3`, below are some expressions that use the `equals` method and the `==` operator, and the values of the expressions:

Expression	Value
`s1.equals(s2)`	true
`s1 == s2`	true
`s1.equals(s3)`	true
`s1 == s3`	false
`s2.equals(s3)`	true
`s2 == s3`	false

For objects other than `Strings`, it is up to the designer of the class to write an `equals` method that returns `true` when the two objects are "the same." By default, every object has an `equals` method that returns `true` only when the `==` operator would return `true`; if the designer of a class doesn't write an `equals` method, the default one will be used.

It is not possible to define a new `equals` method for an array, so if A and B are two array variables, `A.equals(B)` (and `B.equals(A)`) evaluates to `true` if and only if A and B point to the same chunk of memory. If you want to test whether two arrays contain the same values, you must write code that looks at the values; you cannot use the array's `equals` method.

The `toString` method converts an object to a `String`. When you use the plus (+) operator to concatenate a `String` with another object, the other object is converted to a `String` by calling its `toString` method. Although every object has a default `toString` method, those methods usually don't produce a useful string (for example, on my computer, the string returned by the `toString` method of an array of integers was "`[I@7dd0b5aa`"). Therefore, if you want to print an array, you will have to write code to do it rather than using the array's `toString` method.

Two-Dimensional Arrays (AB only)

Here is an example of how to define a two-dimensional array:

```
int[][] A = new int[3][5];
```

When this code is executed, space for a 3-by-5 array (an array with three rows and five columns) is allocated. A common way to initialize an array is to use a `for-loop`. For example, the following code initializes array A so that each row contains the numbers zero to four.

```
int[][] A = new int[3][5];
int num = 0;
for (int row=0; row<3; row++) {
    for (int col=0; col<5; col++) {
        A[row][col] = num;
        num++;
    }
    num = 0;
}
```

To find out how many rows a two-dimensional array A has, you can use A.length; you can use A[0].length to find out the number of columns. Therefore, instead of using the values "3" and "5" as the upper limits of the two for-loop indexes, we could have used A.length and A[0].length, as shown below.

```
for (int row=0; row<A.length; row++) {
    for (int col=0; col<A[0].length; col++) {
        .
        .
        .
```

A two-dimensional array can also be initialized using sequences of values inside curly braces. One sequence of values is provided for each row, and each such sequence contains a value for each column in that row. For example, the following code initializes array A to contain the same values as the for-loop given above:

```
int[][] A = {{0,1,2,3,4},{0,1,2,3,4},{0,1,2,3,4}};
```

Practice Multiple-Choice Questions

1. Consider the following code segment (line numbers are included for reference):

```
1  int[] A = new int[3];
2  int[] B = new int[10];
3  B[9] = 30;
4  A = B;
5  A[9] = 20;
6  B[9] = 10;
7  System.out.println(A[9]);
```

What happens when this code is compiled and executed?

A. Line 5 will cause a compile-time error because of an out-of-bounds array index.

B. Line 5 will cause a runtime error because of an out-of-bounds array index.

C. The code will compile and execute without error. The output will be 10.

D. The code will compile and execute without error. The output will be 20.

E. The code will compile and execute without error. The output will be 30.

2. Which of the following statements is *not* true?

    A. Every object has an `equals` method.

    B. If a programmer does not write an `equals` method for a new class, the default method will return `true` if and only if all fields of the two instances of the class contain the same values.

    C. The `equals` method for `Strings` returns `true` if and only if the two `Strings` contain the same sequence of characters.

    D. The `equals` method for arrays returns `true` if and only if the two arrays point to the same chunk of memory.

    E. The `equals` method for `Strings` will return `false` if one `String` is shorter than the other.

3. Consider the following code segment:

    ```
    String s1 = "abc";
    String s2 = s1;
    String s3 = s2;
    ```

    After this code executes, which of the following expressions would evaluate to `true`?

    I.   `s1.equals(s3)`
    II. `s1 == s2`
    III. `s1 == s3`

    A. I only

    B. II only

    C. III only

    D. I and II only

    E. I, II, and III

4. Consider the following code segment:

    ```
    int[] A = {1, 2, 3};
    int[] B = {1, 2, 3};
    int[] C = A;
    ```

    After this code executes, which of the following expressions would evaluate to `true`?

    I.   `A.equals(B)`
    II. `A == B`
    III. `A == C`

    A. I only

    B. II only

    C. III only

    D. I and III only

    E. I, II, and III

5. (AB only) Consider the following declaration:

    ```
    int[][] arr = new int[5][6];
    ```

    Which of the following is an object?

    A. `arr`
    B. `arr[0][0]`
    C. `arr[0][0] * 2`
    D. `arr.length`
    E. `arr[arr.length-1][arr[0].length-1]`

Answers to Multiple-Choice Questions

1. C
2. B
3. E
4. C
5. A

2

Object-Oriented Features

2.1 Objects, Classes, and Methods

Recall that in Java every variable either has a primitive type (`int`, `double`, or `boolean` for the AP CS subset) or is an *object*. Some objects (e.g., arrays and strings) are built in to the language. When a programmer designs a program, one important question is what new objects to define, and the answer depends on what the program is designed to do. In general, the new objects will represent the things that the program is designed to manipulate. For example, if a programmer designs a program to be used by a bookstore to keep track of the current inventory, the program will probably include the definition of a new kind of object to represent books.

Each new kind of object is defined by defining a new *class*; for example, we could define the following Book class to represent books.

```
public class Book {
/*** fields ***/
    private String title;
    private double price;
    private int numSold;

/*** constructor ***/
    public Book( String theTitle, double thePrice ) {
        title = theTitle;
        price = price;
        numSold = 0;
    }

/*** public methods ***/
    // get the price
    public double getPrice( ) { return price; }

    // get the number sold
    public int getNumSold( ) { return numSold; }
```

```
    // sell k copies
    public void sell(int k) { numSold += k; }


    // set the price
    public void setPrice(double newPrice) { price = newPrice; }


    // put the book on sale
    // take off the given percent from the price, but don't go
    // below the given minimum price
    public void putOnSale( int percent, double minPrice ) {
        setPrice( computeSalePrice(percent, minPrice) );
    }


    // determine which book is the most popular
    public static Book mostPopular( Book[] bookList ) {
    // precondition: bookList.length > 0
    // postcondition: returns the book that has sold the most copies
        int bestNum = bookList[0].numSold;
        int bestIndex = 0;
        for (int j=1; j<bookList.length; j++) {
            if (bookList[j].numSold > bestNum) {
                bestNum = bookList[j].numSold;
                bestIndex = j;
            }
        }
        return bookList[bestIndex];
    }


/*** private methods ***/
    // compute the sale price
    private double computeSalePrice(int percent, double minPrice) {
        double newPrice = price - percent*.01;
        if (newPrice < minPrice) newPrice = minPrice;
        return newPrice;
    }
}
```

Every class has *fields* (also called *instance variables*), *constructors*, and *methods*. The Book class has three fields: title, price, and numSold. It has one constructor: Book. It has seven methods: getPrice, getNumSold, sell, setPrice, putOnSale, mostPopular, and computeSalePrice.

At runtime, there can be many instances of a class (each one created using new). For our example, there can be many instances of the Book class, each of which represents one book. If a field or method is declared static, then there will be just one copy of that field or method for the whole class; otherwise, every instance of the class will have its own copy of the field or method.

2.1.1   Constructors

Whenever a new instance of a class is created, a constructor is called to initialize the nonstatic fields of the new object. The name of a constructor is the same as the name of the class, and, unlike the methods of the class, a constructor has no return type (not even `void`).

The `Book` class defined above has a constructor that initializes all of its fields. It must be called with two arguments (a `String` and a `double`). For example:

```
Book b = new Book("The Cat in the Hat", 5.00);
```

2.1.2   Methods

Each method in a class can be either *static* or *nonstatic*, and can be either *public* or *private*. A method should be nonstatic when it performs a task that is specific to one instance of the class. Most methods are nonstatic. For example, the `getPrice` and `getNumSold` methods of the `Book` class return the price and number sold for one instance of a `Book`, and the `sell` method changes the `numSold` field of one instance of a `Book`. Therefore, none of these methods is static.

A method should be static when it performs a task that is not specific to one instance of a class. For example, the `mostPopular` method finds the book in the given array that has sold the most copies. It makes sense for this method to be part of the `Book` class (since it has to do with books), but since it does not perform a task specific to one book it also makes sense for it to be a static method. Other examples of static methods are the `abs`, `pow`, and `sqrt` methods of the `Math` class (a class provided as part of the Java language, and discussed in Chapter 8). Those methods are static since they provide operations of general use to anyone who wants to perform mathematical calculations; they are not specific to one instance of the `Math` class, and in fact, you don't even need to create an instance of the `Math` class to use the `abs`, `pow`, or `sqrt` methods.

Now let's consider how to call the static and nonstatic methods of the `Book` class from code that is not itself part of the `Book` class. To call a static method of the `Book` class, you use the name of the class (`Book`), followed by a dot, followed by the name of the method. To call a nonstatic method of a `Book` object, you use the name of the object, followed by a dot, followed by the name of the method. For example, the following code illustrates how to call a static method (`mostPopular`) of the `Book` class and a nonstatic method (`sell`) of a `Book` object from code that is not part of the `Book` class. Assume that b is a `Book`, and B is an array of `Books`.

```
b = Book.mostPopular( B );   // call Book's "mostPopular" method
b.sell(5);                   // call b's "sell" method
```

Methods that are intended to be used by clients of a class should be public; other methods should be private. For example, the `computeSalePrice` method performs an operation that is used by the `putOnSale` method but is not intended to be used by clients of the `Book` class. Therefore, the `computeSalePrice` method is a private method. All of the other `Book` methods are public methods.

Parameters

Each method has zero or more *parameters,* sometimes referred to as *formal parameters*. The corresponding values used in a call to the method are called *arguments* or *actual parameters*. A method call must include one argument for each of the method's parameters, and the type of each argument must match the type of the corresponding parameter. For example, in the Book class, the computeSalePrice method has two formal parameters, an int and a double. The putOnSale method calls computeSalePrice with two arguments: percent and minPrice, which are of type int and double, respectively (matching the types of the corresponding parameters).

In Java, all arguments are passed by *value*. This means that what is actually passed is a *copy* of the argument, made when the method is called. Therefore, changes made to the formal parameter by the method have no effect on the argument (since the changes are applied to the copy). For example, suppose we change the computeSalePrice method so that it has three parameters instead of two, where the third parameter is the current price of the book, and instead of returning the sale price, it simply sets the third parameter to that value.

```
private static void computeSalePrice(int percent, double minPrice
                                     double bookPrice) {
    double newPrice = price - percent*.01;
    if (newPrice < minPrice) newPrice = minPrice;
    bookPrice = newPrice;
}
```

And suppose we change the call in the putOnSale method to:

```
computeSalePrice(percent, minPrice, price);
```

In this case, the putOnSale method has no effect on the book's price. This is because when method computeSalePrice is called, the value of the argument price is copied into a new location (called bookPrice), and it is the copy that is assigned to. When method computeSalePrice returns, the book's price field still contains its original value.

However, remember that if an argument is an object, then what is copied is a pointer to the chunk of memory where the object is stored. Changing the formal parameter itself will not affect the corresponding argument, but changing the value *pointed to* by the formal parameter will also change the value pointed to by the argument (since both the argument and the formal parameter point to the same chunk of memory).

Here is some example code to illustrate these ideas:

```
public void changeBook( book b ) {
    b.putOnSale(10, 0.0);
    b = null;
}


public void test( ) {
    Book myBook = new Book("Birds", 10.00);
    changeBook( myBook );
    System.out.println( myBook.getPrice() );
}
```

When this code executes, the Book constructor initializes the price of myBook to $10.00. When method changeBook is called, the value of the argument myBook is copied into a new location (called b). That value is a pointer to the chunk of memory that holds the Book object, including its three fields. When changeBook changes the price of b to $9 (by calling putOnSale), it changes the value of the price field that is part of that chunk of memory. Since argument myBook is pointing to that same chunk of memory, the value of myBook.price is also changed, and so the value "9.0" is printed after changeBook returns. However, the last statement in changeBook (which sets b to null) only changes the value in the location named b; it has no effect on argument myBook, and so there is no NullPointerException when myBook.getPrice is called.

Here are some pictures to illustrate better what happens at runtime:

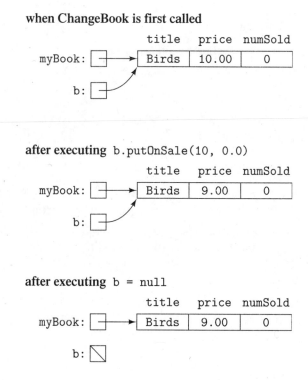

when ChangeBook is first called

after executing b.putOnSale(10, 0.0)

after executing b = null

Since arrays are also objects, the same ideas apply to array parameters, as illustrated at the top of the next page.

Return Type

Every method (except a constructor) has a *return type*. In general, if a method is designed to perform some action rather than to compute a value, its return type should be void; otherwise, its return type should be the type of the value it is intended to compute. For example, in the Book class, method putOnSale has return type void because its purpose is to modify the book's price, not to compute and return a value. In contrast, the purposes of method mostPopular are to determine which book in the given array has sold the most copies and to return that book. Therefore, its return type is Book.

Code

```
public void changeArray( int[] B ) {
    B[0] += 5;
    B = null;
}

public void test( ) {
    int[] A = new int[3];
    A[0] = 1;
    changeArray( A );
    System.out.println( A[0] );
}
```

What Happens at Runtime

when `ChangeArray` is first called

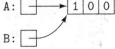

after executing `B[0] += 5`

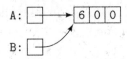

after executing `B = null`

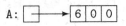

Preconditions and Postconditions

It is a good idea to provide documentation for each method that explains what it does. One good way to do this is to write a precondition and a postcondition for each method. The precondition says what is expected to be true when the method is called, and the postcondition says what will be true when the method returns, assuming that the expectations of the precondition are met. For example, the `mostPopular` method of the `Book` class (shown again below) has a precondition and a postcondition.

```
public static Book mostPopular( Book[] bookList ) {
// precondition: bookList.length > 0
// postcondition: returns the book that has sold the most copies
    int bestNum = bookList[0].numSold;
    int bestIndex = 0;
    for (int j=1; j<bookList.length; j++ ) {
        if (bookList[j].numSold > bestNum) {
            bestNum = bookList[j].numSold;
            bestIndex = j;
        }
    }
    return bookList[bestIndex];
}
```

It is the responsibility of the programmer who includes calls to `mostPopular` to make sure that the method's precondition is satisfied on every call; if the array argument has length 0, the programmer cannot expect the method to work as intended. In this case, an `IndexOutOfBoundsException` would occur. In general, if a method's preconditions are not satisfied, the method might return the wrong value, perform the wrong task, or throw an exception.

Recursion

A method that can call itself, either directly or indirectly (for example, by calling another method that calls another method that calls the first method), is called a *recursive* method.

Recursive methods are sometimes much easier to understand than the equivalent nonrecursive code would be. For example, AB students should have seen examples of operations on binary trees that are much more easily implemented using recursive methods than using nonrecursive methods. Both A and AB students should be familiar with the Merge Sort algorithm, which is also best defined using recursion.

It is important to remember that every recursive method must have a "base case"—a test that can prevent the method from calling itself again; otherwise, a runtime error will occur (for example, a StackOverflowError exception might be thrown). This is usually referred to as an *infinite recursion*, though in fact the limited resources of the computer prevent it from actually being infinite.

Here is an example of a recursive method that does not have a base case:

```
public void printInt( int k ) {
    System.out.print( k + " " );
    printInt( k+1 );
}
```

If printInt is originally called like this:

```
printInt( 1 );
```

the output will be:

```
1  2  3  4  5  6  7  8  9  10  11  ...
```

and eventually there will be a runtime error.

Not only must a recursive method include a base case, but it must also "make progress" toward the base case, so that eventually there are no more recursive calls. Here is another version of printInt:

```
public void printInt( int k ) {
    if (k < 1) {
        System.out.println( );
    }
    else {
        System.out.print( k + " " );
        printInt( k+1 );
    }
}
```

This version *does* include a base case (the recursive call is not made if k is less than one); however, if printInt is originally called with an argument that is greater than or equal to one, the base case is never reached, and there is still an infinite recursion.

Here is a version of `printInt` that never causes an infinite recursion, no matter how it is originally called:

```
public void printInt( int k ) {
// postcondition: prints the numbers from k to 10,
//                    ending with a new line.
    if (k > 10) {
        System.out.println( );
    }
    else {
        System.out.print( k + " " );
        printInt( k+1 );
    }
}
```

It is also important to understand that a recursive method may do some things before the recursive call and may do some more things after the recursive call. The things that are done *after* the recursive call must wait until all of the recursion has finished. For example, consider the two methods shown below (assume that `readInt` reads one integer value).

```
void echoInput( ) {
    int k;
    k = readInt( );
    if (k != 0) {
        System.out.print( k + " " );
        echoInput( );
    }
}

void reverseInput( ) {
    int k;
    k = readInt( );
    if (k != 0) {
        reverseInput( );
        System.out.print( k + " " );
    }
}
```

The only difference between `echoInput` and `reverseInput` is that `echoInput` prints the value of variable k *before* the recursive call, and `reverseInput` prints the value *after* the recursive call. However, that is a very important difference! Because `reverseInput` waits to print the value of k until after the recursive call has finished, the first value read in to k will be the *last* value printed. For example, if the two methods are each called with the input 1 2 3 4 0, the output of `echoInput` will be 1 2 3 4, and the output of `reverseInput` will be 4 3 2 1.

Overloading

In Java it is possible for a class to have multiple versions of a method with the same name. Such methods are called *overloaded* methods. Two versions of a method must have different *signatures*; that is, they must either have a different number of parameters or at least one parameter must have different types in the two versions of the method (it is *not* good enough for the two versions to have different return types).

Overloading is useful when you want to provide the same operation on different kinds of objects. For example, you might want to define a max method for integers and for decimal numbers. You can do this via overloading as follows:

```java
public int max( int x, int y ) {
    if (x >= y) return x;
    return y;
}


public double max( double x, double y ) {
    if (x >= y) return x;
    return y;
}
```

In this example, both versions of max have the same number of parameters, but the types of the two parameters differ in each of the versions, so this is legal overloading.

Another reason for using overloaded methods is to provide the same operation with a different number of parameters. For example, you might want to define another version of max that returns the maximum of *three* given integer values rather than two:

```java
public int max( int x, int y, int z ) {
    if (x >= y) return max(x, z);
    else return max(y, z);
}
```

The constructors for a class can also be overloaded. When an instance of a class is created using new, the number and types of the arguments are used to determine which constructor is called.

For example, the Book class has a constructor with two parameters (the title and price of the new book). That constructor is called when a new Book is created like this:

```java
Book b = new Book( "Happy Days", 22.50);
```

We could define a second constructor, with just one parameter (the title) that initializes the price to some default value. The constructor could be defined like this:

```java
public Book( String theTitle ) {
    title = theTitle;
    price = 20.00;
    numSold = 0;
}
```

This new constructor would be called when a Book was created like this:

```
Book b = new Book("Happy Days");
```

Although it is not appropriate for the Book class, a constructor with *no* parameters can also be defined. (This kind of constructor is called the *default* or *no-argument* constructor.) If the Book class had a default constructor, it would be called like this:

```
Book b = new Book( );
```

Practice Multiple-Choice Questions

Questions 1 and 2 concern the following (incomplete) Point class.

```
public class Point {
  /*** fields ***/
     private int xCoord;  // the current x coordinate
     private int yCoord;  // the current y coordinate


  /*** constructors ***/
   // default constructor: initialize the point to 0,0
     public Point( ) { ... }


   // another constructor: initialize the point to x,y
     public Point(int x, int y) { ... }

  /*** methods ***/
   // set the x coordinate to the given value
     public void setX(int x) { ... }


   // set the y coordinate to the given value
     public void setY(int y) { ... }


   // return the x coordinate
     public int getX( ) { ... }


   // return the y coordinate
     public int getY( ) { ... }


   // move the point horizontally d units
     public void moveHorizontal(int d) { ... }


   // move the point vertically d units
     public void moveVertical(int d) { ... }
}
```

1. Assume that P is a `Point` variable in a method that is *not* in the `Point` class. Which of the following code segments correctly sets P to represent the point (5,5)?

Segment I	**Segment II**	**Segment III**
`P = new Point();`	`P = new Point();`	`P = new Point(5,5);`
`P.xCoord = 5;`	`P.setX(5);`	
`P.yCoord = 5;`	`P.setY(5);`	

A. I only

B. II only

C. III only

D. I and II

E. II and III

2. Assume that P is a `Point` variable that represents the point (x,y) in a method that is *not* in the `Point` class. Which of the following code segments correctly changes P to represent the point (y,x?)

A. ```
P.getX() = P.getY();
P.getY() = P.getX();
```

B.  ```
P.setX(P.getY());
P.setY(P.getX());
```

C. ```
P.moveHorizontal(P.getY());
P.moveVertical(P.getX());
```

D.  ```
int tmp = P.xCoord;
P.xCoord = P.yCoord;
P.yCoord = tmp;
```

E. ```
int tmp = P.getX();
P.setX(P.getY());
P.setY(tmp);
```

3.  Which of the following best describes the purpose of a method's pre- and postconditions?

A.  They provide information to the programmer about what the method is intended to do.

B.  They provide information to the programmer about how the method is implemented.

C.  They provide information to the compiler that permits it to generate better code.

D.  They provide information to the compiler that makes type checking easier.

E.  They permit the method to be in a different file than the code that calls the method.
```

4. Consider the following code segment:

```
public void changeParams( int k, int[] A, String s ) {
    k++;
    A[0]++;
    s += "X";
}

public void print( ) {
    int k = 0;
    int[] A = {10, 20};
    String s = "aaa";

    changeParams(k, A, s);
    System.out.println(k + " " + A[0] + " " + s);
}
```

What is output when method print is called?

A. 0 10 aaa

B. 1 10 aaaX

C. 0 11 aaa

D. 1 11 aaaX

E. 0 11 aaaX

5. Consider the following code segment:

```
public void mystery( int j, int k ) {
    if (j != k) mystery( j+1, k );
}
```

Which of the following best characterizes the conditions under which the call mystery(x, y) leads to an infinite recursion?

A. All conditions

B. No conditions

C. x < y

D. x > y

E. x == y

Answers to Multiple-Choice Questions

1. E
2. E
3. A
4. C
5. D

2.2   Inheritance and Polymorphism

Inheritance is used in a Java program when the objects manipulated by the program form a natural hierarchy using an "*is-a*" relationship. For example, suppose we want to design a program for a bookstore that sells several different kinds of books, including children's books and textbooks. A children's book *is a* book, and so is a textbook. Therefore, we might want to define classes ChildrensBook and TextBook as *subclasses* of the Book class (and the Book class will then be the *superclass* of both the ChildrensBook and TextBook classes).

A subclass is defined using the keyword extends as follows:

```
public class ChildrensBook extends Book {
    .
    .
    .
}


public class TextBook extends Book {
    .
    .
    .
}
```

An advantage of defining classes this way is that subclasses *inherit* all of the fields and methods of their superclasses (but not the constructors, which are discussed below). For example, since every book has a title, a price, and the number of copies sold, there is no need to include those fields in the definitions of the ChildrensBook and TextBook classes; they will be inherited automatically. Similarly, there is no need to redefine the getPrice, getNumSold, sell, setPrice, putOnSale, mostPopular, and computeSalePrice methods; every ChildrensBook and every TextBook will have those methods.

Note that the relationship between a book and a title is a "*has-a*" relationship (a book *has a* title), not an "*is-a*" relationship. That is why title is a field, not a subclass, of a Book.

Usually, a subclass will define some new fields and/or methods that are not defined by its superclass. For example, a ChildrensBook might include the age of the children for whom it is intended, and a TextBook might include the name of the course for which it is required:

```
public class ChildrensBook extends Book {
    /*** new field ***/
        private int childsAge;

    /*** new method ***/
        public int getAge() { return childsAge; }
}

public class TextBook extends Book {
    /*** new field ***/
        private String requiredBy;
```

```
/*** new method ***/
    public String getRequiredBy( ) { return requiredBy; }
}
```

Constructors

As mentioned above, the constructors of a superclass are *not* inherited by its subclasses. However, a subclass's constructors always call a superclass constructor, either explicitly or implicitly. A superclass constructor is called explicitly using super. For example, we could define a constructor for the ChildrensBook class to include an explicit call to the Book constructor like this:

```
public ChildrensBook(String theTitle, double price, int age) {
    super(theTitle, price);
    childsAge = age;
}
```

When this ChildrensBook constructor is called, it first calls the Book constructor to initialize the title, price, and numSold fields; it then initializes the childsAge field itself. Since the title, price, and numSold fields are all *private* fields of the Book class, they can only be initialized using the Book constructor; the ChildrensBook constructor cannot assign to those fields.

Note that if an explicit call to the superclass's constructor is included, it must be the *first* statement in the subclass's constructor. If a subclass's constructor does not include an explicit call to one of its superclass's constructors, then there will be an *implicit* call to the superclass's default constructor (i.e., the compiler will add a call). If the superclass does not have a default constructor, this implicit call will cause a compile-time error. For example, if we failed to include an explicit call to super in the ChildrensBook or TextBook constructors, we would get a compile-time error since the Book class has no default constructor.

Using a Subclass Instead of a Superclass

Another advantage of using inheritance is that you can use a subclass object anywhere that a superclass object is expected. For example, because every textbook *is a* book, any method that has a parameter of type Book can be called with an argument of type TextBook; you do not have to write two versions of the method, one for Book parameters and the other for TextBook parameters. For example, the following method determines whether two books have the same price:

```
public static boolean samePrice( Book b1, Book b2 ) {
    return(b1.getPrice() == b2.getPrice());
}
```

The method will work just fine if both b1 and b2 have type Book, if both have type TextBook, or if one is a Book and the other is a TextBook.

```
Book b1 = ...
Book b2 = ...
TextBook tb1 = ...
```

```
TextBook tb2 = ...
boolean result = samePrice(b1, b2);   // 2 Book arguments
result2 = samePrice(tb1, tb2);        // 2 TextBook arguments
result3 = samePrice(b1, tb1);         // 1 Book and 1 TextBook
```

The fact that you can call the `samePrice` method with Book arguments or with arguments that are any subclass of Book is one example of *polymorphism* in Java: a method whose parameters can have different types on different calls is a *polymorphic method*.

Because you can use a TextBook anywhere that a Book is expected, not only can you pass a TextBook argument to a method with a Book parameter, you can also assign from a TextBook to a Book (because a Book is expected on the right-hand side of the =, and a TextBook *is a* Book). For example:

```
TextBook tb = ...
Book b = tb;              // assign from a TextBook to a Book
```

Although a subclass object can be used anywhere a superclass object is expected, the reverse is not true: in general, you cannot use a superclass object where a subclass object is expected. For example, you cannot call a method that has a TextBook parameter with a Book argument, and you cannot assign from a Book to a TextBook. To illustrate this, assume that the following method has been defined in the TextBook class:

```
public static boolean sameClass( TextBook tb1, TextBook tb2 ) {
    return ((tb1.requiredBy).equals(tb2.requiredBy));
}
```

The following code would cause two compile-time errors, as noted in the comments:

```
Book b = ...
TextBook tb = b; // compile-time error!
                 // can't assign from a Book to a TextBook
if (TextBook.sameClass( b, tb )) ... // compile-time error!
                              // can't use a Book argument
                              // when the corresponding
                              // parameter is a TextBook
```

If you know that a particular Book variable is actually pointing to a TextBook object, then you can use a *class cast* to tell the compiler that it is OK to use that variable where a TextBook is expected. For example:

```
Book b = new TextBook(...);    // b points to a TextBook object
TextBook tb;


tb = (TextBook)b;                              // no compile-time error
if (TextBook.sameClass( (TextBook)b, tb )) ... // no compile-time error
```

Although the use of a class cast prevents a compile-time error, a runtime check is still performed to make sure that the Book variable really is pointing to a TextBook object. If not, an exception is thrown. For example:

```
Book b = new Book(...);  // b points to a Book object
TextBook tb;

tb = (TextBook)b; // runtime error!
                  // b points to a Book, not a TextBook
if (TextBook.sameClass( (TextBook)b, tb )) ... // runtime error!
                                    // b points to a Book,
                                    // not a TextBook
```

Class casts are often required when using the standard Java classes that implement collections of objects. For example, the ArrayList class can be used to represent a list of any kind of object; therefore, the return type of its get method is Object. When you write code to get an object of a particular type from an ArrayList, you need to use a cast. For example, below is code that creates an ArrayList of Books, then prints their prices.

```
// create 3 books and an empty ArrayList
   Book b1 = new Book("Half Magic", 10.95);
   Book b2 = new Book("Magic by the Lake", 15.95);
   Book b2 = new Book("Knights Castle", 12.50);
   ArrayList list = new ArrayList( );

// add the books to the list
   list.add(b1);
   list.add(b2);
   list.add(b3);

// get the books from the list (using casting) and print their prices
   for (int j=0; j<list.size(); j++) {
      Book oneBook = (Book)(list.get(j))      // cast needed here!
      System.out.println(oneBook.getPrice());
   }
```

Overloading Methods

Just as a class can define *overloaded* methods (methods with the same name but different signatures), a subclass can overload a method of its superclass by defining a method with the same name but a different signature. For example, the designer of the ChildrensBook class might want a second version of the putOnSale method that just specifies the percent discount, without any minimum price. It can be implemented by calling the original putOnSale method with a minimum price of 0.0 as shown below.

```
// overload the putOnSale method
public void putOnSale(int percent) {
   putOnSale(percent, 0.0);
}
```

Overriding Methods

In addition to overloading methods defined by its superclass, a subclass can also *override* a superclass method; that is, it can define a new version of the method specialized to work on subclass objects. A superclass method is overridden when the subclass defines a method with exactly the same name, the same number of parameters, the same types of parameters, and the same return type as the method in the superclass.

For example, there might be a rule that textbooks for Physics 101 are never put on sale. In that case, the TextBook class might override the Book class's definition of the putOnSale method as follows:

```
// put the book on sale if it is NOT for Physics 101
public void putOnSale( int percent, double minPrice ) {
    if (requiredBy.equals("Physics 101")) {
        System.out.println("Books for Physics 101 cannot be on sale.");
    else {
        super.putOnSale(percent, minPrice);
    }
}
```

Note that if the textbook is *not* for Physics 101, the TextBook method calls the putOnSale method of the Book class (its superclass) to set the sale price.

As discussed above, a variable of type Book may actually point to a Book object, a TextBook object, or a ChildrensBook object. The type of the object actually pointed to (not the declared type of the variable) is what determines which version of an overridden method is called. For example:

```
Book b = new Book(...);
Book cb = new ChildrensBook(...);
Book tb = new TextBook(...);

b.putOnSale(10, 15.50);   // b points to a Book object, so the Book
                          // class's putOnSale method is called
cb.putOnSale(10, 15.50);  // cb points to a ChildrensBook object;
                          // the putOnSale method was not overridden
                          // in the ChildrensBook class, so the Book
                          // class's putOnSale method is called
tb.putOnSale(10, 15.50);  // tb points to a TextBook object;
                          // the putOnSale method was overridden in
                          // the TextBook class, so the TextBook
                          // class's putOnSale method is called
```

In this example, variables b, cb, and tb are all declared to be of type Book. However, cb is initialized to point to a ChildrensBook, and tb is initialized to point to a TextBook. The calls b.putOnSale(10, 15.50) and cb.putOnSale(10, 15.50) cause the Book class's putOnSale method to be called (because b points to a Book, and because cb points to a ChildrensBook and the ChildrensBook class does not override the putOnSale method). The call tb.putOnSale(10, 15.50) causes the TextBook class's putOnSale method to be called (because tb points to a TextBook, and that class *does* override the putOnSale method).

As illustrated on the previous page, the types of the objects pointed to by variables b, cb, and tb determine which version of the putOnSale method is called. This is an example of *dynamic dispatch,* and it is another aspect of Java that makes it a *polymorphic* language. The first polymorphic aspect of Java, discussed earlier in this section, was that a method's parameters could have different types on different calls. Here we see that a language is also polymorphic if the way an object is processed can depend on its type.

Abstract Methods and Classes

Suppose you want to define a class hierarchy in which some method needs to be provided by all subclasses, but there is no reasonable default version (i.e., it is not possible to define a version of the method in the superclass that makes sense for the subclasses). For example, you might define a Shape class with three subclasses: Circle, Square, and Rectangle. A Circle will have fields that specify the coordinates of its center and its radius. A Square will have fields that specify the coordinates of its upper-left corner and the length of one side. A Rectangle will have fields that specify the coordinates of its upper-left corner, its height, and its width.

It will be useful to have a Draw method for all Shapes; however, there is no reasonable Draw method that will work for a Circle, a Square, and a Rectangle. This is a time to use an *abstract method*: a method that is *declared* in a class but defined only in a subclass. (For our example, the Draw method will be the abstract method; it will be declared in the Shape class, and it will be defined in each of the three subclasses: Circle, Square, and Rectangle.)

Here's the syntax:

```
public abstract class Shape {
    abstract public void Draw();  // no body, just the method header
}


public class Circle extends Shape {
    public void Draw() {
        // code for Circle's Draw method goes here
    }
}


public class Square extends Shape {
    public void Draw() {
        // code for Square's Draw method goes here
    }
}


public class Rectangle extends Shape {
    public void Draw() {
        // code for Rectangle's Draw method goes here
    }
}
```

Note that if a class includes an abstract method, the class *must* be declared abstract, too (otherwise you get a compile-time error). Also, an abstract class cannot be instantiated (you cannot create an instance of the class itself, only of one of its subclasses). For example:

```
Shape s;          // OK -- just a pointer to a Shape,
                  //       no attempt to create a Shape object
s = new Circle(); // OK -- Circle is not an abstract class
s = new Shape();  // Error!  Can't instantiate an abstract class
```

Interfaces

Some objects have more than one "is-a" relationship. For example, consider designing classes to represent some of the people associated with a university. One way to think of the hierarchical relationship among those people is as shown below:

```
        Person
       /      \
 Student    Teacher
     |
    TA
```

This diagram says that a TA (a teaching assistant) is a student, a student is a person, and a teacher is also a person. However, although a TA is certainly a student, in some ways, a TA is also a teacher (e.g., a TA teaches a class and gets paid). Java does not allow you to make the TA class a subclass of both the Student class and the Teacher class. One solution to this problem is to make TA a subclass of the Student class and to use an *interface* to define what TAs and teachers have in common.

An interface is similar to a class, but it can only contain:

- public, static, final fields (i.e., constants)
- public, abstract methods (i.e., just method headers, no bodies)

Here's an example:

```
public interface Employee {
    void raiseSalary( double d );
    double getSalary();
}
```

Note that both methods are implicitly public and abstract (those keywords can be provided, but are not necessary).

A class can *implement* one or more interfaces (in addition to extending one class). It must provide bodies for all of the methods declared in the interface, or else it must be abstract. For example:

```
public class TA implements Employee extends Student {
    public void raiseSalary( double d ) {

        :   actual code here

    }
```

```
public double getSalary() {
    :
    :   actual code here
    :
}
```
}

Many classes can implement the same interface (e.g., both the TA class and the Teacher class can implement the Employee interface). Interfaces provide a way to group similar objects. For example, you could write a method with a parameter named emp of type Employee, and then call that method with either a TA or a Teacher object. The compiler would make sure that the method was never called with a non-Employee argument (e.g., a call with a Student argument would cause a compile-time error), and dynamic dispatch (polymorphism) would ensure that code like emp.raiseSalary(2.0) would correctly call the raiseSalary method of the TA or Teacher class, depending on the type of the object actually pointed to by parameter emp.

If you don't use the Employee interface, it would not be possible to write a single method with a parameter that was either a TA or a Teacher, but not a Person or Student.

Practice Multiple-Choice Questions

1. Consider writing a program to be used by a restaurant to keep track of the items on the menu, which include appetizers, main dishes, and desserts. The restaurant wants to keep track, for every menu item, of the ingredients needed to prepare that item. Some operations will be implemented that apply to all menu items, and there will also be some specialized operations for each of the three different kinds of menu items.

    Which of the following is the best design?

    A. Define one class MenuItem with four fields: Appetizer, MainDish, Dessert, and Ingredients.

    B. Define three unrelated classes: Appetizer, MainDish, and Dessert, each of which has an Ingredients field.

    C. Define a superclass MenuItem with three subclasses: Appetizer, MainDish, and Dessert, and with an Ingredients field.

    D. Define a superclass MenuItem with four subclasses: Appetizer, MainDish, Dessert, and Ingredients.

    E. Define four classes: Appetizer, MainDish, Dessert, and Ingredients. Make Ingredients a subclass of Dessert, make Dessert a subclass of MainDish, and make MainDish a subclass of Appetizer.

2.   Consider the following (incomplete) class definitions:

```
public abstract class Shape {
    public Shape() { ... }

    public abstract void print();
}

public class Square extends Shape {
    public Square() { ... }

    public void print() {
        System.out.println("square");
    }
}
```

Which of the following statements does *not* cause a compile-time error?

I.   `Shape s = new Square();`
II. `Shape s = new Shape();`
III. `Square s = new Shape();`

(A.) I only

B. II only

C. III only

D. I and II only

E. II and III only

Questions 3 and 4 refer to the following (incomplete) class definitions.

```
public class Person {
    public Person() { ... }
    public void print() { System.out.println("person"); }
    public static void printAll( Person[] list ) {
        for (int k=0; k<list.length; k++) list[k].print();
    }
}


public class Student extends Person {
    public void print() { System.out.println("student"); }
}
```

3. Consider the following code:

```
ArrayList L = new ArrayList();
Student s;
Person p = new Person();
L.add(p);
statement
```

Which of the following can be used to replace the placeholder *statement* so that the code will cause neither a compile-time nor a runtime error?

A. p = (Student)(L.get(0));

B. p = (Person)(L.get(0));

C. s = L.get(0);

D. s = (Person)(L.get(0));

E. s = (Student)(L.get(0));

4. Assume that method printAll is called with an array of length 5, and that none of the five elements of the array is null. Which of the following statements best describes what will happen, and why?

A. The word person will be printed five times since the type of the array parameter is Person.

B. The word person will be printed five times since printAll is a method of the Person class.

C. The word student will be printed five times since the print method was overridden by the Student class.

D. For each of the five objects in the array, either the word person or the word student will be printed, depending on the type of the object.

E. If the array actually contains objects of type Person, then the word person will be printed five times; otherwise, a runtime error will occur.

5. Consider the following interface and class definitions:

```
public interface Employee {
    void raiseSalary();
}

public interface Musician {
    void Play();
}

public class Test implements Employee, Musician {
    public void raiseSalary() {
        System.out.println("raising");
    }

    public void Play() {
        System.out.println("playing");
    }
}
```

Which of the following statements about these definitions is true?

A. The code will not compile because class `Test` tries to implement two interfaces at once.

B. The code will not compile because class `Test` only implements interfaces; it does not extend any class.

C. The code will not compile because class `Test` only implements the methods defined in the `Employee` and `Musician` interfaces; it does not define any new methods.

D. The code will compile; however, if class `Test` did not include a definition of the `Play` method, the code would not compile.

E. The code will compile; furthermore, even if class `Test` did not include a definition of the `Play` method, the code would compile.

Answers to Multiple-Choice Questions

1. C
2. A
3. B
4. D
5. D

2.3   Arrays of Objects

The example arrays in Chapter 1 were all arrays of int or String. However, an array can contain any type, including objects other than strings, and it is important to understand how to use such arrays: how to create objects and put them into an array, how to access the objects in an array, how to call the methods of those objects, and how to access the fields of those objects (when appropriate). It is also important to understand the difference between initializing an array of objects and initializing the objects themselves.

To illustrate these ideas we will use the (incomplete) Date and Person classes shown below.

```java
public class Date implements Comparable {
    private int month;
    private int day;
    private int year;

    public Date(int aMonth, int aDay, int aYear) {
        month = aMonth;
        day = aDay;
        year = aYear;
    }

    // return a negative integer, zero, or a positive integer
    // depending on whether this date is earlier than, the same as,
    // or later than other
    public int compareTo(Object other) {
        :
            code not shown
        :
    }
}

public class Person {
    private String firstName;
    private String lastName;
    private Date birthday;
    private Person[] siblings;

    public Person(String first, String last, Date bDay) {
        firstName = first;
        lastName = last;
        birthday = bDay;
        siblings = null;
    }
```

```
public void setSiblings(Person[] sibs) {
   siblings = sibs;
}

public String getFirstName() {
   return firstName;
}

public Person oldestSib() {
// precondition: siblings.length > 0 and
//               siblings contains no nulls
// postcondition: returns the oldest sibling
   int index = 0;
   Date sibDate = siblings[index].birthday;
   for (int k=1; k<siblings.length; k++) {

         missing code

   }

   return siblings[index];
   }
}
```

First, let's consider how to create an array to hold three people. We could start by declaring and initializing an array variable as follows:

```
Person[] personList;
personList = new Person[3];
```

It is important to realize that while this statement initializes the personList array, there are not yet any people in the array (instead, each item in the array is null). In order to fill the array with people, we must use new to create the people, just as we used new above to create the array itself. To illustrate this more clearly, the declaration and initialization of the array are repeated on the next page, followed by code that fills in the first two elements of the array. Each line of code is illustrated to show what happens at runtime.

Now let's consider how to access and use the people in an array by filling in the missing code in the oldestSib method. The code needs to compare the birthday in variable sibDate with the birthday of the kth person in the siblings array; if the birthday of the person in the array is earlier, the index and sibDate variables need to be updated. (Note that since the oldestSib method is part of the Person class, this code can access the private fields of the people in the array.) There are several different ways to write the missing code: we could first get the kth person from the siblings array, then get that person's birthday, and then check whether the birthday comes before

```
Person[] personList;
```

personList: ?

```
personList = new Person[3];
```

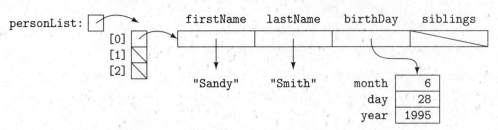

```
personList[0] = new Person("Sandy", "Smith", new Date(6, 28, 1995));
```

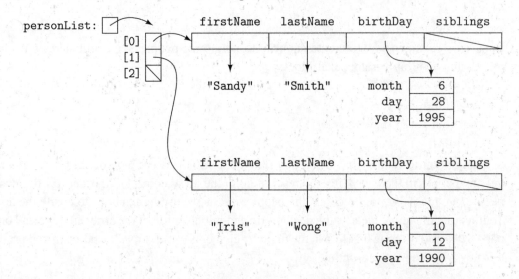

```
personList[1] = new Person("Iris", "Wong", new Date(10, 12, 1990));
```

sibDate (updating index and sibDate if it does). In that case, the *for-loop* would be as shown below (remember that the method call d.compareTo(sibDate) returns a negative integer if d is earlier than sibDate, zero if the two dates are the same, and a positive integer if d is later than sibDate):

```
for (int k=1; k<siblings.length; k++) {
    Person p = siblings[k];
    Date d = p.birthday;
```

```
    if (d.compareTo(sibDate) < 0) {
        index = k;
        sibDate = d;
    }
}
```

We could also compare the two dates using a single expression in the *if* statement like this:

```
for (int k=1; k<siblings.length; k++) {
    if (siblings[k].birthday.compareTo(sibDate) < 0) {
        index = k;
        sibDate = siblings[k].birthday;
    }
}
```

To understand this version of the *if* statement, it helps to think about the types of the subexpressions of `siblings[k].birthday.compareTo(sibDate)`. The type of `siblings[k]` is `Person`, and the type of `siblings[k].birthday` is `Date` (the birthday of the kth person in the array, counting from zero). The whole expression, `siblings[k].birthday.compareTo(sibDate)`, calls the `compareTo` method of the kth person's birthday, so its type is the result type of `compareTo`, which is an `int`. Therefore, it is correct to see if that result is less than zero (i.e., does the kth person's birthday come before `sibDate`).

Now let's consider how to write code that manipulates an array of people but is *not* part of the `Person` class, so the code cannot access the fields of the `Person` class directly. For example, suppose we have an array of people (in a variable named `personList`) and a first name (in a variable named `firstName`), and we want to remove from the array all people who have that first name; i.e., we want to end up with a *smaller* array that only includes people with a different first name. To accomplish this, we could do the following:

- Go through the array, counting how many people have the given first name.
- If the count is zero, then do nothing further. Otherwise, create a new array with just enough space for the people who do not have the given first name; go through the `personList` array again, and copy the people who don't have the given first name into the new array. Then set `personList` to point to the new array.

Here's one way to write the code:

```
int counter = 0;

// count how many people in personList have firstName
for (int k=0; k<personList.length; k++) {
    String oneName = personList[k].getFirstName();
    if (oneName.equals(firstName)) {
        counter++;
    }
}
```

```
    if (counter != 0) {
        // create a new array, fill it with the people who do not
        // have firstName, and set personList to point to the new array
        Person[] newList = new Person[personList.length - counter];
        int newIndex = 0;
        for (int k=0; k<personList.length; k++) {
            String oneName = personList[k].getFirstName();
            if (! oneName.equals(firstName)) {
                newList[newIndex] = personList[k];
                newIndex++;
            }
        }
        personList = newList;
    }
```

We could also write the comparison of the kth person's name with the given name as a single expression, without using local variable oneName:

```
    if (personList[k].getFirstName().equals(firstName)) {
        counter++;
    }
```

In this version of the code, the *if* condition has two method calls: first the kth person's getFirstName method is called, returning a String; then that String's equals method is called to see if it matches firstName. Some people find the first version easier to understand, but both versions of the code are correct, and it would be fine to use either version for a free-response question on the AP CS exam.

Practice Multiple-Choice Questions

Questions 1–4 refer to the following Time class.

```
public class Time {
// a Time represents the time needed to do some task;
// e.g., 4 hours and 20 minutes, or 32 hours and 3 minutes

    private int hours;   // 0 <= hours
    private int minutes; // 0 <= minutes <= 59

    public Time(int hrs, int mins) {
        hours = hrs;
        minutes = mins;
    }
```

```
public int getHours() { return hours; }
public int getMinutes() { return minutes; }
public void setHours(int hrs) { hours = hrs; }
public void setMinutes(int mins) { minutes = mins;}
}
```

1. Consider the following data field and method (*not* part of the Time class).

    ```
    private Time[] myTimes;


    public Time longestTime() {
    // precondition: myTimes.length > 0 and
    //                myTimes contains no nulls
    // postcondition: returns the longest Time in myTimes
        Time t = myTimes[0];
        int index = 0;
        for (int k=1; k<myTimes.length; k++) {
            if (missing condition) {
                t = myTimes[k];
                index = k;
            }
        }
        return t;
    }
    ```

    Which of the following code segments could be used to replace *missing condition* so that `longestTime` works as specified by its pre- and postconditions?

    A. `myTimes[k].hours > t.hours`

    B. `myTimes[k].getHours() > t.hours`

    C. `myTimes[k].getHours() > t.getHours()`

    D. `(myTimes[k].getHours() > t.getHours()) ||`
        `(myTimes[k].getMinutes() > t.getMinutes())`

    E. `(myTimes[k].getHours() > t.getHours()) ||`
        `((myTimes[k].getHours() == t.getHours()) &&`
        `(myTimes[k].getMinutes() > t.getMinutes()))`

2. Assume that variable `timeList` has been declared to be an array of `Time`s as follows:

    ```
    Time[] timeList;
    ```

    Which of the following code segments correctly initializes the array to contain ten `Time`s, each representing the time "3 hours and 20 minutes"?

    I. ```
    timeList = new Time[10];
    ```

    II. ```
    timeList = new Time[10];
    for (int k=0; k<10; k++) {
        timeList[k].setHours(3);
        timeList[k].setMinutes(20);
    }
    ```

    III. ```
    timeList = new Time[10];
    for (int k=0; k<10; k++) {
        timeList[k] = new Time(3, 20);
    }
    ```

    A.  I only

    B.  II only

    C.  III only

    D.  II and III only

    E.  I, II, and III

3.  Consider the following code segment:

    ```
    Time[] myTimes = new Time[N];
    for (int k=0; k<myTimes.length; k+=2) {
        System.out.println(myTimes[k].getHours());
    }
    ```

    Assume that `N` is a positive `int`. Which of the following is true?

    A. The code will not compile because the *for-loop* does not access all of the items in the array.

    B. The code will compile, but there will be a `NullPointerException` when it executes.

    C. The code will compile, but there will be an `IndexOutOfBoundsException` when it executes.

    D. The code will compile and execute without error; it will print the values of the hours in `myTimes[0]`, `myTimes[2]`, `myTimes[4]`, etc.

    E. The code will compile and execute without error; it will print the values of the hours in `myTimes[2]`, `myTimes[4]`, etc.

4. Consider the following code segment:

    ```
    Time[] myTimes = new Time[3];
    Time t = new Time(1, 15);
    myTimes[0] = t;
    myTimes[1] = t;
    ```
    ```

```
myTimes[2] = t;
myTimes[1].setMinutes(43);
for (int k=0; k<3; k++) {
   System.out.print(myTimes[k].getMinutes() + " ");
}
```

What happens when this code executes?

A. There is a `NullPointerException`.

B. There is an `IndexOutOfBoundsException`.

C. There is no exception; 15 15 15 is printed.

D. There is no exception; 15 43 15 is printed.

E. There is no exception; 43 43 43 is printed.

5. Assume that a class XX has been defined that includes a definition of the `equals` method. Consider the following declarations and incomplete method:

```
private XX[] A1;
private XX[] A2;

public boolean arraysEq() {
// precondition: A1.length > 0 and A2.length > 0 and
//               neither A1 nor A2 contains a null
// postcondition: returns true iff A1 and A2 contain
//               the same objects in the same order
   if (A1.length != A2.length) return false;
   .
   :   missing code
   .
}
```

Which of the following code segments could be used to replace *missing code* so that `arraysEq` works as specified by its pre- and postconditions?

A.
```
for (int k=0; k<A1.length; k++) {
    if (! A1[k].equals(A2[k])) return false;
}
return true;
```

B.
```
for (int k=0; k<A1.length; k++) {
    if (! A1[k] == A2[k]) return false;
}
return true;
```

C. `return (A1.equals(A2));`

D. `return (A1 == A2);`

E. `return true;`

Answers to Multiple-Choice Questions

1. E
2. C
3. B
4. E
5. A

3

Design and Analysis
of Data Structures
and Algorithms

3.1 Overview

Designing good data structures and algorithms is a very important part of programming. Data structure design includes defining the set of operations that will be available to the users of the data structure (the *interface*), as well as designing the way the data will actually be stored (the *implementation*). A data structure should be designed with the following goals in mind:

- The code that uses the data structure should be easy to understand.
- The data structure should be easy to modify (for example, by adding new operations).
- The code that implements the data structure should be reasonably efficient.

When designing data structures and algorithms, it is important to consider their space and time requirements (how much computer memory will be required to store the data, and how the running time of each operation is related to the amount of data). Computer Science A students should be able to compare the space and time requirements of different designs, and Computer Science AB students should be able to express those requirements using Big-O notation.

3.2 Big-O Notation (AB only)

Big-O notation is used to express how the space or time required by a particular implementation is related to the amount of data being processed. The table below gives some of the most common Big-O expressions, with explanations and examples.

Expression	Explanation	Example
$O(1)$	Constant. The amount of space or time is independent of the amount of data. If the amount of data doubles, the amount of space or time will stay the same.	An item can be added to the beginning of a linked list in constant time (independent of the number of items already in the list).
$O(\log N)$	Logarithmic. If the amount of data doubles, the amount of space or time will increase by one.	The worst-case time for binary search is logarithmic in the size of the array.

Expression	Explanation	Example
O(N)	Linear. If the amount of data doubles, the amount of space or time will also double.	The time needed to print all of the values stored in an array is linear in the size of the array.
$O(N^2)$	Quadratic. If the amount of data doubles, the amount of space or time will quadruple.	The amount of space needed to store a two-dimensional, square array is quadratic in the number of rows.
$O(2^N)$	Exponential. If the amount of data increases by one, the amount of space or time will double.	The number of moves required to solve the Towers of Hanoi puzzle is exponential in the number of disks used.

Practice Multiple-Choice Questions

Questions 1 and 2 refer to the following information:

A farmer has N barns. Each barn contains cows, sheep, or pigs. The farmer wants a data structure to record the following information for each barn:

- The day of the year the animals in the barn were purchased (a number in the range 1 to 365)
- The kind of animals in the barn
- The number of animals in the barn

The farmer plans to define a class named Barn to hold information about one barn, and to use an array of Barns of length N to store information about each of the N barns.

The farmer is considering two possible ways to define the fields of the Barn class:

Definition 1: Use three fields of type int, String, and int to hold the three pieces of information for each barn.

Definition 2: Use one field that is an int array of length 3. The three elements of the array will hold the three pieces of information for each barn.

1. Which of the following is the best reason for preferring Definition 1 over Definition 2?

   A. Definition 2 will not work, since the kind of animal in the barn cannot be represented using an integer.

   B. Less space will be used by Definition 1 than by Definition 2.

   C. Less time will be needed to determine the number of animals in a given barn using Definition 1 than using Definition 2.

   D. Using three named fields, rather than a single array, makes it clearer how the data are to be stored in each instance of a Barn.

   E. Since the information about all N barns is to be stored in an array, it is better not to use an array in the definition of the Barn class.

2. (AB only) Assume that Definition 1 has been chosen. Which of the following best characterizes the time needed to print all of the information about the kth barn?

    A. $O(1)$

    B. $O(k)$

    C. $O(\log N)$

    D. $O(k * N)$

    E. $O(N^2)$

Questions 3 and 4 refer to the following information:

A teacher needs a data structure to store information about student absences each day of the 80-day semester. There are N students in the class. Two different designs are being considered.

  Design 1: A one-dimensional array with 80 elements. Each element of the array is an `ArrayList` of N strings. Each string is either "absent" or "present."

  Design 2: A two-dimensional array with 80 rows and N columns. Each element of the array contains a boolean value (`true` or `false`).

Assume that more space is required to store a string than to store a boolean value.

3. Which of the following statements about the space requirements of the two designs is true?

    A. Design 1 will require more space than Design 2.

    B. Design 2 will require more space than Design 1.

    C. Designs 1 and 2 will require the same amount of space.

    D. Which design will require more space depends on how many students are actually absent during the semester.

    E. Which design will require more space depends on the value of N.

4. Assume that Design 2 is chosen and that the following operation is implemented as efficiently as possible.

    > Given a student number j (between 1 and N) and a day number k (between 1 and 80), look in the data structure to see whether student j was absent on day k.

    Which of the following statements is true?

    A. The time required to perform the operation is proportional to the size of the array.

    B. The time required to perform the operation is proportional to the number of students absent on the given day.

    C. The time required to perform the operation is proportional to the total number of students.

    D. The time required to perform the operation is proportional to the number of days in the semester.

    E. The time required to perform the operation is independent of the number of students absent on the given day, the total number of students, and the number of days in the semester.

5. (AB only) Consider the following code segment:

```
int N = some positive integer value;
for (int k=1; k<=N; k++) {
    for (int j=1; j<=k; j++) {
        System.out.print("*");
    }
}
```

Which of the following best characterizes the number of stars printed when this code segment executes?

A. $O(1)$

B. $O(\log N)$

C. $O(N)$

D. $O(N^2)$

E. $O(2^N)$

Answers to Multiple-Choice Questions

1. D
2. A
3. A
4. E
5. D

4

Lists

Computer Science A students should be familiar with the `ap.java.util.ArrayList` class; AB students should also be familiar with *linked lists* and the `ap.java.util.LinkedList` class, as well as the `ap.java.util.Iterator`, `ap.java.util.ListIterator`, and `ap.java.util.List` interfaces. Those topics are discussed in this chapter.

4.1   The ap.java.util.ArrayList Class

An `ArrayList` is a "built-in" class that gives you a way to store an ordered list of objects. Note that "ordered" doesn't mean that the objects are in *sorted* order, it just means that each object has a *position* in the list, starting with position zero. Both A and AB students should be familiar with the methods that allow you to add an object (at a particular position in the list), get the object at a particular position, remove an object from a particular position (returning the removed object), replace the object at a particular position with another one, and see how many objects are currently in the list:

Method	Explanation
`boolean add(Object x)`	Adds x to the end of this list and returns `true`.
`void add(int n, Object x)`	If index n is out of bounds (n < 0 or n > `size()`), throws an `IndexOutOfBoundsException`. Otherwise, moves the elements in positions n (counting from zero) to the end of this list over one place to the right to make room for new element x, then inserts x at position n in this list.
`Object get(int n)`	If index n is out of bounds (n < 0 or n >= `size()`), throws an `IndexOutOfBoundsException`. Otherwise, returns the element at position n (counting from zero) in this list.
`Object remove(int n)`	If index n is out of bounds (n < 0 or n >= `size()`), throws an `IndexOutOfBoundsException`. Otherwise, removes the element at position n (counting from zero) in this list, then shifts the remaining elements over one place to the left to fill in the gap. Returns the removed element.

Method	Explanation
`void set(int n, Object x)`	If index n is out of bounds (n < 0 or n >= size()), throws an `IndexOutOfBoundsException`. Otherwise, replaces the element at position n (counting from zero) in this list with x.
`int size()`	Returns the number of elements in this list.

AB students should also be familiar with the two methods that return iterators for the list (iterators are discussed in Section 4.4):

Method (AB only)	Explanation
`Iterator iterator()`	Returns an iterator for this list.
`ListIterator listIterator()`	Returns a list iterator for this list.

The main advantage of an `ArrayList` compared to a plain array is that, whereas the size of an array is fixed when it is created (e.g., `int[] A = new int[10]` creates an array of integers of size 10, and you cannot store more than 10 integers in that array), the size of an `ArrayList` can change: the size increases by one each time a new item is added (using either version of the `add` method), and the size decreases by one each time an item is removed (using the `remove` method).

One disadvantage of an `ArrayList` compared to a plain array is that, whereas you can create an array of any size, and then you can fill in any element in that array, a new `ArrayList` always has size zero, and you can never add an object at a position greater than the size. For example, the following code is fine:

```
Object[] obList = new obList[10];
obList[5] = "hello";
```

but this code will cause a runtime exception:

```
ArrayList obList = new ArrayList();
obList.add(5, "hello");          // error! can only add at position 0
```

Below is code that uses an `ArrayList` to create a list of the integers from 1 to 10, and to print them in order.

```
ArrayList list = new ArrayList();
for (int k=1; k<=10; k++) {
   list.add(new Integer(k));
}
for (int k=0; k<list.size(); k++) {
   Integer tmp = (Integer)list.get(k);
   System.out.println(tmp.intValue());
}
```

Note that the `ArrayList`'s get method returns an `Object`, not an `Integer`. Because of this, if the second `for`-loop in the code above were written as follows, without casting the result of get on the second line:

```
for (int k=0; k<list.size(); k++) {
    Integer tmp = list.get(k);
    System.out.println(tmp.intValue( ));
}
```

we would get a compile-time error because the type of the right-hand side of the assignment—
Object—is not compatible with the type of the left-hand side—Integer. However, since we know
that the result of calling get is in fact an Integer, we can use casting to change the type of the
right-hand side from Object to Integer, thus preventing the compile-time error.[1]

An ArrayList is implemented using an array. This means, for example, that adding an item to the
end of an ArrayList of length N is very efficient (does not depend on N), but adding or removing an
item at position k requires moving $N-k$ items (all of the items to the right of the one that was added
or removed), so the time required is proportional to $N-k$. Getting or replacing any item from an
ArrayList is also very efficient, because the get and set methods require using just one indexing
operation in the array used to implement the ArrayList (no items need to be moved).

To further demonstrate how to use an ArrayList, we'll use the Date and Person classes defined
in Chapter 2, but we'll change the siblings field to be an ArrayList instead of an array. This
requires changing method oldestSib, too. The new field declaration and the code for that method
are given below, with line numbers included for reference.

```
 1  private ArrayList siblings;

 2  public Person oldestSib() {
 3  // precondition: siblings.size() > 0 and
 4  //               siblings contains no nulls
 5  // postcondition: returns the oldest sibling
 6      int index = 0;
 7      Date sibDate = ((Person)siblings.get(index)).birthday;
 8      for (int k=1; k<siblings.size(); k++) {
 9          Person p = (Person)siblings.get(k);
10          Date d = p.birthday;
11          if (d.compareTo(sibDate) < 0) {
12              index = k;
13              sibDate = d;
14          }
15      }
16      return (Person)siblings.get(index);
17  }
```

---

1. In the new version of Java, JDK 5.0, it will be possible to say in the declaration of an ArrayList what
kind of objects it contains. For example, in the code above we could say ArrayList<Integer> list = new
ArrayList<Integer>;. In that case, it would not be necessary to cast the result of the call list.get(k).

Note that there are several differences between this version of the oldestSib method and the one that uses an array of people:

- On lines 7, 9, and 16, we use the ArrayList's get method to get a person from the list, while in the previous version we used indexing.

- On line 8 we use the ArrayList's size method to find out how many people are in the list, while in the previous version we used the array's length field.

- Each time we call the ArrayList's get method we need to use a cast to tell the compiler that the item we're getting from the ArrayList is a Person, not just an Object (which is the return type of the get method). If we left out those casts, we'd get compile-time errors, because on line 7 we're accessing the birthday of the person from the ArrayList (and an Object has no birthday field), on line 9 we're assigning the person from the ArrayList to a variable of type Person (not type Object), and on line 16 we're returning the item we get from the ArrayList, and the return type of this method is Person, not Object.

Now let's consider the code we'd need to create either an *array* or an ArrayList containing N people (where N is some positive integer). We'll assume that method createPerson creates and returns one Person, using information from a file.

Array Version	ArrayList Version
```Person[] personList;```	```ArrayList personList;```

```
Person[] personList;                 ArrayList personList;
personList = new Person[N];          personList = new ArrayList();
for (int k=0; k<N; k++) {            for (int k=0; k<N; k++) {
  Person p = createPerson();           Person p = createPerson();
  personList[k] = p;                   personList.add(p);
}                                    }
```

In the two versions, the first two lines (the declaration and initialization of variable personList) and the last lines (the code that adds a new person to the list) are different.

In the ArrayList version of the code given above, we used the add method that has just one Object parameter, and that adds that object to the end of the list. We could also have used the version that has two parameters, the index at which to add and the object to be added:

```
personList.add(k, p);
```

In either case, the ArrayList is filled in from left to right; i.e., the first person gets added at position 0, the second person at position 1, and so on. Let's think about what we'd have to do to fill in an array or an ArrayList from right to left. For an array, we could simply let our *for-loop* index run from N–1 down to 0 as follows:

```
Person[] personList = new Person[N];
for (int k=N-1; k>=0; k--) {
  Person p = createPerson();
  personList[k] = p;
}
```

However, if we tried to do something similar with an `ArrayList`, we'd get a runtime error:

```
ArrayList personList = new ArrayList();
for (int k=N-1; k>=0; k--) {
   Person p = createPerson();
   personList.add(k, p);  // causes a runtime error!
}
```

The problem is that you can't call an `ArrayList`'s add method with an index greater than its size; i.e., you can only add a new item at the end of the list or at a position in the list that already contains an item (in which case that item and all of the items to its right are moved over one place to make room for the new item).

To fill in an `ArrayList` from right to left, we need to add each new person to the *front* of the `ArrayList` (i.e., add it at position 0) like this:

```
ArrayList personList = new ArrayList();
for (int k=0; k<N; k++) {
   Person p = createPerson();
   personList.add(0, p);
}
```

Is it equally efficient to store the N people in an array or in an `ArrayList`? If we add them left-to-right, then the answer is yes, because putting a person anywhere in an array is a constant-time operation, and so is adding a person to the end of an `ArrayList`. However, if we add the people right-to-left, then while adding each of them to the array is still constant time (so creating the whole array of N people takes time proportional to N), each call to the `ArrayList`'s add method takes time proportional to the current size of the list, and so the total time to create the `ArrayList` is proportional to N^2.

Finally, let's rewrite the code that removes from a list all of the people with a given first name. Since we can use the `ArrayList`'s remove method (which changes the size of the list), this code is easier to write when variable `personList` is an `ArrayList` instead of an array. It is no longer necessary to count the number of people with the given first name, nor to create a new `ArrayList`; instead we simply call the `ArrayList`'s remove method each time we find a person with the given first name:

```
int k = 0;
while (k<personList.size()) {
   Person p = (Person)personList.get(k);
   String oneName = p.getFirstName();
   if (oneName.equals(firstName)) {
      personList.remove(k);
   } else {
      k++;
   }
}
```

Note that when the kth person in the list has the given first name we do *not* increment k. This is because calling the remove method causes a new person to move into the kth position, and we need to check whether that person needs to be removed from the list, too. For example, if the first names of the people in the list are:

```
Deborah    Sarah    Sarah    Mary    Sarah
```

and the given name is Sarah, then the first call to remove will happen when k is 1. That will change the list so that the first names of the remaining people are:

```
Deborah    Sarah    Mary    Sarah
```

and k will still be 1. If we increment k to 2, the next first name we'll check will be Mary; i.e., we'll fail to check the first name of the second Sarah in the (original) list. Clearly, that is not correct, so we should only increment k when the first name of the kth person does *not* match firstName.

Although this code is simpler than the code we wrote when personList was an array, there is a disadvantage in terms of efficiency. The array version of the code required going through the personList array twice: once to count the number of people with the given first name, and once to copy those people to the new array. Therefore, the time required to execute the array version of the code will be proportional to the size of the original array. The ArrayList version of the code only goes through the ArrayList once, but each time the remove method is called, all of the items to the right of the one being removed have to be moved over one position in the list. This means that, in the worst case, the time for the ArrayList version will be proportional to N^2, where N is the original size of the list.

Practice Multiple-Choice Questions

1. Assume that variable myList is an ArrayList containing at least two objects. Which of the following code segments moves the first object in the list to the end of the list?

    A. `myList.add(myList.get(0));`

    B. `myList.add(myList.remove(0));`

    C. `myList.add(0, myList.remove(0));`

    D. `myList.add(myList.size(), myList.get(0));`

    E. `myList.add(myList.remove(myList.size()-1));`

2. Consider the following code segment:

```
ArrayList L = new ArrayList();
for (int k=0; k<9; k++) {
   L.add(new Integer(k));
}
for (int k=0; k<5; k++) {
   Object tmp = L.get(k);
   L.set(k, L.get(8-k));
   L.set(8-k, tmp);
}
for (int k=0; k<9; k++) {
   System.out.print(L.get(k) + " ");
}
```

What is printed when this code executes?

A. 0 1 2 3 4 5 6 7 8

B. 8 7 6 5 4 3 2 1 0

C. 0 1 2 3 4 3 2 1 0

D. 0 0 0 0 0 0 0 0 0

E. 8 8 8 8 8 8 8 8 8

3. Assume that variable L is an `ArrayList` and that the method call `L.size()` returns 10. Which of the following method calls does *not* cause a runtime error?

A. `L.add(10, "hello")`

B. `L.add(20, "hello")`

C. `L.get(10)`

D. `L.set(10, "hello")`

E. `L.remove(10)`

4. Consider the following code segment:

```
ArrayList L = new ArrayList();
L.add("one");
L.add("two");
L.add("three");
System.out.println((Integer)L.get(L.size()-1));
```

Which of the following statements about this code is true?

A. The code will not compile because the last line casts the result of the call to get to an Integer, but the values stored in the list are of type String.

B. The code will compile but there will be a runtime error because the last line casts the result of the call to get to an Integer, but the values stored in the list are of type String.

C. The code will compile but there will be a runtime error because the last line calls get with a value that is too large.

D. The code will compile and run without error and will print 3.

E. The code will compile and run without error and will print three.

5. Assume that variable strList is an ArrayList of strings. Consider the following two code segments, both of which are intended to add an exclamation point to the end of each string in the list.

Segment 1	Segment 2
```for (int k=0; k<strList.size(); k++) { Str tmp = (String)strList.remove(k); strList.add(k, tmp + "!"); }```	```for (int k=0; k<strList.size(); k++) { String tmp = (String)strList.get(k); strList.set(k, tmp + "!"); }```

Which of the following statements about these two code segments is true?

A. Both will work as intended, and they will be equally efficient.

B. Both will work as intended; Segment 1 will be more efficient than Segment 2.

C. Both will work as intended; Segment 2 will be more efficient than Segment 1.

D. Only Segment 1 will work as intended.

E. Only Segment 2 will work as intended.

Answers to Multiple-Choice Questions

1. B
2. B
3. A
4. B
5. C

4.2 Linked Lists (AB only)

Arrays and `ArrayLists` are two examples of data structures that store sequences of values. Another way to store a sequence of values is to use a *linked list*.

A linked list can be either *singly linked* or *doubly linked*. It addition, the list can be either *circular* or *noncircular*. In all cases, a linked list is implemented using a sequence of nodes. Each node contains a value (e.g., in a list of `Integers`, each node would contain one `Integer`) as well as one or more pointers.

In a singly linked, noncircular list, each node contains one pointer, which points to the next node in the list. The last node's pointer is `null`. In a doubly linked, noncircular list, each node contains two pointers: one pointer points to the next node in the list, and the other pointer points to the previous node in the list. The "next" pointer of the last node in the list and the "previous" pointer of the first node in the list are both `null`.

In a circular, singly linked list, the "next" field of the last node points to the first node. In a circular, doubly linked list, the "next" field of the last node points to the first node, and the "previous" field of the first node points to the last node.

Below are pictures of four different linked lists that all represent the list of integers: 1, 2, 3, 4, 5.

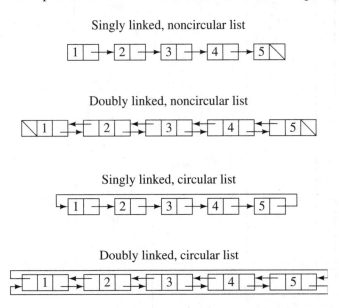

Singly linked, noncircular list

Doubly linked, noncircular list

Singly linked, circular list

Doubly linked, circular list

One way to implement linked lists is to define a `ListNode` class to be used for each node in the list. The AP CS exam assumes that AB students are familiar with the following definition of the `ListNode` class (this definition will be provided in the exam booklet).

```java
public class ListNode {
    public ListNode(Object initValue, ListNode initNext) {
        value = initValue;
        next = initNext;
    }
```

```
        public Object getValue() { return value; }
        public ListNode getNext() { return next; }
        public void setValue(Object theNewValue) { value = theNewValue; }
        public void setNext(ListNode theNewNext) { next = theNewNext; }

        private Object value;
        private ListNode next;
    }
```

Note that the value field of a ListNode has type Object. This allows the ListNode class to be used to implement lists of arbitrary objects; however, it means that lists cannot "directly" contain primitive values (e.g., int and double); those values must be "packaged up" using the wrapper classes Integer and Double.

Note also that the ListNode class can be used to implement only singly linked lists (either circular or noncircular), but not doubly linked lists. To implement a doubly linked list we would need to define a DblListNode class with a previous field as well as a next field (and with methods to get and set the value of the previous field).

Here is code that creates a singly linked list of ten integers and prints each value in the list in order:

```
ListNode L;          // the first node in the list
ListNode lastNode;   // the last node in the list

// create a list of the integers 1 to 10
L = new ListNode(new Integer(1), null);
lastNode = L;
for (int k=2; k<=10; k++) {
    ListNode newNode = new ListNode(new Integer(k), null);
    lastNode.setNext(newNode);
    lastNode = newNode;
}

// print the values in the list
ListNode tmp = L;
while (tmp != null) {
    System.out.print(tmp.getValue() + " ");
    tmp = tmp.getNext();
}
System.out.println();
```

Some common operations on linked lists are:

- Add a new node to the front of a list.
- Add a new node to the end of a list.
- Determine whether a list contains a particular value.
- Remove a given node n from a list.

- Given a value v and a node n in a list, add a new node containing v just after node n.

- Given a value v and a node n in a list, add a new node containing v just before node n.

AB students should be able to understand and implement code that performs these and similar operations. This includes understanding the complexity of the operations and understanding which versions of linked lists allow which operations to be implemented more efficiently. For example, given a (pointer to a) node n in a singly linked list that contains N values, removing node n requires $O(N)$ time in the worst case. This is because the list must be traversed, starting with the first node, to find the node that comes immediately before n (because that node's "next" pointer needs to be updated when node n is removed). On the other hand, the same operation can be done in $O(1)$ time in a doubly linked list (because node n includes a pointer to its predecessor).

To illustrate the difference between removing a node from a singly linked and a doubly linked list, two "remove" methods are given below. The first method removes node n from the singly linked list whose first node is pointed to by L. The second method removes node n from the *doubly* linked list whose first node is pointed to by L. For the second method, we assume that we have a DblListNode class as discussed above.

```java
public static ListNode removeSinglyLinked(ListNode n, ListNode L) {
// precondition: n points to a node in the list pointed to by L
// postcondition: returns a pointer to the first node of the list
//                with n removed
   if (L == n) {
      ListNode tmp = L.getNext();
      L.setNext(null);
      return tmp;
   } else {
      ListNode tmp = L;
      while (tmp.getNext() != n) tmp = tmp.getNext();

      // now tmp points to the node just before n
      tmp.setNext(n.getNext());
      n.setNext(null);
      return L;
   }
}

public static DblListNode removeDoublyLinked( DblListNode n,
                                        DblListNode L) {
// precondition: n points to a node in the list pointed to by L
// postcondition: returns a pointer to the first node of the list
//                with n removed
   if (L == n) {
      ListNode tmp = L.getNext();
      L.setNext(null);
      tmp.setPrevious(null);
      return tmp;
```

```
    } else {
        DblNode prev = n.getPrevious();
        DblNode nxt = n.getNext();
        prev.setNext(nxt);
        n.setPrevious(null);
        if (nxt != null) nxt.setPrevious(prev);
        n.setNext(null);
        return L;
    }
}
```

The reason the two methods given above need to return a value (rather than just modifying the list pointed to by L) is because node n may be the *first* node in the list; i.e., n may point to the same node as L. We can't just change parameter L to point to the second node in the list, because (as discussed in Chapter 2), L was passed by value. This means that changing L in the remove method has no effect on the argument passed to that method. Therefore, if n is the first node in the list, we set its next field to null and return a pointer to the second node in the list; if n is not the first node in the list, we modify the list by removing n, and return L.

If we have a list pointed to by a variable L, and we want to remove the node pointed to by variable n, we would use the following statement (for a singly linked list):

```
L = removeSinglyLinked(n, L);
```

Practice Multiple-Choice Questions

For questions 1–3, assume that the following method has been added to the standard ListNode class (line numbers are included for reference).

```
1  public void printList( ) {
2      System.out.print(value);
3      if (next != null) next.printList();
4  }
```

Assume that variable L is a ListNode and has been initialized as illustrated below:

1. What is output as the result of the call L.printList( )?

    A. HELLO

    B. OLLEH

    C. HLO

    D. OLH

    E. HHHHH

2. Which of the following best characterizes the running time of method `printList` when it is called for a list containing *N* nodes?

    A. O(1)
    B. O(log *N*)
    C. O(*N*)
    D. O(*N* log *N*)
    E. O(*N*²)

3. Assume that lines 2 and 3 of method `printList` are reversed. Now what is output as the result of the call `L.printList( )`?

    A. HELLO
    B. OLLEH
    C. HLO
    D. OLH
    E. HHHHH

4. Assume that a class `MyListNode` has been defined to represent the nodes of some kind of linked list of `Integers`. `MyListNode` has the same methods as the standard `ListNode` class, but you don't know whether it defines nodes for a singly linked or doubly linked list, or whether the list is circular or noncircular.

    Assume that the following is a method of the `MyListNode` class:

    ```
    public boolean listMember(Integer K) {
    // precondition: this node is the first node in a linked list
    // postcondition: returns true if K is in the list;
    //                false otherwise
       if (getValue().equals(K)) return true;
       MyListNode n = getNext();
       while (n != null) {
          if (n.getValue().equals(K)) return true;
          n = n.getNext();
       }
       return false;
    }
    ```

    For which of the following kinds of linked lists will method `listMember` work as specified by its pre- and postcondition?

    I.   singly linked, noncircular
    II. doubly linked, noncircular
    III. doubly linked, circular

    A. I only
    B. II only
    C. III only
    D. I and II
    E. II and III

5. Consider adding the following (incomplete) method to the ListNode class:

```
public boolean listEq(ListNode L) {
// precondition: this node is the first node of a
//               linked list and
//               L is the first node of another linked list
// postcondition: returns true if the two lists are the same
//               (they contain the same values in the same
//               order); otherwise returns false.
   if ((next == null && L.getNext() != null) ||
       (next != null && L.getNext() == null)) return false;
   if ( condition ) return false;
   if (next == null && L.getNext() == null) return true;
   return expression;
}
```

Which of the following can be used to replace *condition* and *expression* so that method listEq works as intended?

	condition	*expression*
A.	this != L	next.listEq(L.getNext())
B.	this != L	value.listEq(L.getValue())
C.	!value.equals(L.getValue())	listEq(L)
D.	!value.equals(L.getValue())	value.listEq(L.getValue())
E.	!value.equals(L.getValue())	next.listEq(L.getNext())

Answers to Multiple-Choice Questions

1. A
2. C
3. B
4. D
5. E

4.3   The ap.java.util.LinkedList Class (AB only)

As their names suggest, the ArrayList and LinkedList classes both implement the List interface (discussed in Section 4.4); the main difference is that the ArrayList class is implemented using an array, while the LinkedList class is implemented using a (doubly) linked list. Both classes provide methods to add, get, remove, and replace (set the values of) objects in a list, to see how many objects are currently in the list, and to get iterators for the list. The AP CS LinkedList class is somewhat more restricted than the ArrayList class, however, in that objects can only be added and removed from the front or the end of a list, rather than at an arbitrary position. Here are the LinkedList methods:

Method	Explanation
boolean add(Object x)	Adds x to the end of this list and returns *true*.
void addFirst(Object x)	Adds x at the beginning of this list.
void addLast(Object x)	Adds x to the end of this list.
Object get(int n)	If index n is out of bounds (n < 0 or n >= size()), throws an IndexOutOfBoundsException. Otherwise, returns the element at position n (counting from zero) in this list.
Object getFirst()	If this list is empty, throws a NoSuchElementException. Otherwise, returns the first element in this list.
Object getLast()	If this list is empty, throws a NoSuchElementException. Otherwise, returns the last element in this list.
Iterator iterator()	Returns an iterator for this list.
ListIterator listIterator()	Returns a list iterator for this list.
Object removeFirst()	If this list is empty, throws a NoSuchElementException. Otherwise, removes and returns the first element in this list.
Object removeLast()	If this list is empty, throws a NoSuchElementException. Otherwise, removes and returns the last element in this list.
Object set(int n, Object x)	If index n is out of bounds (n < 0 or n >= size()), throws an IndexOutOfBoundsException. Otherwise, replaces the element at position n (counting from zero) in this list with x, and returns the object that was previously at position n.
int size()	Returns the number of elements in this list.

Because a LinkedList is implemented using a doubly linked list rather than an array, the times required for some of its methods are quite different from the times required for the corresponding methods of the ArrayList class. Here is a table that summarizes the worst-case times required for the methods for a list of size N.

Method	ArrayList Time	LinkedList Time
add to the front	O(N)	O(1)
add to the end	O(1)	O(1)
get the kth object	O(1)	O(N)
remove from the front	O(N)	O(1)
remove from the end	O(1)	O(1)
set the kth object	O(1)	O(N)
size	O(1)	O(1)

The reason the get and set methods can be O(N) for a LinkedList is that it is necessary to follow a sequence of pointers (starting either at the front or at the end of the list) to get to a node in the middle of the list; the same operations can be done in constant time using indexing for an ArrayList.

Because some of the method times differ for an ArrayList and a LinkedList, you need to consider which operations will be used the most in order to decide whether to use an ArrayList or a LinkedList in a particular piece of code. For example, if you expect to add or remove many items at the front of the list, then a `LinkedList` is preferable to an `ArrayList`; however, if you expect to replace or get many items from places in the list other than the front or the end, then an `ArrayList` is preferable to a `LinkedList`.

Practice Multiple-Choice Questions

1. Consider the following code segment, which copies the objects from list L1 to list L2 in reverse order. Assume that L1 contains N objects, and that L2 is initially empty.

    ```
    for (int k=L1.size()-1; k>=0; k--) {
        L2.add( L1.get(k) );
    }
    ```

    Which of the following best characterizes the running times of this code when the lists are both `ArrayLists` and when they are both `LinkedLists`?

	L1 and L2 are `ArrayLists`	L1 and L2 are `LinkedLists`
A.	$O(1)$	$O(1)$
B.	$O(N)$	$O(N)$
C.	$O(N^2)$	$O(N)$
D.	$O(N)$	$O(N^2)$
E.	$O(N^2)$	$O(N^2)$

2. Consider the following code segment:

    ```
    LinkedList L = new LinkedList();
    int k = 0;
    while (k<11) {
        L.add(new Integer(k));
        k++;
    }
    k = 0;
    while (k<L.size()) {
        L.removeFirst();
        System.out.print( L.get(k) + " " );
        k++;
    }
    ```

    What happens when this code executes?

    A. A call to `removeFirst` causes a `NoSuchElementException`.

    B. A call to `get` causes an `IndexOutOfBoundsException`.

    C. There is no exception; 1 2 3 4 5 is printed.

    D. There is no exception; 6 7 8 9 10 is printed.

    E. There is no exception; 1 3 5 7 9 is printed.

3. Assume that a `Person` class has been defined, including a public `getName` method that returns a person's name (as a `String`). Also assume that variable `L` is a `LinkedList` that contains ten people.

    Which of the following statements correctly tests whether the name of the first person in the list has fewer than `N` characters?

    A. `((String)L.getFirst()).length() < N`
    B. `L.getFirst().getName.length() < N`
    C. `((Person)L.getFirst()).name.length() < N`
    D. `L.getFirst().(String)getName().length() < N`
    E. `((Person)L.getFirst()).getName().length() < N`

4. Under which of the following circumstances would it be most advantageous to use a `LinkedList` rather than an `ArrayList`?

    A. Items will frequently be added and removed from both the front and the end of the list.
    B. Items will frequently be added and removed from just the end of the list.
    C. Items will frequently be replaced at both the front and the end of the list.
    D. Items will frequently be replaced at just the end of the list.
    E. Items will frequently be replaced in the middle of the list.

5. Consider the following declaration and method:

    ```
    private LinkedList L;

    public void changeList() {
        int k = L.size();
        while (k > 0) {
            if (L.getFirst() == null) {
                L.removeFirst();
            } else {
                Object tmp = L.removeFirst();
                L.addLast(tmp);
            }
            k--;
        }
    }
    ```

    Assume that `L` represents the following list before the call `changeList(L)` is made:

    ```
    XX    null    YY    null    null    ZZ
    ```

    What list does `L` represent after the call?

    A. The empty list.
    B. The list XX YY ZZ.
    C. The list ZZ YY XX.
    D. The list XX YY null ZZ.
    E. The list ZZ XX YY null.

Answers to Multiple-Choice Questions

1. D
2. E
3. E
4. A
5. B

4.4   The ap.java.util.Iterator, ap.java.util.ListIterator, and ap.java.util.List Interfaces (AB only)

4.4.1   Iterators and ListIterators

When you use a data structure like an `ArrayList` or a `LinkedList` that represents a list of items, you often need a way to *iterate* through the list, that is, to access each of the items in turn. One way to do this is to use the `get` method. Given a list L, we can iterate through the items in the list as follows (whether L is an `ArrayList` or a `LinkedList`):

```
for (int k=0; k<L.size(); k++) {
    Object ob = L.get(k);
    .
    :    do something to ob here
    .
}
```

However, a more standard way to iterate through a list is to use an `Iterator`. This is especially important for a `LinkedList`, because the time to iterate through a `LinkedList` of size N using an iterator is $O(N)$, while the time to iterate through the list using get is $O(N^2)$; this is because an individual call to get that accesses an item toward the middle of the list is $O(N)$.

In addition to providing a way to iterate through a list of objects one at a time, you can use an `Iterator` to remove an object from the list after it has been visited during an iteration. Here are the `Iterator` methods:

Method	Explanation
`boolean hasNext()`	Returns `true` if the list has more elements; otherwise, returns `false`.
`Object next()`	Returns the next element in the list. Throws a `NoSuchElementException` if there are no elements in the list that have not already been visited on this iteration.
`void remove()`	Removes the last element returned by `next` from the list (throws an exception if there is no such element).

The way to think about an `Iterator` is that it is a finger that points to each item in the list in turn. When an `Iterator` is first created, it is pointing to the first item; the next method lets you get the item pointed to, also advancing the pointer to point to the next item, and the `hasNext` method lets you ask whether you've run out of items. For example, assume that we have the following list of words:

```
apple     pear     banana     strawberry
```

If we create an `Iterator` for the list, we can picture it as follows, pointing to the first item in the list:

```
apple     pear     banana     strawberry
  ↑
```

If we call the iterator's `next` method we'll get back the word `apple`, and the picture will change to:

```
apple     pear     banana     strawberry
           ↑
```

After two more calls to `next` (returning `pear` and `banana`) we'll have:

```
apple     pear     banana     strawberry
                                ↑
```

A call to `hasNext` now returns `true` (because there's still one more item we haven't accessed yet). A call to `next` returns `strawberry`, and our picture looks like this:

```
apple     pear     banana     strawberry
                                          ↑
```

The iterator has fallen off the end of the list. Now a call to `hasNext` returns `false`, and if we call `next`, we'll get a `NoSuchElementException`.

Either a *while-loop* or a *for-loop* can be used with an iterator to visit the items in a list. For example, assume that variable `L` is a list:

```
// version 1: use a while loop
Iterator it = L.iterator();
while (it.hasNext()) {
   Object ob = it.next());

   .
   :   do something to ob here
   .

}

// version 2: use a for loop
for (Iterator it = L.iterator(); it.hasNext();) {
   Object ob = it.next();

   .
   :   do something to ob here
   .

}
```

Note that the *update-expression* part of the for-loop is empty. That is because the call to it.next inside the loop not only returns the next value in the list but also "advances" the iterator.

In general, you should not modify a list by calling its add, remove, or set methods during an iteration. If you do, a subsequent call to one of the iterator's methods may throw an exception. To allow modification of a list during an iteration, the Iterator interface includes a remove method, which removes the last element returned by next from the list (or throws an exception if there is no such element).

Below is some code that illustrates using the remove method on a list of non-null Strings. The code finds all strings in the list that start with an "x" and removes those strings from the list.

```
for (Iterator it = L.iterator(); it.hasNext();) {
   String tmp = (String)it.next( );
   if (tmp.length() > 0) {
      tmp = tmp.substring(0,1);
      if (tmp.equals("x")) it.remove( );
  }
}
```

The ListIterator interface is an extension of the Iterator interface. In the AP CS Java subset, both lists and sets have Iterators, but only lists have ListIterators. To allow elements to be replaced or added to a list during an iteration, the ListIterator interface provides the following methods in addition to the methods provided by the Iterator interface:

Method	Explanation
void add(Object x)	Inserts x into the list immediately before the element that would be returned by next (if there is no such element, inserts x at the end of the list). This does not affect the value returned by a subsequent call to next.
void set(Object x)	Replaces the last element returned by next with x (throws an exception if there is no such element).

Below are two code segments that illustrate the use of the add and set methods, respectively. In both segments, variable L is a list of non-null strings. The first code segment looks for instances of the string "happy" in the list, and adds the string "birthday" after each of them. The second code segment replaces each instance of the string "happy" with the string "hilarious".

```
// Segment 1: add "birthday" after each instance of "happy" in L
for (ListIterator it = L.listIterator(); it.hasNext();) {
   String tmp = (String)it.next();
   if (tmp.equals("happy") {
      it.add("birthday");
   }
}

// Segment 2: replace each instance of "happy" in L with "hilarious"
for (ListIterator it = L.listIterator(); it.hasNext();) {
   String tmp = (String)it.next();
```

```
    if (tmp.equals("happy") {
        it.set("hilarious");
    }
}
```

4.4.2   The List Interface

Both the ap.java.util.ArrayList class and the ap.java.util.LinkedList class implement the ap.java.util.List interface. That interface includes the following methods:

Method	Explanation
void add(Object x)	Adds x to the end of this list.
Object get(int n)	If index n is out of bounds (n < 0 or n >= size()), throws an IndexOutOfBoundsException. Otherwise, returns the element at position n (counting from zero) in this list.
Iterator iterator())	Returns an iterator for this list.
ListIterator listIterator()	Returns a list iterator for this list.
Object set(int n, Object x)	If index n is out of bounds (n < 0 or n >= size()), throws an IndexOutOfBoundsException. Otherwise, replaces the element at position n (counting from zero) in this list with x and returns the object that was previously at position n.
int size()	Returns the number of elements in this list.

Note that the List interface provides fewer methods than either the ArrayList or the LinkedList class (there is only one add method that adds to the end of the list, and there is no remove method). However, it is possible to add items at positions other than the end of the list using the list's ListIterator, and to remove items using either its ListIterator or its Iterator.

If you want to implement an operation on lists that would use the same code whether that list is an ArrayList or a LinkedList, then it makes sense to define that operation using a method with a List parameter, instead of writing two copies, one with an ArrayList parameter and one with a LinkedList parameter. Examples of operations that you might want to use on either an ArrayList or a LinkedList include printing the list and searching for a particular object in the list (using sequential search). Below are methods that implement those two operations; both of them could be called with either an ArrayList or a LinkedList argument.

```
// Example 1: Print the items in a list
public static void printList(List L) {
// precondition: L is not null
    Iterator it = L.iterator();
    while (it.hasNext()) {
        System.out.println( it.next() );
    }
}
```

```
// Example 2: Search for an object in a list
public static boolean searchList(List L, Object ob) {
// precondition: neither L nor ob is null
// postcondition: returns true iff ob is in list L
   Iterator it = L.iterator();
   while (it.hasNext()) {
      if (ob.equals(it.next())) return true;
   }
   return false;
}
```

Practice Multiple-Choice Questions

1. Assume that variable L is a List containing 3 strings:

    ```
    "Mon"    "Tues"    "Wed"
    ```

    Consider the following code segment:

    ```
    Iterator it = L.iterator();
    for (int k=0; k<4; k++) {
       System.out.println( it.next() );
    }
    ```

    What happens when this code segment executes?

    A. An exception is thrown because of a call to it.next when there are no more items to be visited.
    B. No exception is thrown; the output is: Mon Tues Wed.
    C. No exception is thrown; the output is: Mon Tues Wed Wed.
    D. No exception is thrown; the output is: Mon Tues Wed Mon.
    E. No exception is thrown; the output is: Mon Tues Wed null.

2. Consider writing a method named largestVal whose header is given below.

    ```
    public static Integer largestVal( List L ) {
    // precondition: L contains non-null Integers
    // postcondition: returns the largest Integer in the list
    ```

    Two different ways to write the body of the method are being considered:
    Version 1: Use L's get method to iterate through the list.
    Version 2: Use L's iterator method to get an Iterator, and use that Iterator to iterate through the list.

    Assume that largestVal may be called with a list of size N that is either an ArrayList or a LinkedList. Which of the following statements about the two ways to write the method body is true?

A. The two versions will be O(N) whether parameter L is an `ArrayList` or a `LinkedList`.

B. The two versions will be O(N) if parameter L is an `ArrayList`, but only version 1 will be O(N) if parameter L is a `LinkedList`.

C. The two versions will be O(N) if parameter L is an `ArrayList`, but only version 2 will be O(N) if parameter L is a `LinkedList`.

D. The two versions will be O(N) if parameter L is a `LinkedList`, but only version 1 will be O(N) if parameter L is an `ArrayList`.

E. The two versions will be O(N) if parameter L is a `LinkedList`, but only version 2 will be O(N) if parameter L is an `ArrayList`.

3. Which of the following statements is *not* true?

A. Every `List` has both an `iterator` and a `listIterator` method.

B. An `Iterator` for an `ArrayList` will visit the objects in the list in the *same* order as the `ListIterator` for that `ArrayList`.

C. If a method has a parameter of type `Iterator`, the method can be called with an argument of type `ListIterator`.

D. If a method has a parameter of type `ListIterator`, the method can be called with an argument of type `Iterator`.

E. The `hasNext` method of an `Iterator` for a `LinkedList` of size 0 will always return `false`.

4. Consider the following data field and method:

```
private List L;

public boolean mystery() {
    Iterator it1 = L.iterator();
    Iterator it2 = L.iterator();
    if (it2.hasNext()) it2.next();
    while (it2.hasNext()) {
        if (it1.next().compareTo(it2.next()) > 0) return false;
    }
    return true;
}
```

Which of the following best describes the circumstances under which method `mystery` returns true?

A. When the objects in L are in sorted order.

B. When the objects in L are *not* in sorted order.

C. When L contains no duplicates.

D. When L *does* contain duplicates.

E. When L is the same forwards and backwards.

5. Which of the following statements will compile without error?

    A. `ArrayList L = new List();`

    B. `ArrayList L = new LinkedList();`

    C. `List L = new ArrayList();`

    D. `LinkedList L = new List();`

    E. `LinkedList L = new ArrayList();`

Answers to Multiple-Choice Questions

1. A
2. C
3. D
4. A
5. C

5
Sorting and Searching

5.1 Sorting

Both A and AB students should be familiar with a number of sorting algorithms. Students should understand that some algorithms are more efficient than others, and they should be able to reason about the efficiency of an algorithm, given a description of how it works.

This section is divided into two parts. The first part reviews two quadratic sorting algorithms: Selection Sort and Insertion Sort. The second part reviews two more efficient algorithms: Quick Sort and Merge Sort. In all cases, it is assumed that the values to be sorted are in an array.

5.1.1 Quadratic Sorting Algorithms

Selection Sort

Selection Sort works by finding the smallest element in the array and swapping it with the value in the first position, then finding the second smallest element and swapping it with the value in the second position, and so on. If there are N values to be sorted, Selection Sort will make N passes through the array of values. The first time, it will look at all N values; the second time, it will look at $N - 1$ values; the third time, it will look at $N - 2$ values; and so on. So the time required by Selection Sort is proportional to:

$$N + (N - 1) + (N - 2) + \cdots + 3 + 2 + 1$$

This is proportional to N^2. If the values in the array are already in sorted order, Selection Sort will still make the same passes through the array (although it will not do any swaps). Therefore, the time for Selection Sort is proportional to N^2 regardless of how close to sorted the values are initially.

Insertion Sort

Insertion Sort works by making one pass through the array of values; each time it considers an element, it goes *back* through the array to find the appropriate place for that element. In the worst case (when the array of values is initially in *reverse* sorted order), it will have to go all the way back to the beginning of the array every time it considers an element. In that case, for the first element it will look at 0 previous values; for the second element, it will look at 1 previous value; for the third element, it will look at 2 previous values; and so on. So the time required by Insertion Sort in this case is proportional to:

$$0 + 1 + 2 + \cdots + (N - 2) + (N - 1)$$

Again, this is proportional to N^2.

However, in the best case (when the array of values is already in sorted order), Insertion Sort will only look at one previous value each time it moves on to the next element. In this case, it will only require time proportional to N.

5.1.2   More Efficient Sorting Algorithms

Quick Sort

Quick Sort starts by partitioning the array around a "pivot" value, so that all of the values that are less than or equal to the pivot come first, then the pivot itself, then all of the values that are greater than the pivot. For example, assume that the array initially contains the following values:

    4   6   7   0   3   9   3   6

If 4 is chosen as the pivot value, then after partitioning, the array might look like this (with the pivot value shown in bold):

    3   3   0   **4**   7   9   6   6

After partitioning the array, Quick Sort makes two recursive calls: the first call sorts the portion of the array to the left of the pivot, and the second call sorts the portion of the array to the right of the pivot. The recursion ends when the portion of the array to be sorted has length zero or one.

The efficiency of Quick Sort depends on the choice of the pivot value. It is least efficient when the value chosen as the pivot is either the smallest or the largest value in the array. In that case, Quick Sort requires time proportional to N^2 (i.e., it is no more efficient than Selection Sort or Insertion Sort). However, if the number of values that are less than or equal to the pivot is about the same as the number of values greater than the pivot, then Quick Sort is much more efficient. AB students should realize that, in this case, Quick Sort takes $O(N \log N)$ time.

Merge Sort

Merge Sort works by recursively sorting the two halves of the given array into some auxiliary data structures (e.g., two other arrays, each half the size of the original array) and then merging the sorted values back into the original array. (As for Quick Sort, the recursion ends when there is just one value to be sorted.) For example, assume that the array initially contains the following eight values:

    4   6   7   0   3   9   3   6

The first recursive call would sort the left half of the array, producing the following sorted array (of size four):

    0   4   6   7

And the second recursive call would produce the following sorted array:

3   3   6   9

The two sorted arrays would be merged to produce the following final array:

0   3   3   4   6   6   7   9

AB students should recognize that Merge Sort requires $O(N \log N)$ time. A students should simply understand that Merge Sort is always more efficient than Selection Sort and usually more efficient than Insertion Sort (except when the array is already sorted or is close to being sorted). However, a disadvantage of Merge Sort is that it requires more space than the other sorting algorithms, because of the auxiliary data structures that it uses.

5.2   Searching

All AP Computer Science students should understand how to search for a given value in an array using sequential or binary search. In addition, AB students should understand searching using a hashtable and using a binary search tree. Sequential search and binary search are reviewed below; hashing and binary search trees are discussed in Chapter 6.

Sequential Search

A *sequential search* simply involves looking at each item in the array in turn until either the value being searched for is found or it can be determined that the value is not in the array. If the array is unsorted, then it is necessary to keep searching as long as the value is not found. However, if the array is sorted, it may be possible to quit searching without examining all of the elements in the array. If the array is sorted from low to high, the search can stop as soon as the current array value is greater than the value being searched for.

In the worst case, a sequential search will require looking at the whole array, so the time required to search an array of size N is proportional to N.

Binary Search

If the array is sorted, a *binary search* can be performed and is usually more efficient than a sequential search. A binary search first looks at the middle element, m. If m matches the value being searched for, the search is finished. Otherwise, if m is greater than the value being searched for, we know that if the value being searched for is in the array at all, it must be to the left of m in the array. A new binary search is done on the half of the array to the left of m. Similarly, if m is less than the value being searched for, we know that if the value being searched for is in the array at all, it must be to the right of m in the array. A new binary search is done on the half of the array to the right of m. If the value being searched for is not in the array, a new binary search will eventually be done on a portion of the array of size zero. At that point, the search will end (knowing that the value being searched for was not in the original array).

Binary search is proportional to the log (base 2) of the size of the array.[1] AB students should recognize that the worst-case time for binary search is $O(\log N)$.

Practice Multiple-Choice Questions

1. Consider searching for a given value in an array. Which of the following must be true in order to use binary search?

   I.   The values in the array must be integers.
   II. The values in the array must be in sorted order.
   III. The array must not contain any duplicate values.

   A. I only

   B. II only

   C. I and II only

   D. II and III only

   E. I, II, and III

2. Consider searching for a given value in a sorted array. Under which of the following circumstances will sequential search be *faster* than binary search?

   A. The value is not in the array.

   B. The value is in the first element of the array.

   C. The value is in the last element of the array.

   D. The value is in the middle element of the array.

   E. Sequential search will never be faster than binary search.

Questions 3 and 4 refer to the following code segment (line numbers are included for reference). Assume that variable A is an array of `ints` of length N.

```
1 for (int k=0; k<N; k++) {
2    for (int j=k+1; j<N; j++) {
3       if (A[j] < A[k]) {
4          swap(A, j, k);
5       }
6       System.out.println(k);
7    }
8 }
```

---

1. The log base 2 of N is the number of doublings it takes to get N, starting with 1. For example, the log of 2 is 1, because only one doubling is required: one times two equals two. The log of 8 is 3, because three doublings are required: one times two equals two, two times two equals four, and four times two equals eight.

3. Assume that `swap` correctly swaps the jth and k^{th} values in array `A`. Which of the following assertions is true every time line 6 is executed?

   A. The values in array `A` are sorted from low to high.
   B. The values in `A[k]` through `A[N]` are sorted from low to high.
   C. The values in `A[k]` through `A[N]` are sorted from high to low.
   D. The values in `A[0]` through `A[k]` are sorted from low to high.
   E. The values in `A[0]` through `A[k]` are sorted from high to low.

4. (AB only) Assume that `swap` takes constant time. Which of the following best characterizes the runtime of the entire code segment?

   A. O(1)
   B. O(log N)
   C. O(N)
   D. O(N log N)
   E. O(N^2)

5. (AB only) Consider searching for a given value in an unsorted array. Which of the following will be the most efficient?

   A. Use sequential search.
   B. Sort the array using *selection sort*, then use binary search.
   C. Sort the array using *merge sort*, then use binary search.
   D. Copy the values into an `ArrayList`, then use the list's iterator to look for the value.
   E. Copy the values into a `LinkedList`, then use the list's iterator to look for the value.

Answers to Multiple-Choice Questions

1. B
2. B
3. D
4. E
5. A

6

Hashtables, Trees, Sets, and Maps (AB only)

Computer Science AB students should be familiar with the concepts of hashtables, trees, sets, and maps. Hashtables and trees are both interesting data structures in their own right, and are used to implement the `ap.java.util.HashSet`, `ap.java.util.TreeSet`, `ap.java.util.HashMap`, and `ap.java.util.TreeMap` classes, which in turn implement the `ap.java.util.Set` and `ap.java.util.Map` interfaces.

6.1 Hashtables

A hashtable is a data structure that stores an unordered collection of objects. A hashtable can provide very efficient methods to add an object to the collection, determine whether a particular object is in the collection, and remove an object from the collection. The key to the efficiency of those operations is to store the objects in an array, taking advantage of the fact that indexing into an array is a constant-time operation. It is also reasonably efficient to iterate over all of the objects in a hashtable.

To decide which element of the array will hold a particular object, we use a *hash function:* a method that takes an object as its parameter and returns the array index where that object should be stored; that is, the returned value is an `int` in the range 0 to $k-1$, where k is the length of the array. Although the objects can be stored directly in the array, a better approach is to make each element of the array a linked list, and to store the objects as the list elements.

To insert an object into a hashtable, the hash function is applied to the object, returning an integer k, and then the object is added to the front of the list that is in the kth element of the array. Since an object can be added to the front of a linked list in constant time, the time for the insert operation is independent of the number of values already in the hashtable. If the hash function is O(1), then the time for the insert operation is also O(1).

To look up an object, that is, to determine whether that object is in the hashtable, the hash function is applied to the object, returning integer k, and then the list in the kth element of the array is searched. If the array is sufficiently large and if the hash function distributes the objects evenly, then no list will contain more than one object, and the look-up operation will be independent of the number of values in the hashtable. Given these assumptions, if the hash function is O(1), then the time for the look-up operation is also O(1). However, if the array is of a fixed, small size and/or the hash function does not distribute the objects evenly, then the time to look up an object in a hashtable that contains N values can be as bad as O(N).

Below is an example that illustrates using a hashtable to store names. In this example, the hashtable is an array of size 5 and each element of the hashtable is a linked list of names. The hash function first finds the middle letter of the name (if the name has an even number of letters, the hash function uses the letter to the left of the middle). It then computes the position of that letter in the alphabet (1 for a, 2 for b, and so on), and returns the position mod 5. For example, given the name `Ellen`, the hash function would return 2, because the middle letter of `Ellen` is `l`, which is the twelfth letter in the alphabet, and 12 mod 5 = 2.

The names to be inserted into the hashtable are:

    `Ellen`   `Ann`   `George`   `Fred`   `Susan`

The corresponding hash values (the integers returned by the hash function) are:

    2   4   0   3   4

After inserting the first four names, the hashtable looks like this:

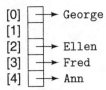

```
[0] |--+--> George
[1] |  |
[2] |--+--> Ellen
[3] |--+--> Fred
[4] |--+--> Ann
```

The name `Susan` hashes to the same place as the name `Ann`, so after inserting `Susan` the hashtable looks like this:

```
[0] |--+--> George
[1] |  |
[2] |--+--> Ellen
[3] |--+--> Fred
[4] |--+--> Susan ---> Ann
```

Removing an object from a hashtable is very similar to searching for it: apply the hash function to get the array index k, and then search for the object in the list in the kth element of the array, removing it if it is found. As for the look-up operation, if the array is sufficiently large, and the hash function is O(1) and distributes the objects evenly, then the remove operation will also be O(1).

A straightforward way to iterate over the objects in a hashtable is to go through the array, iterating through each linked list in turn. This requires time proportional to the size of the array plus the number of objects in the hashtable.

An important question when implementing a hashtable is how to define the hash function. There are two important issues to consider when choosing a hash function:

1. The computation of the hash function should be efficient, preferably O(1).

2. The hash function should spread the objects as evenly as possible (i.e., should map different keys to different locations in the hashtable).

Since the result of the hash function will be used as an array index, it must be no smaller than 0 and no larger than the array length minus one. Therefore, for an array of length N, it is reasonable for the hash function to convert the key to an integer k and to return k mod N. Often, the objects being inserted into a hashtable are integer values or strings. If they are integers, the hash function can simply return the value mod N; if they are strings, the hash function can convert some or all of the characters to positive integers, combine those values (e.g., by computing the sum or the product), and return the result mod N.

Deciding *which* characters to convert to integers is an interesting problem. Remember that we want our hash function to be efficient, and to map different keys to different locations in the hashtable. Unfortunately, there tends to be tension between those two goals; for example, a hash function that only uses the first and last characters in a key will be faster to compute than a hash function that uses all of the characters in the key, but it will also be more likely to map different keys to the same hashtable location. This is why it is not always easy to design an O(1) hash function or one that distributes keys evenly across the hashtable.

Although it is a good idea to understand the issues involved in choosing a hash function, if you program in Java, you can simply use the `hashCode` method that is supplied for every `Object` (including `Strings`). The method returns an integer j, and you can just use j mod N for your hash function. Of course, if the objects being inserted into the hashtable are members of a class that you define, you will need to implement the `hashCode` method for that class yourself. Every `hashCode` method should guarantee both of the following:

- If an `Object`'s `hashCode` method is called more than once during the execution of a Java program, the same integer value is returned every time.

- If two `Objects` are equal according to the `equals` method, then the same integer value is returned by the `hashCode` methods of the two `Objects`.

If you write a `hashCode` method for a class, you should make sure that it provides the two guarantees given above.

Practice Multiple-Choice Questions

1. Consider implementing a hash function called `hash` for a hashtable of size N. The values to be stored in the hashtable are strings. Which of the following should be true of the value returned by the call `hash("hello")`?

   A. The value should be in the range 0 to $N-1$.

   B. The value should be 5, since `"hello"` contains five characters.

   C. The value should be less than the value returned by the call `hash("yellow")`, since `"hello"` comes before `"yellow"` in alphabetical order.

   D. The value should be the same as the value returned by the call `hash("olleh")`, since `"hello"` and `"olleh"` contain the same characters.

   E. The value should be a prime number.

2. Suppose you decided to implement a hashtable using `ArrayLists` as the array elements instead of linked lists. Which of the following changes to the implementation should be made?

    A. When inserting a new value into the hashtable, the value should be added at the end of the list instead of at the front of the list.

    B. When looking up a value, the list should be searched from right to left instead of from left to right.

    C. When removing a value, the list should be searched from right to left instead of from left to right.

    D. The method that computes the hash function for an object should never return a value greater than the length of the longest `ArrayList`.

    E. The method that computes the hash function for an object should never return a value less than the length of the longest `ArrayList`.

3. Consider implementing a hashtable to store `Integers`. Assume that the hashtable is implemented using an array of size 5, and that each element of the array contains a linked list. Also assume that the hash function returns the `Integer`'s value mod 5. If the hashtable is initially empty, what does it look like after inserting the values 103 452 48 150 25?

A.
```
0 ┤├─► 25
1 ┤├─► 48
2 ┤├─► 103
3 ┤├─► 150
4 ┤├─► 452
```

D.
```
0 ┤├─► 103 ──► 150
1 ┤├─► 25
2 │  │
3 │  │
4 ┤├─► 48 ──► 452
```

B.
```
0 ┤├─► 103
1 ┤├─► 452
2 ┤├─► 48
3 ┤├─► 150
4 ┤├─► 25
```

E.
```
0 ┤├─► 25 ──► 48
1 ┤├─► 103 ──► 150 ──► 452
2 │  │
3 │  │
4 │  │
```

C.
```
0 ┤├─► 25 ──► 150
1 │  │
2 ┤├─► 452
3 ┤├─► 48 ──► 103
4 │  │
```

Questions 4 and 5 refer to the following information.

Three different hash functions are being considered for a hashtable of size N that will be used to store names:

Hash Function 1: Compute the position in the alphabet of the first letter in the name (1 for a, 2 for b, etc.) and return that position mod N.

Hash Function 2: For each letter in the name, compute the position in the alphabet of that letter (1 for a, 2 for b, etc.) and return the sum of those positions mod N.

Hash Function 3: For each letter in the name, compute the position in the alphabet of that letter (1 for a, 2 for b, etc.) and return the product of those positions mod N.

4.   Which of the following best describes the running times of the three hash functions?

   A. All three hash functions have $O(1)$ running time.

   B. All three hash functions have $O(N)$ running time.

   C. All three hash functions have running time proportional to the length of the name whose hash function is being computed.

   D. Hash Function 1 has $O(1)$ running time, and the other two have $O(N)$ running time.

   E. Hash Function 1 has $O(1)$ running time, and the other two have running times proportional to the length of the name whose hash function is being computed.

5.   Which of the following statements about Hash Function 1 is (are) true?

   I.   It will not distribute the names across the hashtable well if a lot of the names start with the same letter.
   II.   It will not distribute the names across the hashtable well if a lot of the names end with the same letter.
   III. It will not distribute the names across the hashtable well if N is a very large number.

   A. I only.
   B. I and II only.
   C. I and III only.
   D. II and III only.
   E. I, II, and III.

Answers to Multiple-Choice Questions

1. A
2. A
3. C
4. E
5. C

6.2   Trees

Trees are an important abstract data type with many applications in computer science. AB students should be familiar with *binary trees* and with a special kind of binary tree called a *binary search tree.* AB students should also be familiar with *preorder, inorder,* and *postorder* traversals of binary trees.

A tree is a collection of nodes and edges. Every nonempty tree includes a special node called the *root,* which has no parent (no incoming edges); every node other than the root has exactly one parent. Every nonempty tree also has one or more *leaves:* nodes with no children (no outgoing edges). A binary tree is a tree in which no node has more than two children. The *height* of an empty tree is 0; the height of a nonempty tree is the number of nodes in the longest path from the root to a leaf. For example:

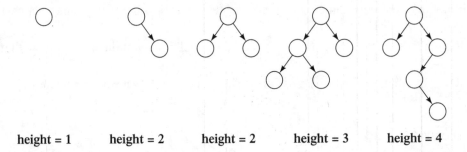

height = 1   height = 2   height = 2   height = 3   height = 4

Usually, each node of a tree contains a value (in addition to containing pointers to its children). Binary trees in which the values stored at the nodes are objects can be implemented as follows (this class definition will be provided in the AP CS exam booklet):

```
public class TreeNode {
    public TreeNode(Object initValue,
                    TreeNode initLeft, TreeNode initRight) {
        value = initValue;
        left = initLeft;
        right = initRight;
    }
    public Object getValue() { return value; }
    public TreeNode getLeft() { return left; }
    public TreeNode getRight() { return right; }
```

```
       public void setValue(Object theNewValue) { value = theNewValue; }
       public void setLeft(TreeNode theNewLeft) { left = theNewLeft; }
       public void setRight(TreeNode theNewRight) { right = theNewRight; }

       private Object value;
       private TreeNode left;
       private TreeNode right;
   }
```

Preorder, inorder, and postorder traversals of a binary tree all involve visiting all of the nodes of the tree. The difference is the order in which the nodes are visited:

Preorder	Inorder	Postorder
visit the root;	visit the left subtree in inorder;	visit the left subtree in postorder;
visit the left subtree in preorder;	visit the root;	visit the right subtree in postorder;
visit the right subtree in preorder.	visit the right subtree in inorder.	visit the root.

Here is an example of a binary tree of characters and the sequences of characters that would be produced by each of the three traversals if visiting a node means printing its value:

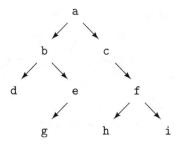

Preorder traversal:	a b d e g c f h i
Inorder traversal:	d b g e a c h f i
Postorder traversal:	d g e b h i f c a

If we decide to add code to the TreeNode class for a preorder traversal (where visiting a node means printing its value followed by a space), this is the method we'd add:

```
public void doPreorder() {
    System.out.print(value + " ");
    if (left != null) left.doPreorder();
    if (right != null) right.doPreorder();
}
```

The code for the other traversals (inorder and postorder) would be similar, except that for the inorder traversal the call to System.out.print would go between the two recursive calls, and for the posorder traversal the call to System.out.print would go after those two calls.

Some common operations on binary trees are:

- Find the largest (or smallest) value in the tree.
- Count the number of nodes, leaves, or nonleaves in the tree.
- Determine the height of the tree.
- Determine whether the tree is a binary *search* tree.
- Compute the sum of the values stored in the tree.

AB students should be able to understand and implement code that performs these and similar operations, and they should understand the complexity of the operations. Usually, the best way to implement operations that involve visiting all of the nodes in a binary tree is to use recursion. If the operation involves computing a value (like the number of nodes, leaves, or non-leaves in the tree), a recursive call to the left child's method would be used to get the value computed for the left subtree, then a recursive call to the right child's method would be used to get the value computed for the right subtree, then those two values would be combined to compute the final value.

For example, below is a method with one `TreeNode` parameter n that computes and returns the sum of the `Integer` values stored in the binary tree rooted at n.

```
public static int nodeSum( TreeNode n ) {
// precondition: the nodes in the tree rooted at n contain Integer values
    if (n == null) return 0;
    int val = ((Integer)n.getValue()).intValue();
    return nodeSum(n.getLeft()) + nodeSum(n.getRight()) + val;
}
```

Note that the method given above is *not* part of the `TreeNode` class. We could also have written it as a member of the `TreeNode` class as follows:

```
public int nodeSum( ) {
// precondition: the nodes in the tree rooted at this node contain
//               Integer values
    int leftVal, rightVal;
    if (left == null) leftVal =  0;
    else leftVal =  left.nodeSum();
    if (right == null) rightVal =  0;
    else rightVal =  right.nodeSum();
    return leftVal + rightVal + ((Integer)value).intValue();
}
```

Given a non-null `TreeNode` named n that is the root of a binary tree that stores `Integer` values, and the two methods defined above, we could print the sum of those values using either of the following statements:

```
System.out.println( nodeSum(n) );


System.out.println( n.nodeSum() );
```

The first statement calls the method that is *not* part of the `TreeNode` class, and the second statement calls the method that *is* part of that class.

A *binary search tree* is a special kind of binary tree with the following properties:

- The values stored in the tree are of type `Comparable`; that is, it is possible to determine whether one value is less than, equal to, or greater than another value.
- For all nodes *n*, all of the values in *n*'s left subtree are less than or equal to the value at node *n*.
- For all nodes *n*, all of the values in *n*'s right subtree are greater than the value at node *n*.

(It is sometimes useful to consider only binary search trees that contain no duplicate values; in that case, all of the values in *n*'s left subtree are strictly less than the value at node *n*.) Some examples of binary trees that are and are not binary search trees are shown below.

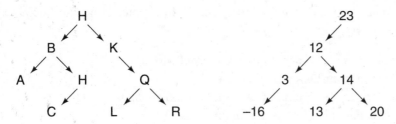

These two trees are binary search trees.

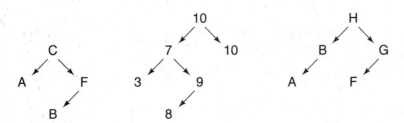

These three trees are not binary search trees; can you find the mistakes?

An advantage of using a binary search tree to store values is that inserting or deleting a value, as well as searching for a value, can be implemented quite efficiently. The average time for each of the operations is O(log N), where N is the number of values in the tree. In the worst case, however, the time for each of the operations is O(N). This happens when the height of the tree is O(N) rather than O(log N); that is, when the tree is tall and skinny instead of short and fat.

It is possible to implement trees like binary search trees that are kept *balanced*; that is, the length of the longest path from the root to a leaf is always O(log N), where N is the number of nodes in the tree. For those trees (which are used to implement the `TreeSet` and `TreeMap` classes), the insert, delete, and look-up operations are always O(log N).

Searching for a value v in a binary search tree is similar to performing a binary search in a sorted array. At each step, there is a current subtree to be considered. If the subtree is empty, the search fails. Otherwise, the value d in the root node of the current subtree is examined, and one of three actions is taken:

1. If $d == v$, the search succeeds.
2. If $d > v$, the search continues in the left subtree.
3. If $d < v$, the search continues in the right subtree.

Similarly, in a binary search, at each step there is a current part of the array to be considered. If the current part of the array is empty, the binary search fails. Otherwise, the middle value d in the current part of the array is considered, and one of three actions is taken:

1. If $d == v$, the search succeeds.
2. If $d > v$, the search continues in the left half of the current part of the array.
3. If $d < v$, the search continues in the right half of the current part of the array.

Below is a method that searches for value v in the binary search tree rooted at node n (the method is not part of the TreeNode class).

```
public static boolean search( Comparable v, TreeNode n ) {
// precondition: v is not null,
//                and n is the root of a binary search tree
// postcondition: returns true if v is in the tree;
//                otherwise returns false
   if (n == null) return false;
   int comp = v.compareTo(n.getValue());
   if (comp < 0) return search(v, n.getLeft());
   if (comp > 0) return search(v, n.getRight());
   return true;
}
```

New values are inserted into a binary search tree in new leaf nodes. The insert method finds the node that will be the parent of the new leaf using code similar to the code that searches for a value: it starts at the root of the tree and works its way down, going left or right depending on how the new value compares to the value at the current node. Here is the insert code.

```
public static void insert(Comparable v, Treenode n) {
// precondition: n is not null
// postcondition: v has been inserted into the correct place
//                in the tree rooted at n
   int comp = v.compareTo(n.getValue());
   if (comp <= 0) {
      if (n.getLeft() == null) {
         n.setLeft(new TreeNode(v, null, null));
      } else {
         insert(v, n.getLeft());
      }
   } else {
```

```
        if (n.getRight() == null) {
            n.setRight(new TreeNode(v, null, null);
        } else {
            insert(v, n.getRight());
        }
    }
}
```

Note that this code allows duplicate values to be inserted in the tree: if value v is the same as the value in node n, variable comp will be zero and v will be inserted into the left subtree of node n.

Here are pictures illustrating how the insert method works.

We'll start with this tree, and we'll insert the value 13.

```
        23
       /
      12
     / \
    3   14
```

We start by comparing 13 with the value at the root.

```
       [23]
       /
      12
     / \
    3   14
```

13 is less than 23, so we'll insert it into the left subtree.

```
        23
       /
     [12]
     / \
    3   14
```

13 is greater than 12, so we'll insert it into the right subtree.

```
        23
       /
      12
     / \
    3  [14]
```

13 is less than 14, and 14 has no left child, so we'll add 13 in a new left leaf node here.

The final tree.

```
        23
       /
      12
     / \
    3   14
       /
      13
```

Practice Multiple-Choice Questions

1. Assume that the following method has been added to the standard `TreeNode` class.

    ```java
    public int treeCount( ) {
        if (left == null && right == null) return 1;
        if (left == null) return right.treeCount();
        if (right == null) return left.treeCount();
        return(left.treeCount( ) + right.treeCount( ));
    }
    ```

    Which of the following best describes what method `treeCount` does?

    A. Always returns 0.
    B. Always returns 1.
    C. Returns the number of nodes in the tree.
    D. Returns the number of leaf nodes in the tree.
    E. Returns the number of nonleaf nodes in the tree.

2. Consider adding a method that returns the smallest value in a binary search tree to the `TreeNode` class. An incomplete version of the method is given below.

    ```java
    public Object smallest( ) {
    // precondition: this node is the root of a binary search tree
        if ( condition ) return(value);
        else return( expression );
    }
    ```

    Which of the following replacements for *condition* and *expression* correctly complete this method?

	condition	expression
A.	`left != null`	0
B.	`left == null`	`left.smallest()`
C.	`right == null`	`left.smallest()`
D.	`(left == null) && (right == null)`	`left.smallest()`
E.	`(left == null) && (right == null)`	`right.smallest()`

Questions 3 and 4 concern the tree shown below.

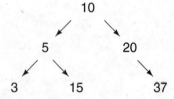

3. Recall that the height of a nonempty tree is the number of nodes in the longest path from the root to a leaf. Which of the following statements about this tree is (are) true?

    I.   It is a binary tree.
    II. It is a binary search tree.
    III. Its height is 3.

    A. I only

    B. III only

    C. I and II only

    D. I and III only

    E. I, II, and III

4. Which of the following corresponds to an inorder traversal of this tree?

    A. 3   5 15 10 20 37
    B. 10   5 20   3 15 37
    C. 3   5 10 15 20 37
    D. 10   5   3 15 20 37
    E. 3 15   5 37 20 10

5. Consider the following binary search tree:

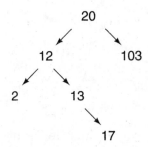

    Which of the following could be the order in which the values were inserted into this tree?

    A.   2 12   13 17 20 103
    B.   20 12 103 17 13   2
    C.   20 12 103 13   2   17
    D. 103 20   17 13 12   2
    E. 103 17   2 13 12   20

Answers to Multiple-Choice Questions

    1. D
    2. B
    3. D
    4. A
    5. C

6.3   Sets and Maps

6.3.1   Sets

A *set* is a collection of objects with no duplicates, and in no particular order. In the AP CS Java subset, the Set interface includes methods to add objects to a set, to see if a particular object is in a set, to iterate through a set, to remove a particular object from a set, and to find out how many objects are currently in a set:

Method	Explanation
boolean add(Object x)	Adds x to this set if it is not already there. Returns true if x was not already in this set; otherwise, returns false.
boolean contains(Object x)	Returns true if this set contains x; otherwise, returns false.
Iterator iterator()	Returns an iterator for this set.
boolean remove(Object x)	Removes x from this set if it is there. Returns true if x was in this set; otherwise, returns false.
int size()	Returns the number of objects in this set.

Sets and lists are somewhat similar in that both can be used to store collections of objects, but they have some important differences; the most important differences are as follows:

- A list can contain duplicates, but a set cannot.
- A list is an *ordered* collection, but the items in a set are *unordered*.

The fact that a set cannot contain duplicates means that the add method may or may not actually increase the size of the set: an attempt to add an object x that is already in the set will not change the set and will return false (x is considered to be in the set if there is some object ob in the set such that ob.equals(x)).

The fact that a list is an ordered collection means that we can talk about the first item in the list, the second item, and so on. This is why the add, get, set, and remove methods for lists include versions that have an index parameter (where to add the new item, or which item in the list to get/set/remove). Also, list iterators visit items in order (first the first item, then the second, and so on). Since a set is an unordered collection, when we add an item to a set it just becomes a member of that set in no particular place within the set, and we cannot ask to remove the kth item, we can only ask to remove a particular item if it is in the set. Also, unless we know how the set is implemented, we cannot predict the order in which a set's iterator will visit the objects in the set; it is guaranteed to visit all of them, but in no particular order.

Deciding whether to store a collection of objects in a list or a set depends on whether ordering is important, whether you want to allow duplicates in the collection, and what operations will be performed most frequently. As we'll see below, the different ways to implement a set lead to different running times for the set operations and for the corresponding operations on lists.

To illustrate the use of some of the Set methods, let's write a method that determines whether every object in one set is also in another set (that is, whether the first set is a *subset* of the second set). The data field declarations and the method are given on the next page:

```
private Set S1, S2;

public boolean isSubset() {
// precondition: neither S1 nor S2 is null
// postcondition: returns true iff S1 is a subset of S2
    if (S1.size() > S2.size()) return false;
    Iterator it = S1.iterator();
    while (it.hasNext()) {
       if (! S2.contains(it.next())) return false;
    }
    return true;
}
```

6.3.2 Maps

A *map* is an unordered collection of unique keys (that is, there are no duplicates), each of which has an associated object. In the AP CS Java subset, the Map interface includes methods to determine whether a particular key is in the collection, to get the object associated with a particular key, to get a set containing all of the keys in the collection, to add a new key and its associated object to the collection or to replace the object associated with a key, to remove a key and its associated object from the collection, and to find out how many keys (and their objects) are currently in the collection.

Method	Explanation
boolean containsKey(Object key)	Returns true if this map contains key; otherwise, returns false.
Object get(Object key)	Returns the value associated with key in this map. Returns null if this map does not contain key.
Set keySet()	Returns a set view of the keys contained in this map.
Object put(Object key, Object val)	If this map already contains value val associated with key, then does nothing and returns null. Otherwise, if this map already contains a value v associated with key, then replaces it with val and returns v. Otherwise, adds val to the map associated with key and returns null.
Object remove(Object key)	Removes the mapping for key from this map if it is there, and returns the value previously associated with key (returns null if key was not in the map).
int size()	Returns the number of key-value mappings in this map.

You should use a map when you have a collection of unique keys with associated objects and accessing the objects based on the values of their keys is a common operation. For example, a university might want to keep track of information about all of its students (the student's name, year of enrollment, classes taken, grades received, etc.). If each student has a unique ID number, we could define a Student class to store the student information, and we could use a map in which the keys are ID numbers and the associated objects are Students. Although you could also include the ID number in the Student class and then store the collection of students in a list or a set, the advantage of a map is that its get method provides an efficient way to get an object based on its key—if you used a list or a set, then to look up the information for a student with a particular ID, you'd have to search through the collection to find the student with that ID.

One (small) disadvantage of a map (compared to a list or a set) is that maps do not have iterators. However, we can use the keySet method to get the set of keys stored in the collection, and then we can use the set's iterator to visit each key. If we want the keys' associated objects, we can use the map's get method.

To illustrate some of the map methods, we'll assume that we have a Student class with the following methods:

String getName(): returns this student's name

double getGPA(): returns this student's grade-point average

void addGrade(int grade): adds the given grade to this student's list of grades (updating the student's grade-point average)

We'll also assume that we have a University class with two Map fields, both of which have ID numbers (Strings) as their keys and Students as the associated objects. The first map is for Honors students, and the second map is for all other students. Honors students are those students whose grade-point averages are 3.5 or higher. Here are the two field declarations:

```
private Map honorsStudents;  // maps IDs (Strings) to Students
private Map otherStudents;   // maps IDs (Strings) to Students
```

We'll write two methods for the University class. The first method adds a new grade to one student's list of grades and uses the new GPA to make sure the student is in the correct list (the Honors list or the non-Honors list):

```
public void addGrade( String oneId, int grade ) {
    // get the student; keep track of whether it is an Honors student
    boolean wasHonors = true;
    Student oneStudent = (Student)honorsStudents.get(oneId);
    if (oneStudent == null) {
        wasHonors = false;
        oneStudent = (Student)otherStudents.get(oneId);
    }
    oneStudent.addGrade(grade);

    // if the student's Honors status has changed, switch lists
    double newGpa = oneStudent.getGPA();
    if (wasHonors) {
        if (newGpa < 3.5) {
            honorsStudents.remove(oneId);
            otherStudents.put(oneId, oneStudent);
        }
```

```
    } else {
        if (newGpa >= 3.5) {
            otherStudents.remove(oneId);
            honorsStudents.put(oneId, oneStudent);
        }
    }
}
```

The second method prints the names and GPAs of all Honors students:

```
public void printHonors() {
    // get a set containing the ID numbers of all Honors students
    Set honorsStudentIDs = honorsStudents.keySet();

    // iterate through the set; for each ID, get the student and
    // print the student's name and GPA
    Iterator it = honorsStudentIDs.iterator();
    while (it.hasNext()) {
        String oneId = (String)it.next();
        Student oneStudent = (Student)honorsStudents.get(oneId);
        System.out.println(oneStudent.getName() + ": " +
                            oneStudent.getGPA());
    }
}
```

Sometimes the objects stored in a map are themselves collections (e.g., lists, sets, or maps). For example, assume that we have a Recipe class. We could define a map whose keys are the names of ingredients (e.g., "chocolate", "cheese", "eggs", "carrots"), and whose associated objects are sets of the recipes that include those ingredients (so, for example, "chocolate" would be mapped to recipes for all of the desserts that use chocolate).

Below is a declaration for the map, and a method that uses the map to determine whether there is any recipe that contains both of two given ingredients.

```
private Map ingredientMap;

public boolean hasBothIngredients( String ing1, String ing2 ) {
    // get the sets of recipes for each of the two ingredients
    // if either has no recipes, return false
    Set S1 = (Set)ingredientMap.get(ing1);
    Set S2 = (Set)ingredientMap.get(ing2);
    if (S1==null || S1.size() == 0 || S2==null || S2.size() == 0) {
        return false;
    }
```

```
// for each recipe that uses ingredient 1, see if the same
// recipe is in ingredient 2's set of recipes
Iterator it = S1.iterator();
while (it.hasNext()) {
    if (S2.contains(it.next())) return true;
}
return false;
}
```

6.3.3   The ap.java.util.HashSet, ap.java.util.TreeSet, ap.java.util.HashMap, and ap.java.util.TreeMap classes

Now that we understand sets and maps, as well as hashtables and search trees, we can put everything together to consider the `ap.java.util` classes that use hashtables and search trees to implement sets and maps.

Our discussions of hashtables and trees assumed that individual objects were being stored. That is fine for implementing sets, but doesn't work for implementing maps, which involve keys and associated objects. Here's one way to use a hashtable to implement a map:

- Apply the hash function to the key (not the associated object) to find out where in the array to store the key and the object.

- Have *two* lists in every array element; a list of keys and a list of their associated objects.

- To insert key *k* and object *ob* into the array, add *k* to the front of the first list, and add *ob* to the front of the second list.

- To determine whether key *k* is in the hashtable (that is, to implement the `containsKey` method), search for *k* in the first list.

- To get the object associated with a given key, *k*, search for *k* in the first list, and keep track of its position in that list; if it is found, iterate through the second list to the corresponding position, and return the object at that position.

Using a search tree to implement a map is more straightforward: just change the `TreeNode` class to have two `Object` fields, one for the key and one for the associated object. Of course, since a search tree can only be implemented if the values stored there are `Comparable`, a map can only be implemented using a search tree if the keys are `Comparable` (and a set can only be implemented using a search tree if the objects in the set are `Comparable`).

The following two tables give the running times for the set and map operations (for a set or map containing *N* objects), assuming they are implemented using hashtables, and assuming they are implemented using balanced trees. Note that the time for the `iterator` method is the time to *get* an iterator for a set, not the time to iterate over the set. Iterating over a set implemented using a hashtable takes time proportional to the size of the set plus the length of the hashtable's array (and the objects are visited in no particular order); iterating over a set implemented using a tree takes time proportional to the size of the set (and the objects are visited in sorted order).

Set Operations

Method	Time Using a HashSet	Time Using a TreeSet
add	O(1)	O(log N)
contains	O(1)	O(log N)
iterator	O(1)	O(1)
remove	O(1)	O(log N)
size	O(1)	O(1)

Map Operations

Method	Time Using a HashMap	Time Using a TreeMap
containsKey	O(1)	O(log N)
get	O(1)	O(log N)
keySet	O(N + array length)	O(N)
put	O(1)	O(log N)
size	O(1)	O(1)

Looking at these tables, you might think that it's always better to use a `HashSet` than a `TreeSet`, and always better to use a `HashMap` than a `TreeMap`. Remember, however, that the running times given above for the hashtable implementations make some important assumptions:

- The running time of the hash function is O(1).

- The length of the hashtable's array is at least N, where N is the number of objects in the hashtable.

- The hash function distributes the objects evenly, so that the lengths of the lists in the array are independent of N.

As discussed above, it is not always easy to guarantee that these assumptions hold, so in the *worst* case, the hashtable operations (and thus the `HashSet` and `HashMap` operations) are O(N) instead of O(1).

Practice Multiple-Choice Questions

1.   Assume that variable S is a Set. Consider the following code segment:

```
for (int k=0; k<10; k++) {
   S.add(new Integer(k));
}
for (int k=1; k<10; k+=2) {
   S.add(new Integer(k));
}
```

If S.size() returns 0 before the code segment executes, what does it return after the code segment executes?

A.   0

B.   5

C.   10

D.   15

E.   20

2.   Suppose that we have a set of strings and we don't know how it is implemented. If we use the set's iterator to print the strings in the set, in what order will they be printed?

A.   The strings will be printed in alphabetical order.

B.   The strings will be printed in *reverse* alphabetical order.

C.   The strings will be printed in the order in which they were added to the set.

D.   The strings will be printed in the *reverse* of the order in which they were added to the set.

E.   It is not possible to predict the order in which the strings will be printed.

3.   Assume that variable M is a Map. Consider the following code segment:

```
M.put( "1", "apple" );
M.put( "2", "banana" );
M.put( "3", "orange" );
M.put( "1", "orange" );
M.put( "2", "plum" );
M.put( "4", "banana" );
```

If M is empty before the code segment executes, which of the following best shows what it contains after the code segment executes?

A.   (1, apple) (1, orange) (2, banana) (2, plum) (3, orange) (4, banana)

B.   (1, orange) (2, plum) (3, orange) (4, banana)

C.   (1, orange) (2, plum) (4, banana)

D.   (1, apple, orange) (2, banana, plum) (3, orange) (4, banana)

E.   (1, 3, apple, orange) (2, 4, banana, plum)

4. Given two sets, $S1$ and $S2$, the set difference $S1 - S2$ is defined to be a set that includes an object x iff x is in $S1$ but not $S2$.

   Consider the following code segment, which is intended to make S3 be the set difference $S1 - S2$, without modifying S1 or S2.

   ```
   Set S3 = S1;
   Iterator it = S2.iterator();
   while (it.hasNext()) {
       S3.remove(it.next());
   }
   ```

   Assume that S1 and S2 are properly initialized Sets, containing $N1$ and $N2$ items, respectively, and that the `iterator`, `hasNext`, `contains`, `next`, and `remove` methods are all constant-time methods.

   Which of the following statements about the code segment is true?

   A. The code segment does *not* work as intended, because it modifies S1.

   B. The code segment does *not* work as intended, because it modifies S2.

   C. The code segment works as intended; when it executes it will take $O(N1 + N2)$ time (because copying from S1 to S3 takes $O(N1)$ time, and iterating through S2 takes $O(N2)$ time).

   D. The code segment works as intended; when it executes it will take $O(N2)$ time (because copying from S1 to S3 takes $O(1)$ time, and iterating through S2 takes $O(N2)$ time).

   E. The code segment works as intended; when it executes it will take $O(N1*N2)$ time (because copying from S1 to S3 takes $O(N1)$ time, and iterating through S2 takes $O(N2)$ time).

5. Assume that variable `members` is a Map with the names of people who belong to a club as the keys, and lists of their siblings' names as the associated objects.

   Consider the following code segment:

   ```
   List L = (List)members.get("Sandy Brown");
   if (L == null) return false;
   for (Iterator it = L.iterator(); it.hasNext();) {
       if (members.containsKey(it.next())) return true;
   }
   return false;
   ```

   Which of the following best describes the circumstances under which this code returns `true`?

   A. When Sandy Brown is a member of the club.

   B. When Sandy Brown is a sibling of some member of the club.

   C. When one of Sandy Brown's siblings is a member of the club.

   D. When Sandy Brown and one of Sandy Brown's siblings are members of the club.

   E. When Sandy Brown and all of Sandy Brown's siblings are members of the club.

Answers to Multiple-Choice Questions

1. C
2. E
3. B
4. A
5. D

7

Stacks, Queues, Priority Queues, and Heaps (AB only)

A *stack* is a last-in-first-out collection of objects. The AP CS exam assumes that AB students are familiar with the following definition of the Stack interface:

```
public interface Stack {
    boolean isEmpty();
    // postcondition: Returns true if stack is empty, false otherwise.

    void push(Object x);
    // precondition: stack is [e_1, e_2, ..., e_n] with n >= 0
    // postcondition: stack is [e_1, e_2, ..., e_n, x]

    Object pop();
    // precondition: stack is [e_1, e_2, ..., e_n] with n >= 1
    // postcondition: Throws an unchecked exception if the
    //                stack was empty.
    //                Otherwise, stack is [e_1, e_2, ..., e_{n-1}]
    //                and returns e_n.

    Object peekTop();
    // precondition: stack is [e_1, e_2, ..., e_n] with n >= 1
    // postcondition: Throws an unchecked exception if the
    //                stack was empty.
    //                Otherwise, returns e_n. (The stack is unchanged.)
}
```

Queues are similar to stacks in that both have operations that add objects to the collection of objects, that remove objects from the collection, that return one object from the collection (without removing it), and that tell whether the collection is empty; however, a queue is a first-in-first-out collection of objects, whereas a stack is last-in-first-out.

The AP CS exam assumes that AB students are familiar with the following definition of the `Queue` interface:

```
public interface Queue {
    boolean isEmpty();
    // postcondition: Returns true if queue is empty, false otherwise.

    void enqueue(Object x);
    // precondition: queue is [e_1, e_2, ..., e_n] with n >= 0
    // postcondition: queue is [e_1, e_2, ..., e_n, x]

    Object dequeue();
    // precondition: queue is [e_1, e_2, ..., e_n] with n >= 1
    // postcondition: Throws an unchecked exception if the
    //                queue was empty.
    //                Otherwise, queue is [e_2, ..., e_n]
    //                and returns e_1.

    Object peekFront();
    // precondition: queue is [e_1, e_2, ..., e_n] with n >= 1
    // postcondition: Throws an unchecked exception if the
    //                queue was empty.
    //                Otherwise, returns e_1. (The queue
    //                is unchanged.)
}
```

A *priority queue* is a data structure that stores a collection of `Comparable` objects; that is, objects that implement the `Comparable` interface, so that they can be compared to determine which is the smallest.

To understand the difference between a priority queue and a "plain" queue, recall that a plain queue is a first-in-first-out collection of objects. This means that if you add N objects to a queue (using the enqueue method) and then you remove N objects from the queue (using the dequeue method), the objects will come out in the same order they went in. By contrast, if you add N objects to a *priority* queue (using the add method) and then you remove N objects from the priority queue (using the removeMin method), the objects will come out in *sorted* order (from low to high).

The AP CS exam assumes that AB students are familiar with the following definition of the `PriorityQueue` interface:

```
public interface PriorityQueue {
    boolean isEmpty();
    // postcondition: Returns true if the number of elements in the
    //                priority queue is 0;
    //                otherwise, returns false.
```

```
    void add(Object x);
    // postcondition: x has been added to the priority queue;
    //                 the number of elements in the priority queue
    //                 is increased by 1.
    Object removeMin();
    // postcondition: Throws an unchecked exception if the priority
    //                 queue is empty.
    //                 Otherwise, the smallest item in the priority
    //                 queue is removed and returned, and the number
    //                 of elements in the priority queue is decreased
    //                 by 1.

    Object peekMin();
    // postcondition: Throws an unchecked exception if the priority
    //                 queue is empty.
    //                 Otherwise, the smallest item in the priority
    //                 queue is returned.  (The priority queue is
    //                 unchanged.)
}
```

The AP CS Java subset does not supply implementations of the Stack, Queue, or PriorityQueue interfaces. Questions about these data structures will include code like the following (which defines a class used to represent stacks of Integers):

```
public class IntStack implements Stack {
    .
    .   implementation omitted
    .
}


Stack s = new IntStack();
```

AB students should have experience implementing stacks, queues, and priority queues. For example, an ArrayList or LinkedList can be used to hold the items in the stack, queue, or priority queue.

AB students should also be aware that an efficient way to implement priority queues is to use a *heap* (sometimes called a *min-heap*). A heap is a binary tree with two special properties:

1. **Order Property:** For every node in the tree, the value stored at that node is smaller than all of the values in its subtrees (note that this means that the smallest value is at the root).

2. **Shape Property:** This property has three parts:

    i.   Every leaf is either at depth d or $d - 1$ (where the depth of a leaf is the length of the path from the root).

    ii. All leaves at depth d are to the left of all leaves at depth $d - 1$.

    iii. There is at most one node that has just one child; that child is a *left* child, and it is the *rightmost* leaf at depth d.

Below are some example binary trees; some are heaps and some are not.

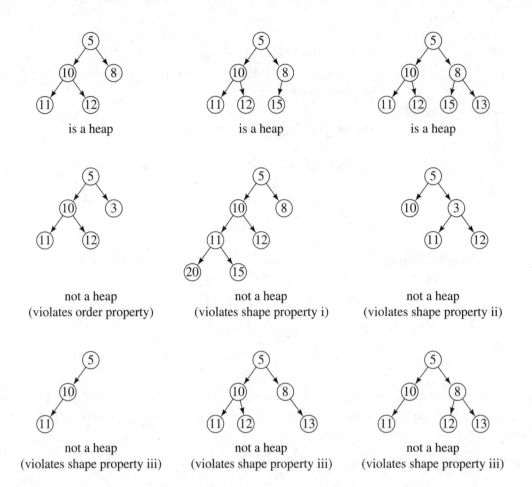

A heap is an interesting data structure because two useful operations can be performed in time O(log *N*), where *N* is the number of items in the heap:

- Insert a value
- Remove and return the smallest value (so that the binary tree is still a heap)

Clearly, if a heap is used to implement a priority queue, the `add` and `removeMin` operations can be implemented to run in O(log *N*) time (and the other operations can be implemented to run in constant time).

Practice Multiple-Choice Questions

1. Assume that stacks of `Integers` are implemented using the following (incomplete) class definition:

    ```
    public class IntStack implements Stack {
          :
          implementation omitted
          :
    }
    ```

Consider the following code segment:

```
Stack S = new IntStack();
for (int k=1; k<=5; k++) {
    S.push(new Integer(k));
}
while (!S.isEmpty()) {
    System.out.print(S.peekTop() + " ");
    int k = ((Integer)S.pop()).intValue();
    System.out.print(k + " ");
}
System.out.println();
```

What happens when this code segment is executed?

A. A runtime error occurs due to an attempt to pop an empty stack.

B. The while-loop never terminates.

C. The code executes without error; the output is 1 2 3 4 5.

D. The code executes without error; the output is 5 4 3 2 1.

E. The code executes without error; the output is 5 5 4 4 3 3 2 2 1 1.

2. Assume that stacks are implemented by using a linked list to store the items in the stack. How should the push and pop operations be implemented?

push(Object x)	pop()
A. add x to the list in sorted order	remove and return the item at the front of the list
B. add x to the list in sorted order	remove and return the item at the end of the list
C. add x to the front of the list	remove and return the item at the front of the list
D. add x to the front of the list	remove and return the item at the end of the list
E. add x to the end of the list	remove and return the item at the front of the list

3. Consider writing a program to simulate grocery shoppers waiting in check-out lines at a grocery store with ten cash registers. Assume that a Shopper class has been defined (to represent one grocery shopper). Which of the following data structures would be the most appropriate for that program?

A. Ten Shoppers

B. Ten arrays of Shoppers

C. Ten stacks of Shoppers

D. Ten queues of Shoppers

E. Ten linked lists of Shoppers

4. Assume that S is a String and that stacks and queues of Strings are implemented using the following (incomplete) class definitions:

```
public class StringStack implements Stack {

    :  implementation omitted

}

public class StringQueue implements Queue {

    :  implementation omitted

}
```

Consider the following three code segments:

<u>Segment I</u>
```
String newS = "";
for (int k=0; k<S.length(); k++) newS += S.substring(k, k+1);
S = newS;
```

<u>Segment II</u>
```
Stack X = newStringStack();
for (int k=0; k<S.length(); k++)  X.push(S.substring(k, k+1));
S = "";
while (! X.isEmpty()) S += X.pop();
```

<u>Segment III</u>
```
Queue Q = new StringQueue();
for (int k=0; k<S.length(); k++)  Q.enqueue(S.substring(k, k+1));
S = "";
while (! Q.isEmpty())  S += Q.dequeue();
```

Which of these code segments reverses the characters in S?

A. I only

B. II only

C. III only

D. I and II

E. II and III

5. Assume that a priority queue is implemented using a linked list to store the items in the priority queue. The add operation adds the new value at the front of the list, and the `peekMin` operation looks at all of the values in the list to find (and return) the smallest value.

Which of the following best characterizes the worst-case running times of the two operations for a priority queue with N items?

	add	peekMin
A.	O(1)	O(1)
B.	O(1)	O(N)
C.	O(log N)	O(log N)
D.	O(log N)	O(N)
E.	O(N)	O(N)

Answers to Multiple-Choice Questions

1. E
2. C
3. D
4. B
5. B

8

AP Computer Science Standard Interfaces and Classes

The AP exams will make use of a set of standard interfaces and classes defined in the packages ap.java.lang, ap.java.util, and ap. The interfaces and classes in ap.java.lang and ap.java.util are also defined in the Java packages java.lang and java.util; however, the Java versions generally include more methods than the AP versions. The interfaces and classes in the ap package have no analog in Java; they are defined specially for use in the AP courses and on the AP exams.

The standard AP interfaces and classes are summarized briefly below. Some of them (the Array-List, LinkedList, List, HashSet, TreeSet, HashMap, TreeMap, Set, and Map classes) were discussed in more detail in earlier chapters. A "quick reference" guide that summarizes the AP interfaces and classes (possibly containing just the names of the classes, interfaces, and methods with no explanations) will be provided as part of the AP CS exams.

8.1 Interface and Classes from the ap.java.lang Package

8.1.1 The ap.java.lang.Comparable Interface

This interface is used for objects that have a "natural ordering"; that is, objects for which it makes sense to say that one is "less than" or "comes before" another. For example, the String, Integer, and Double classes all implement the Comparable interface.

The AP CS Java subset includes only one Comparable method.

The Comparable Interface

Method	Explanation
int compareTo(Object other)	Returns a negative integer, zero, or a positive integer depending on whether this Object is less than, equal to, or greater than other.

8.1.2 The ap.java.lang.Double and ap.java.lang.Integer Classes

Both the Double class and the Integer class implement the ap.java.lang.Comparable interface (described above). Each Double represents a double value, and each Integer represents an int value. The AP CS Java subset includes the following Double and Integer methods.

The Double and Integer Classes

Method	Explanation
`Double(double d)`	Constructs a new `Double` that represents d.
`double doubleValue()`	Returns the double represented by this `Double`.
`Integer(int k)`	Constructs a new `Integer` that represents k.
`int intValue()`	Returns the int represented by this `Integer`.
`int compareTo(Object other)`	Returns a negative integer, zero, or a positive integer depending on whether this `Double`/`Integer`'s value is less than, equal to, or greater than other's value.
`boolean equals(Object other)`	Returns true if other is the same kind of `Object` (`Double` or `Integer`) as this one and has the same value; otherwise, returns false.

The `Double` and `Integer` classes are provided so that you can use objects that represent ints and doubles. For example, you might want to create a list of integer values using the `ArrayList` class. Since an `ArrayList` can only store objects, not primitive values, you would create an `Integer` for each integer value that you wanted to store, and add that `Integer` to the `ArrayList`. To get the (plain) integer values back, you would use the `Integer`'s `intValue` method.

Below is code that uses an `ArrayList` called `dblList` that coutains nonnegative `Doubles`. It creates a new `ArrayList` called `intList` that contains the same values rounded to the nearest integer.

```
// precondition: dblList is an ArrayList of non-null,
//               non-negative Doubles
// postcondition: creates ArrayList intList containing the
//               corresponding integer values
ArrayList intList = new ArrayList();
for (int k=0; k<dblList.size(); k++) {
    Double dbl = (Double)dblList.get(k);
    intList.add(new Integer(dbl.doubleValue() + .5));
}
```

8.1.3   The ap.java.lang.Math Class

The `Math` class provides a number of standard mathematical functions. The AP CS Java subset includes the following `Math` methods.

The Math Class

Method	Explanation
`static int abs(int x)`	Returns the absolute value of int x.
`static double abs(double x)`	Returns the absolute value of double x.
`static double pow(double base, double exponent)`	Returns the value of base raised to the power of exponent.
`static double sqrt(double x)`	Returns the square root of x.

Note that all of the `Math` methods are *static*. This means that when you want to use a `Math` method, you use the class name followed by a dot followed by the method name, instead of using the name of a `Math` object followed by a dot followed by the method name. For example, the code segment below includes a use of the abs (absolute value) method of the `Math` class:

```
double d = -2.0;
double posd = Math.abs(d);  // posd is 2.0
```

8.1.4   The ap.java.lang.Object Class

As discussed in Chapter 1, objects are the basic building blocks of object-oriented programs. The AP CS Java subset includes the following `Object` methods.

The Object Class

Method	Explanation
boolean equals(Object other)	Returns true if this `Object` is the same as other; otherwise, returns false. (Note that the default version returns true if and only if the == operator returns true; i.e., if and only if this `Object` points to the same chunk of memory as other.)
int hashCode() (AB only)	Returns a hashcode value for this `Object`. (See Chapter 6 for more information about the hashCode method.)
String toString()	Returns a string representation of this `Object`.

Remember that every class is a subclass of `Object`, so every class inherits the `equals`, `toString`, and `hashCode` methods of the `Object` class. However, it is often a good idea to redefine these methods when you define a new class so that you get more suitable versions.

For example, consider the following (partial) definition of the `Person` class:

```
public class Person {
  /*** fields ***/
    private String name;
    private String address;

  /*** constructor ***/
    public Person(String initName, String initAddress) {
      name = initName;
      address = initAddress;
    }

  /*** methods ***/
      .
      .
      .
}
```

Now consider the following code segment:

```
Person p1 = new Person("Chris Smith", "123 Willow St");
Person p2 = new Person("Chris Smith", "123 Willow St");
if (p1.equals(p2)) System.out.println("equal");
else System.out.println("not equal");
```

If the Person class does not redefine the default equals method (inherited from the Object class), "not equal" will be printed, because p1 and p2 point to different chunks of storage. If we want two People objects with the same name and the same address to be considered equal, we must include a new definition of the equals method in the Person class:

```
public boolean equals(Person p) {
    return (name.equals(p.name) && address.equals(p.address));
}
```

8.1.5 The ap.java.lang.String Class

The String class implements the ap.java.lang.Comparable interface (described in Section 8.1.1). An instance of the String class represents a sequence of zero or more characters. The AP CS Java subset includes the following String methods.

The String Class

Method	Explanation
int compareTo(Object other)	If other is not a String, throws an exception. Otherwise, returns a negative number if this string comes before other in lexicographic order; returns a positive number if this string comes after other in lexicographic order; returns zero if the two strings are the same.
boolean equals(Object other)	Returns true if other is a string with the same sequence of characters as this one; otherwise, returns false.
int indexOf(String s)	Returns the position of the first occurrence of s in this string, or −1 if s does not occur in this string.
int length()	Returns the number of characters in this string.
String substring(int from, int to)	Returns the substring that starts with the character in position from and ends with the character in position to − 1 (counting from zero).
String substring(int from)	Returns the substring that starts with the character in position from (counting from zero) and ends with the last character in the string.

Practice Multiple-Choice Questions

1. Consider the following code segment:

```
String S = "razzle-dazzle"
int k;
k = S.indexOf("z");
while (k != -1) {
   S = S.substring(0, k) + "p" + S.substring(k+1);
   k = S.indexOf("z");
}
System.out.println(S);
```

What is output when this code segment is executed?

A. `rapple-dapple`

B. `rapzle-dazzle`

C. `razzle-dazple`

D. `razzle-dazzle`

E. `ra`

2. Assume that variable A is an array of `Strings` and that variable S is a `String`. Consider the following code segment:

```
for (int k=0; k<A.length; k++) {
   if (A[k].compareTo(S) < 0) return false;
}
return true;
```

When does this code segment return `true`?

A. When all of the strings in A come before S in lexicographic order

B. When no string in A comes before S in lexicographic order

C. When no string in A comes after S in lexicographic order

D. When some string in A comes before S in lexicographic order

E. When some string in A comes after S in lexicographic order

Questions 3 and 4 concern the following code segment (line numbers are included for use in question 4). Assume that variable S is a String.

```
1  int k = 0;
2  for (int j = S.length()-1; j>=0; j--) {
3      if (! (S.substring(k,k+1).equals(S.substring(j,j+1)))) return false;
4      k++;
5  }
6  return true;
```

3. Which of the following best describes what this code segment does?

   A. Always returns true

   B. Always returns false

   C. Determines whether S is the same forwards and backwards

   D. Determines whether S contains any duplicate characters

   E. Determines whether the characters in S are in sorted order

4. Consider changing the code segment to make it more efficient. Which of the following changes would accomplish that without changing what the method does?

   A. Change line 2 to:

   ```
   for (int j = S.length()-1; j>=S.length()/2; j--)
   ```

   B. Change line 2 to:

   ```
   for (int j=0; j<=S.length(); j++)
   ```

   C. Change line 3 to:

   ```
   if (S.substring(k, k+1).equals(S.substring(j, j+1))) return true;
   ```

   and change line 6 to:

   ```
   return false;
   ```

   D. Change line 3 to:

   ```
   if (!(S.substring(k, k+1).equals(S.substring(j, j+1))) ||
       !(S.substring(k+1, k+2).equals(S.substring(j-1, j))))
       return false;
   ```

   E. Change line 3 to:

   ```
   if (!(S.substring(k, k+1).equals(S.substring(j, j+1))) ||
       (j < k)) return false;
   ```

5. Consider the following methods:

```
public static void trySwap(int k, Integer K) {
    int tmp = K.intValue( );
    K = new Integer(k);
    k = tmp;
}

public static void test( ) {
    int n = 5;
    Integer N = new Integer(10);
    trySwap(n, N);
    System.out.println(n + " " + N);
}
```

What is output when method `test` executes?

A. 10 5

B. 5 5

C. 5 10

D. 10 10

E. Nothing is output; a `NullPointerException` is thrown when `trySwap` is called.

Answers to Multiple-Choice Questions

1. A
2. B
3. C
4. A
5. C

8.2   Interfaces and Classes from the ap.java.util Package

8.2.1   The ap.java.util.Iterator and ap.java.util.ListIterator Interfaces (AB only)

These two interfaces (discussed in more detail in Chapter 4) are used to provide a way to iterate through the objects in some collection of objects, one at a time. They also allow an object to be removed from the collection after it has been "visited" during an iteration.

Every class that implements the `Set` interface (e.g., the `HashSet` and `TreeSet` classes) has a method called `iterator` that returns an `Iterator`, and every class that implements the `List` interface (e.g., the `ArrayList` and `LinkedList` classes) includes both an `iterator` method (that returns an `Iterator`) and a `listIterator` method (that returns a `ListIterator`).

The basic iteration methods (provided by both interfaces) are as follows.

The Iterator and ListIterator Interfaces

Method	Explanation
`boolean hasNext()`	Returns `true` if the collection has more elements; otherwise, returns `false`.
`Object next()`	Returns the next element in the collection.
`void remove()`	Removes the last element returned by the iterator from the collection.

The AP CS Java subset includes the following additional methods for the `ListIterator` interface.

The ListIterator Interface

Method	Explanation
`void add(Object x)`	Inserts x into the list immediately before the element that would be returned by `next` (if there is no such element, inserts x at the end of the list).
`void set(Object x)`	Replaces the last element returned by `next` with x (throws an exception if there is no such element).

8.2.2 The ap.java.util.List Interface (AB only)

This interface (discussed in more detail in Chapter 4) is used for sequences of objects (possibly containing duplicates). For example, the `LinkedList` and `ArrayList` classes both implement the `List` interface.

The AP CS Java subset includes the following `List` methods.

The List Interface

Method	Explanation
`void add(Object x)`	Adds x to the end of this list.
`Object get(int n)`	If index n is out of bounds (n < 0 or n >= `size()`), throws an `IndexOutOfBoundsException`. Otherwise, returns the element at position n (counting from zero) in this list.
`Iterator iterator())`	Returns an iterator for this list.
`ListIterator listIterator()`	Returns a list iterator for this list.
`Object set(int n, Object x)`	If index n is out of bounds (n < 0 or n >= `size()`), throws an `IndexOutOfBoundsException`. Otherwise, replaces the element at position n (counting from zero) in this list with x and returns the object that was previously at position n.
`int size()`	Returns the number of elements in this list.

8.2.3 The ap.java.util.Map Interface (AB only)

This interface (discussed in more detail in Chapter 6) is used for sets of unique keys, each with an associated object. For example, the `HashMap` and `TreeMap` classes both implement the `Map` interface.

The AP CS Java subset includes the following `Map` methods.

The Map Interface

Method	Explanation
boolean containsKey(Object key)	Returns `true` if this map contains key; otherwise, returns `false`.
Object get(Object key)	Returns the value associated with key in this map. Returns `null` if this map does not contain key.
Set keySet()	Returns a set view of the keys contained in this map.
Object put(Object key, Object val)	If this map already contains value val associated with key, then does nothing and returns `null`. Otherwise, if this map already contains a value v associated with key, then replaces it with val and returns v. Otherwise, adds val to the map associated with key and returns `null`.
Object remove(Object key)	Removes the mapping for key from this map if it is there, and returns the value previously associated with key (returns `null` if key was not in the map).
int size()	Returns the number of key-value mappings in this map.

8.2.4   The ap.java.util.Set Interface (AB only)

This interface (discussed in more detail in Chapter 6) is used for sets of objects (with no duplicates, and in no particular order). For example, the `HashSet` and `TreeSet` classes both implement the `Set` interface.

The AP CS Java subset includes the following `Set` methods.

The Set Interface

Method	Explanation
boolean add(Object x)	Adds x to this set if it is not already there. Returns `true` if x was not already in this set; otherwise, returns `false`.
boolean contains(Object x)	Returns `true` if this set contains x; otherwise, returns `false`.
Iterator iterator()	Returns an iterator for this set.
boolean remove(Object x)	Removes x from this set if it is there. Returns `true` if x was in this set; otherwise, returns `false`.
int size()	Returns the number of elements in this set.

8.2.5   The ap.java.util.ArrayList Class

The `ArrayList` class implements the `ap.java.util.List` interface (defined above in Section 8.2.2). Both the `ArrayList` class and the `List` interface are discussed in more detail in Chapter 4.

An instance of the `ArrayList` class represents a list of objects (i.e., an ordered sequence). Like an array, elements can be accessed using their position in the list. The AP CS Java subset includes the following `ArrayList` methods.

The ArrayList Class

Method	Explanation
`boolean add(Object x)`	Adds x to the end of this list and returns `true`.
`void add(int n, Object x)`	If index n is out of bounds (n < 0 or n > size()), throws an `IndexOutOfBoundsException`. Otherwise, moves the elements in positions n (counting from zero) to the end of this list over one place to the right to make room for new element x, then inserts x at position n in this list.
`Object get(int n)`	If index n is out of bounds (n < 0 or n >= size()), throws an `IndexOutOfBoundsException`. Otherwise, returns the element at position n (counting from zero) in this list.
`Iterator iterator() (AB only)`	Returns an iterator for this list.
`ListIterator listIterator() (AB only)`	Returns a list iterator for this list.
`Object remove(int n)`	If index n is out of bounds (n < 0 or n >= size()), throws an `IndexOutOfBoundsException`. Otherwise, removes the element at position n (counting from zero) in this list, then shifts the remaining elements over one place to the left to fill in the gap. Returns the removed element.
`void set(int n, Object x)`	If index n is out of bounds (n < 0 or n >= size()), throws an `IndexOutOfBoundsException`. Otherwise, replaces the element at position n (counting from zero) in this list with x.
`int size()`	Returns the number of elements in this list.

8.2.6   The ap.java.util.HashMap and ap.java.util.TreeMap Classes (AB only)

The `HashMap` class and the `TreeMap` class both implement the `ap.java.util.Map` interface (defined above in Section 8.2.3). The `HashMap` and `TreeMap` classes, as well as the `Map` interface are discussed in more detail in Chapter 6.

Instances of these classes represent sets of objects, each with a unique key and some associated information. The AP CS Java subset includes the following methods for the two classes.

The HashMap and TreeMap Classes

Method	Explanation
`boolean containsKey(Object key)`	Returns `true` if this map contains key; otherwise, returns `false`.
`Object get(Object key)`	Returns the value associated with key in this map. Returns `null` if this map does not contain key.

`Set keySet()`	Returns a set view of the keys contained in this map.
`Object put(Object key, Object val)`	If this map already contains value `val` associated with `key`, then does nothing and returns `null`. Otherwise, if this map already contains a value v associated with `key`, then replaces it with `val` and returns v. Otherwise, adds `val` to the map associated with `key` and returns `null`.
`int size()`	Returns the number of key-value mappings in this map.

The AP standard classes provide a number of different ways to store collections of data. The `HashMap` and `TreeMap` classes are two examples. It is usually a good idea to use one of these classes when

- The data to be stored consist of a unique key plus some associated information.
- Accessing one piece of data based on the value of its key is a common operation.

Although other classes (e.g., a `List` or `Set`) could be used, the advantage of the `Map` classes is that they provide efficient methods to add a new piece of data and to look up a piece of data based on its key (the `put` and `get` methods).

For example, a teacher might want to design a data structure to keep track of the homework and exam grades for each of the students in her class. A `Map` would be a good choice for the data structure, because she could use the students' names as the key values and the lists of grades as the associated information. The `Map` would allow her to find a particular student's list of grades quickly (using the `get` method), as well as to add information about a new student quickly (using the `put` method).

8.2.7   The ap.java.util.HashSet and ap.java.util.TreeSet Classes (AB only)

The `HashSet` class and the `TreeSet` class both implement the `ap.java.util.Set` interface (defined above in Section 8.2.4). The `HashSet` and `TreeSet` classes, as well as the `Set` interface are discussed in more detail in Chapter 6.

Instances of these classes represent sets of objects (with no duplicates, and in no particular order). The AP CS Java subset includes the following methods for the two classes.

The HashSet and TreeSet Classes

Method	Explanation
`boolean add(Object x)`	Adds x to this set if it is not already there. Returns `true` if x was *not* already in this set; otherwise, returns `false`.
`boolean contains(Object x)`	Returns `true` if this set contains x; otherwise, returns `false`.
`Iterator iterator()`	Returns an iterator for this set.
`boolean remove(Object x)`	Removes x from this set if it is there. Returns `true` if x was in this set; otherwise, returns `false`.
`int size()`	Returns the number of elements in this set.

A `Set`, like a `Map`, provides a data structure that can be used to store a collection of items. A `Set` is a better choice than a `Map` when the items to be stored consist only of unique values with no associated information. For example, suppose you want a data structure to keep track of the names of all of the movies you've ever seen, and you plan to implement only the following operations:

- Add a new name to the data structure (each time you see a new movie)
- Look up a name in the data structure (each time you want to know whether you've already seen a particular movie)

In this case, a Set would be a good choice for the data structure, since it provides efficient methods for both operations (the add and contains methods).

8.2.8   The ap.java.util.LinkedList Class (AB only)

The LinkedList class implements the ap.java.util.List interface (defined above in Section 8.2.2).

An instance of the LinkedList class represents a list of objects (i.e., an ordered sequence) that is implemented using a linked list (see Chapter 4 for more about linked lists, the LinkedList class, and the List interface). The AP CS Java subset includes the following LinkedList methods.

The LinkedList Class

Method	Explanation
boolean add(Object x)	Adds x to the end of this list and returns *true*.
void addFirst(Object x)	Adds x at the beginning of this list.
void addLast(Object x)	Adds x to the end of this list.
Object get(int n)	If index n is out of bounds (n < 0 or n >= size()), throws an IndexOutOfBoundsException. Otherwise, returns the element at position n (counting from zero) in this list.
Object getFirst()	If this list is empty, throws a NoSuchElementException. Otherwise, returns the first element in this list.
Object getLast()	If this list is empty, throws a NoSuchElementException. Otherwise, returns the last element in this list.
Iterator iterator()	Returns an iterator for this list.
ListIterator listIterator()	Returns a list iterator for this list.
Object removeFirst()	If this list is empty, throws a NoSuchElementException. Otherwise, removes and returns the first element in this list.
Object removeLast()	If this list is empty, throws a NoSuchElementException. Otherwise, removes and returns the last element in this list.
Object set(int n, Object x)	If index n is out of bounds (n < 0 or n >= size()), throws an IndexOutOfBoundsException. Otherwise, replaces the element at position n (counting from zero) in this list with x, and returns the object that was previously at position n.
int size()	Returns the number of elements in this list.

8.2.9   The ap.java.util.Random Class

The Random class provides methods for generating pseudorandom numbers. The numbers can be integers (covering the full range of possible integer values) or doubles (in the range 0.0 to 1.0). The AP CS Java subset includes the following Random methods.

The Random Class

Method	Explanation
double nextDouble()	Returns the next pseudorandom double value between 0.0 and 1.0.
int nextInt(int n)	Returns the next pseudorandom integer value between 0 (inclusive) and n (exclusive).

Practice Multiple-Choice Questions

1. Consider writing code to simulate flipping a coin ten times. An outline of the code is given below.

```
Random ran = new Random();
for (int k=1; k<=10; k++) {
    if (expression == 0) System.out.println("heads");
    else System.out.println("tails");
}
```

Which of the following is the best replacement for *expression*?

A. ran.nextInt(0)

B. ran.nextInt(1)

C. ran.nextInt(2)

D. ran.nextInt(10)

E. ran.nextInt(k)

Questions 2 and 3 assume that variable a is an ArrayList that has been initialized to contain a list of ten strings.

2. Which of the following statements correctly adds the string "the end" to the end of the list?

Statement I	Statement II	Statement III
a.add("the end");	a.add(10, "the end");	a.set(10, "the end");

A. I only

B. II only

C. I and II

D. I and III

E. II and III

3. Which of the following code segments correctly replaces the first string in the list with the string "start"?

   A. `a.set(0, "start");`

   B. `a.get(0, "start");`

   C. `a.add("start");`

   D. `a.add(0, "start");`

   E. `a.remove(0); a.add("start");`

Questions 4 and 5 (for AB students only) concern the following situation: Consider writing a program to keep track of information about the students enrolled in a class. The information for each student is the student's (unique) ID number, and the student's name. Assume that variable m is a Map that has been initialized to store the information for the class (using a string that represents the ID number as the key, and another string that represents the student's name as the associated object).

4. (AB only) Which of the following code segments prints the names of all of the students in the class?

   A. `System.out.println(m);`

   B. `System.out.println(m.get());`

   C. ```
      for (int k=1; k<m.size(); k++) {
          System.out.println(m.get(k));
      }
      ```

   D. ```
      Set keys = m.keySet();
      for (Iterator it = keys.iterator(); it.hasNext(); ) {
        System.out.println(it.next());
      }
      ```

   E. ```
      Set keys = m.keySet();
        for (Iterator it = keys.iterator(); it.hasNext();) {
          Object oneKey = it.next();
          System.out.println(m.get(oneKey));
        }
      ```

5. (AB only) Which of the following expressions evaluates to true if and only if there is a student with ID number 12345 in the class?

   A. `m.get("12345")`

   B. `m.containsKey("12345")`

   C. `m.size() > 0`

   D. `m.keySet().iterator().hasNext()`

   E. `m.keySet().iterator().next()`
      ```

Answers to Multiple-Choice Questions

1. C
2. C
3. A
4. E
5. B

8.3   Interfaces and Classes from the ap Package (AB only)

The interfaces and classes from the *ap* package are discussed in Chapter 7, which also provides practice multiple-choice questions. A summary of the methods defined for each interface and class is given here.

8.3.1   The ap.PriorityQueue Interface (AB only)

Method	Explanation
`void add(Object x)`	Inserts x into this priority queue.
`boolean isEmpty()`	Returns `true` if this priority queue is empty; otherwise, returns `false`.
`Object peekMin()`	If this priority queue is empty, throws an exception. Otherwise, returns the smallest item in this priority queue without removing it.
`Object removeMin()`	If this priority queue is empty, throws an exception. Otherwise, removes and returns the smallest item in this priority queue.

8.3.2   The ap.Queue Interface (AB only)

Method	Explanation
`Object dequeue()`	If this queue is empty, throws an exception. Otherwise, removes and returns the first item from this queue.
`void enqueue(Object x)`	Adds x to the end of this queue.
`boolean isEmpty()`	Returns `true` if this queue is empty; otherwise, returns `false`.
`Object peekFront()`	If this queue is empty, throws an exception. Otherwise, returns the first item in this queue without removing it.

8.3.3   The ap.Stack Interface (AB only)

Method	Explanation
boolean isEmpty()	Returns true if this stack is empty; otherwise, returns false.
Object peekTop()	If this stack is empty, throws an exception. Otherwise, returns the item on the top of this stack without removing it.
Object pop()	If this stack is empty, throws an exception. Otherwise, removes and returns the item on top of this stack.
void push(Object x)	Adds x to the top of this stack.

8.3.4   The ap.ListNode Class (AB only)

Method	Explanation
ListNode getNext()	Returns the next node in the list.
Object getValue()	Returns the value in this node.
void setNext(ListNode n)	Sets the pointer to the next node to n.
void setValue(Object x)	Sets the value in this node to x.

8.3.5   The ap.TreeNode Class (AB only)

Method	Explanation
Object getValue()	Returns the value in this tree node.
TreeNode getLeft()	Returns a pointer to this node's left child.
TreeNode getRight()	Returns a pointer to this node's right child.
TreeNode setLeft (TreeNode n)	Sets the pointer to this node's left child to n.
TreeNode setRight (TreeNode n)	Sets the pointer to this node's right child to n.
void setValue(Object x)	Sets the value in this node to x.

9

Case Studies

Case studies are included in the AP Computer Science curriculum to give students the opportunity to study the development of a nontrivial piece of software; to understand how an expert would go about designing, implementing, and testing such software; and to practice the skills needed to understand and modify code written by someone else.

Each year, the AP Computer Science exams include both multiple-choice and free-response questions about a particular case study. Although a copy of the case study is available to students during the exam, it is absolutely vital that they already be familiar with the case study; there is not enough time during the exam to learn enough about the case study to be able to answer the questions.

If students have not worked with the current year's case study (the Marine Biology Simulation), they should obtain a copy from the College Board Web site or by calling AP Order Fulfillment at (800) 323-7155.

A summary of the Marine Biology Simulation is given below.

9.1   Overview

The Marine Biology Simulation is a large program designed to simulate the movements of fish in a body of water (an environment). Each step of the simulation involves asking each fish in turn to "act," then displaying the current state of the environment. A fish acts by first attempting to breed; if that is unsuccessful, it attempts to move. Finally, the fish determines whether or not it is time to die. The Marine Biology Simulation includes several different kinds of fish, whose actions are governed by somewhat different rules, as well as several different kinds of environments.

The most important classes defined in the case study are Fish and Simulation. The Environment interface is also key to understanding the case study. In addition, there are some important utility classes: Debug, Direction, EnvDisplay, Locatable, Location, and RandNumGenerator. There are two Fish subclasses: DarterFish and SlowFish, and several different implementations of the Environment interface.

All students should have a general understanding of how these classes and interfaces are used in the simulation, and should be able to describe what each method of the class does, what are appropriate values for the parameters of each of the methods of the class, and how to use those methods in a larger problem. A students should be familiar with the `Environment` interface, but only AB students need to understand the details of the `Environment` implementations.

9.2 The Fish Class

The `Fish` class is the heart of the Marine Biology Simulation. Each fish keeps track of the following information:

1. its environment
2. its location in the environment
3. the direction in which it is currently facing
4. its color
5. its probabilities of breeding and dying.

Each `Fish` has several methods that implement its basic behaviors, using a number of helper methods. The `Fish` constructors and methods are described below.

Constructors The `Fish` class has three constructors that allow the user of the simulation to specify different things about a `Fish`. All constructors require `Environment` and `Location` parameters; `Direction` and `Color` parameters are optional. All of the constructors use a private helper method named `initialize`, which initializes the internal state of the `Fish` object. If a `Direction` or `Color` is not passed as a parameter to the constructor, a default `Direction` and random `Color` are chosen by the constructor and passed to the `initialize` method.

void initialize(Environment env, Location loc, Direction dir, Color col) As discussed above, the `initialize` method is used to assign initial values to the instance variables of the `Fish`. The constructors call this method rather than assigning the values directly.

void act() The `act` method is a public method that causes the `Fish` to do whatever it is supposed to do during one timestep of the simulation. While the original `act` method (in Chapters 1 and 2) only moves the `Fish`, the `act` method introduced in Chapter 3 also causes the `Fish` to breed and/or die based on the state of its environment and its own internal state (its probabilities of breeding or dying).

void move() The `move` method uses the helper method `nextLocation` to determine where the `Fish` should move. It also uses the helper methods `changeLocation` and `changeDirection` to update the state of the `Fish`.

boolean breed() The `breed` method uses its probability of breeding and the helper method `emptyNeighbors` to determine whether the `Fish` can breed. If it can breed, it uses the `generateChild` method to fill its empty neighboring locations with new instances of `Fish`. The `breed` method returns a `boolean` value: `true` if it was able to create at least one child, and `false` otherwise.

void generateChild(Location loc) The `generateChild` method creates a new instance of a `Fish` in location `loc`.

void die() The `die` method removes the `Fish` from the environment, which causes it to no longer be a part of the simulation.

Location nextLocation() The `nextLocation` method uses helper method `emptyNeighbors` to retrieve a list of the `Fish`'s empty neighboring locations. The `nextLocation` method then removes from that list the `Location` directly behind the `Fish` (as determined using the `Fish`'s `Direction` method), because `Fish` are not allowed to move backward. Finally, it returns one of the remaining empty `Locations`, chosen randomly, or its current location if the list is empty.

ArrayList emptyNeighbors() The `emptyNeighbors` helper method is used by both `nextLocation` and `breed` to retrieve a list of the `Fish`'s neighboring locations that are currently unoccupied.

void changeLocation(Location newLoc) The `changeLocation` method is used to update the state of the `Fish` to reflect the move chosen by the `nextLocation` method.

void changeDirection(Direction newDir) One of the private instance variables of a `Fish` is a `Direction` that represents which way the `Fish` has most recently moved. The `changeDirection` method updates this variable to represent the direction represented by parameter `newDir`.

Accessor Methods The `Fish` class includes a number of accessor methods to access the state of the `Fish` (e.g., its environment, location, and direction). When writing a method that is not part of the `Fish` class, these methods must be used rather than trying to access the private instance variables of the `Fish`.

9.3   The Environment Interface

All of the implementations of the `Environment` interface provided in the case study model an environment as a two-dimensional grid of locations (cells), each of which either is empty or contains a single fish. The locations are square; that is, locations that are not at the edge of the environment have four neighbors (above, below, left, and right; diagonal cells are not considered to be neighbors). AB students should be prepared to answer questions that change the environment model; for example, locations could be defined to be triangular, in which case they would have only three neighbors.

The `Environment` interface is implemented by several classes including `BoundedEnvironment`, `SquareEnvironment`, and `UnboundedEnvironment` (only AB students need to understand the details of these implementations). Each of the implementations includes the same set of methods, and through most of the simulation it does not matter which implementation is chosen. AB students need to be able to discuss the Big-O running times of each of the `Environment` methods based on the different implementations and what data structures they use.

The `Environment` interface has methods that provide information about the structure of the environment, methods that provide information about the state of the environment, and methods that modify the state of the environment.

Here are the methods that provide information about the structure of the environment.

boolean isValid(Location loc) The `isValid` method is used to determine whether the `Location` passed as a parameter is a valid `Location` in the environment.

int numCellSides() This method returns the number of sides around each cell in the environment. As discussed above, the environments that are defined as part of the case study have four sides (i.e., they have square cells). However, it is possible to define environments whose cells have any number of sides, and questions might be asked about such environments.

int numAdjacentNeighbors() This method returns the number of neighbors each cell in the environment has. For the `Environment` implementations defined in the case study, the `num-AdjacentNeighbors` method always returns 4, since each cell in the environment has four sides, and cells that are diagonally adjacent are not considered neighbors. However, it is possible to define an `Environment` in which diagonal cells *are* considered neighbors, and/or to have more (or fewer) neighbors if a cell has more (or fewer) sides.

Direction randomDirection() This method returns a random `Direction` that represents a direction from a cell in the environment to one of its neighbors.

Direction getDirection(Location fromLoc, Location toLoc) This method returns the `Direction` one must travel to get from `fromLoc` to `toLoc`.

Location getNeighbor(Location fromLoc, Direction compassDir) This method returns the neighbor of the given `Location` in the given `Direction`.

java.util.ArrayList neighborsOf(Location loc) This method returns an `ArrayList` that contains all of the locations that are neighbors of `loc`. Note that this method will not return four locations if `loc` is on the edge of the environment, or if the number of adjacent neighbors for the environment is not four.

The following methods tell us about the state of the environment.

int numObjects() This method returns the number of `Locatable` objects currently stored in the `Environment`.

Locatable[] allObjects() This method returns an array containing all of the `Locatable` objects that are currently stored in the `Environment`.

boolean isEmpty(Location loc) This method returns `true` if `loc` is a valid location in this environment and is empty, `false` otherwise.

Locatable objectAt(Location loc) This method returns the `Locatable` object stored at location `loc`, or `null` if `loc` is not in the environment or is empty.

The following methods are modifiers that change the state of the environment.

void add(Locatable obj) This method adds `obj` to the environment at the location that it specifies.

void remove(Locatable obj) This method removes `obj` from the environment.

void recordMove(Locatable obj, Location oldLoc) This method updates the environment to reflect moving `obj` from `oldLoc` to the location that it specifies.

9.4   The Simulation Class

The `Simulation` class handles the interaction between the environment and the display, and therefore its constructor has two parameters: an `Environment` and an `EnvDisplay`. It has one method called `step` that retrieves a list of all of the objects in the `Environment`, casts each to a `Fish`, and calls the `act` method of each `Fish`. It then displays the current state of the environment.

9.5   Utility Classes and Interfaces

The Marine Biology Simulation includes a number of utility classes, described below.

The Debug class The Debug class has methods that cause debugging statements to be printed by the simulation as it runs.

The Direction class The Direction class defines constants (NORTH, NORTHEAST, EAST, etc.) that represent the possible directions available in an Environment. Methods are also included to return directions that are a quarter turn, or a specified number of degrees away from the current direction. For example, if we have a Direction called currDir that represents north, then the calls currDir.toRight() and currDir.toRight(45) would each return a Direction that represents east, since east is a quarter turn to the right of north, and is also 45 degrees to the right of north.

The EnvDisplay interface This interface has only one method, showEnv, which is used by the Simulation class to display the updated environment after each timestep.

The Locatable interface The Locatable interface has only one method, location, which returns the location of the object whose method is called.

The Location class Not to be confused with the Locatable interface, the Location class is used to represent one location in the environment. In the implementations of the Environment interface included in the case study, locations are represented as a row and column within a rectangular grid.

The RandNumGenerator class This class has a single static method, getInstance, which returns an instance of a Random class. This is very useful when you need to create multiple Random objects in a row: When a Random object is created by calling the no-argument constructor, the computer's clock time is used as a seed. If several Random objects are created rapidly, they will all have the same seed value. Using the getInstance method of the RandNumGenerator class avoids this problem.

9.6   Specialized Fish Subclasses

The Marine Biology Simulation includes two subclasses of the Fish class: DarterFish and SlowFish.

The DarterFish class reimplements the nextLocation and move methods to implement different motion than the original Fish class. A DarterFish moves in a single row or column until it reaches the edge of the environment; at that point it reverses direction and moves to the opposite end of the row or column.

The SlowFish class also reimplements the nextLocation method so that a SlowFish has only a 1-in-5 probability of moving during each timestep.

9.7 What Happens During One Timestep

To understand better how the Marine Biology Simulation works, we now describe what happens during each timestep of the simulation.

For each timestep, the step method of the Simulation object is called. The step method calls the allObjects method of its Environment to retrieve a list of the objects (the Fish) currently in the environment. It then iterates through that list, casting each item to a Fish, and calling the Fish's act method.

The act method calls the move method, which calls the nextLocation method to determine where the Fish will move during this timestep. The nextLocation method calls the emptyNeighbors method to get a list of the empty neighboring locations. The emptyNeighbors method works by calling the Environment's neighborsOf method to get a list of *all* neighboring locations, and then it traverses that list, removing locations that are not empty.

Once the emptyNeighbors method has returned the list of empty neighbors to the nextLocation method, the Location behind the fish is removed from that list, and one of the remaining locations in the list is chosen at random and returned. If there are no locations remaining in the list the current Location of the Fish is returned.

Once the nextLocation method has returned a location to the move method, the move method makes the following calls:

- It calls the changeLocation method to update the Fish's Location.
- It calls the changeDirection method to update the Fish's Direction.
- It calls its Environment's recordMove method to update the state of the Environment.

Finally, the move method returns true if it was able to move, and false otherwise.

In Chapters 1–2 the act method ends here (after calling move); however, in later chapters the act method attempts to breed and/or die at this point. The act method then returns control to the simulation.

9.8 Test-Taking Hints

Following are some simple suggestions that can be helpful when answering multiple-choice or free-response questions based on the case study.

- Use the Case-Study Quick Reference. Do not assume that you remember the exact names of methods, the order of their parameters, or the classes to which they belong. Double-checking in the quick reference can help eliminate small errors that could cost you points.
- If you are asked to reimplement a method that already exists, look up that method in the quick reference. You will find the code from the original implementation, and it could help you in implementing a change.

- Read the directions carefully. The question may tell you to assume that some methods other than the ones you are being asked to write have been modified. Your code must take those other modifications into account.

- Double-check your code to make sure you have satisfied all of the requirements of the question. Often there is a final step that updates either the current object or another object; be sure not to omit that final step.

Practice Multiple-Choice Questions

1. Assume that variable `env` is a properly initialized `Environment`. Which of the following expressions evaluates to the number of locations in environment `env`?

    A. `env.numAdjacentNeighbors()`

    B. `env.numRows() * env.numCols()`

    C. `env.numObjects()`

    D. `env.allObjects().length`

    E. `env.toString().size()`

2. Assume that variable `oneFish` represents a fish in the Marine Biology Simulation. Which of the following is a direction that `oneFish` would *not* swim in one timestep?

    A. `oneFish.direction().toLeft()`

    B. `oneFish.direction().toLeft(270)`

    C. `oneFish.direction().toLeft(90)`

    D. `oneFish.direction().toRight()`

    E. `oneFish.direction().reverse()`

3. Which of the following methods is defined in the `SlowFish` class because it is required to correctly extend the `Fish` class?

    A. `nextLocation`

    B. `generateChild`

    C. `move`

    D. `act`

    E. No methods are required to be implemented in the `SlowFish` class to correctly extend the `Fish` class.

4. (AB only) Assume that the `UnboundedEnvironment` class is changed so that `objectList` is a `LinkedList` instead of an `ArrayList`. Which other classes would need to be changed?

    A. `Fish`

    B. `Simulation`

    C. `Location`

    D. `Direction`

    E. No other class would need to be changed.

5. (AB only) Consider changing the return type of the `emptyNeighbors` method of the `Fish` class from `ArrayList` to `HashSet`, and changing the type of variable `emptyNbrs` from `ArrayList` to `HashSet`. Assume that each location has n neighbors, that the `isEmpty` method takes constant time, and that the `neighborsOf` method takes $O(n)$ time. Which of the following best characterizes the running time of the new version of `emptyNeighbors`?

    A. $O(n)$

    B. $O(1)$

    C. $O(\log n)$

    D. $O(n \log n)$

    E. $O(n^2)$

Answers to Multiple-Choice Questions

    1. B
    2. E
    3. E
    4. E
    5. A

PRACTICE EXAMINATIONS

Hints for Students

This section contains a few practical hints that may help you improve your performance on the AP Computer Science exam.

Multiple-Choice Questions

Hint 1

When the multiple-choice questions are graded, one-quarter of a point is subtracted for each wrong answer to compensate for guessing. Therefore, if you have no idea what the answer to a multiple-choice question is, you are probably better off skipping the question than just guessing. However, if you are able to eliminate one or more responses as definitely not the right answer, it is a good idea to make a guess among the remaining responses.

Hint 2

Many multiple-choice questions involve some code. It is usually better to look first at the question itself, rather than studying the code. Knowing what is being addressed by the question (e.g., what does the code do, what value is produced by executing the code on a particular input, or which line of code contains an error) will help you to focus on the important aspects of the code without wasting time trying to understand every detail.

Hint 3

Sometimes multiple-choice questions are grouped: two or three questions are asked about a common "preamble," which might, for example, be a piece of code or an explanation of a choice of data structures. Do not give up on the whole group of questions just because you are not able to answer the first question in the group! The second question may be easier; it may even give you a new insight that will help you answer the first question. (And remember, as suggested in hint 2 above, it is usually best to look at the actual questions before spending a lot of time reading the preamble.)

Free-Response Questions

Hint 1

The criteria for grading the free-response questions are determined by the chief faculty consultant, so some changes may occur from year to year. The current philosophy is that the score for a free-response question depends on whether the code works correctly. Syntactic details, programming style, and efficiency are very minor issues. Leaving out a few semicolons will not affect the score; neither will using one-character variable names. Comments are not necessary; however, including brief comments may help you to organize your thoughts and may make it easier for you to check your work. Unless the question specifically addresses the issue of efficiency, it is better to write simple, clear code than to write complicated, super-efficient code.

Note that code written in a language other than Java will probably receive no credit.

Hint 2

Free-response questions are often divided into several parts, each of which involves writing a method. The instructions for one part of the question may include something like this:

> In writing method XXX, you may include calls to method YYY, specified above in part (a).

It will usually (though not always) be easier for you to write method XXX if you do indeed include calls to method YYY. If it isn't immediately obvious to you how to use method YYY, spend a few minutes thinking about a different approach to writing method XXX that involves calls to YYY. This may save you time in the long run, because the version of XXX that uses YYY may be easier to write than the version you originally thought of.

Hint 3

If you are asked to write a method with a non-void return type, don't forget to return a value of the correct type.

Hint 4 (AB only)

Methods that implement operations on binary trees are almost always easier to write using recursion than using iteration.

Practice Examination A-1

Section I

Time: 1 hour and 15 minutes
Number of questions: 40
Percent of total grade: 50

1. The expression

        !(a || b)

    is equivalent to which of the following expressions?

    A. (a || b)
    B. (!a) || (!b)
    C. (!a) && (!b)
    D. !(a && b)
    E. (a || b) && (a && b)

2. Which of the following statements about classes and interfaces is true?

    A. A class can extend at most one other class, but can implement more than one interface.
    B. A class can extend more than one other class, and can implement more than one interface.
    C. A class can extend more than one other class, but can implement at most one interface.
    D. A class *must* extend another class and *must* implement at least one interface.
    E. A class need not extend another class but *must* implement at least one interface.

Questions 3–5 concern the following (incomplete) definition of the PosSeq class, which will be used to represent a sequence of positive integer values. Line numbers for the search method are included for reference for question 5.

```java
public class PosSeq {
    private int[] seq;

    // constructor
    public PosSeq( int seqLength ) {
        int val;
        seq = new int[seqLength];
        for (int k=0; k<seqLength; k++) {
            System.out.print("Enter a positive number: ");

            .
            :    missing code
            .

            seq[k] = val;
        }
    }


    public int getMax() {
    // precondition: seq.length > 0
        int final = value;
        for (int k=1; k<seq.length; k++) {
            if (seq[k] > final) statement
        }
        return final;
    }


1   public boolean search(int key) {
2       int k=0;
3       while ((k < seq.length) && (seq[k] != key)) k++;
4       if (seq[k] == key) return true;
5       return false;
6   }

}
```

3. The constructor for the `PosSeq` class is supposed to be an *interactive* method that initializes the `seq` array using positive numbers typed in by the person running the program. Assume that the method `readInt` reads and returns one integer value typed in by the user. Which of the following is the best replacement for the placeholder *missing code* in the `PosSeq` constructor?

    A. `val = readInt();`

    B. `val = readInt();`
       `if (val <= 0) val = 1;`

    C. `val = readInt();`
       `if (val <= 0) System.out.println("Bad input.");`

    D. `val = readInt();`
       `while (val <= 0) {`
       `   val = readInt();`
       `}`

    E. `val = readInt();`
       `while (val <= 0) {`
       `    System.out.println("Bad input");`
       `    System.out.print("Enter a positive number: ");`
       `    val = readInt();`
       `}`

4. Which of the following replacements for *value* and *statement* could be used to complete the `getMax` method so that it returns the largest value in the `seq` array?

	value	*statement*
A.	0	`final = k;`
B.	0	`final = seq[k];`
C.	`seq[0]`	`final = k;`
D.	`seq[0]`	`final = seq[k];`
E.	`k`	`final = k;`

5. The `search` method was intended to return `true` if and only if the given key value is in the `seq` array. However, the method is not written correctly. Which of the following statements about this method is true?

    A. There will be an error when the method is compiled because the `&&` operator used on line 3 is applied to a nonboolean expression.

    B. The test "`(seq[k] != key)`" on line 3 will cause an `IndexOutOfBoundsException` whenever `seq` contains the value key.

    C. The test "`(seq[k] != key)`" on line 3 will cause an `IndexOutOfBoundsException` whenever `seq` does *not* contain the value key.

    D. The test "`seq[k] == key`" on line 4 will cause an `IndexOutOfBoundsException` whenever `seq` contains the value key.

    E. The test "`seq[k] == key`" on line 4 will cause an `IndexOutOfBoundsException` whenever `seq` does *not* contain the value key.

6. Consider writing a method whose sole purpose is to write an error message using `System.out.print`. Which of the following best characterizes the choice between making the method's return type void and making it int?

(A.) The return type should be `void` because the method performs an operation and does not compute a value.

B. The return type should be `int` because that is the default return type for Java methods.

C. The return type should be `void` because `void` methods are more efficient than `int` methods.

D. The return type should be `int` because `int` methods are more efficient than `void` methods.

E. The return type should be `void` because the method does not need to be recursive.

7. Consider the following data field and method:

```
private ArrayList myList;

public boolean compare(ArrayList A) {
    for (int j=0; j<myList.size(); j++) {
        Object ob = myList.get(j);
        int k = A.size()-1;
        while (k >= 0 && !ob.equals(A.get(k))) k--;
        if (k < 0) return false;
    }
    return true;
}
```

Which of the following best describes when method `compare` returns true?

(A.) When A includes at least one copy of every object in `myList`.

B. When A contains the same objects as `myList` in the same order.

C. When A contains the same objects as `myList` in reverse order.

D. When A contains the same objects as `myList` either in the same order or in reverse order.

E. Never.

Questions 8 and 9 refer to the following definition of the `Person` class.

```
public class Person {
    private String firstName;
    private String lastName;
    private int age;

    // constructor
    public Person( String fn, String ln, int a ) {
        firstName = fn;
        lastName = ln;
        age = a;
    }
    public String getFirstName() { return firstName; }
    public String getLastName() { return lastName; }
    public int getAge() { return age; }
}
```

8. Assume that a variable P has been declared as follows:

    ```
    Person[] P;
    ```

    and that P has been initialized with data for twenty people. Which of the following correctly tests whether the third person's age is greater than 10?

    A. `P.getAge[2] > 10`

    B. `P.Person[2] > 10`

    C. `P[2].Person.getAge() > 10`

    D. `P[2].getAge() > 10`

    E. `P.Person.getAge[2] > 10`

9. Assume that variables p1 and p2 have been declared as follows:

    ```
    Person p1, p2;
    ```

    Which of the following is the best way to test whether the people represented by p1 and p2 have the same first name?

    A. `p1 == p2`

    B. `p1.getFirstName().equals(p2.getFirstName())`

    C. `p1.getFirstName() == p2.getFirstName()`

    D. `p1.equals(p2)`

    E. `p2.equals(p1)`

Questions 10 and 11 concern the design of a data structure to store information about which seats on an airplane are reserved. The airplane has N rows (where N is some large number); each row has four seats. Two data structures are being considered:

Data Structure 1: An array of Rows, where a Row is a class with four boolean fields, one for each seat in the row. The length of the array is N. The fields of the kth element in the array are `true` if and only if the corresponding seats in row k are reserved.

Data Structure 2: An array of Reservations, where a Reservation is a class with two integer fields: a row number and a seat number. The length of the array is initially 0. Each time a seat is reserved, a new array is allocated, containing one more element than the previous array; the old array is copied over into the new array, and then the last element of the array is filled in with the newly reserved seat's row and number.

10. Under which of the following conditions does Data Structure 1 require less storage than Data Structure 2?

    A. No seats are reserved.
    B. All seats are reserved.
    C. Only the seats in the first row are reserved.
    D. Only the seats in the last row are reserved.
    E. Data Structure 1 never requires less storage than Data Structure 2.

11. Which of the following operations can be implemented more efficiently using Data Structure 1 than using Data Structure 2?

    Operation I: Determine how many seats are reserved.
    Operation II: Determine whether all seats in a particular row (given the row number) are reserved.
    Operation III: Reserve a seat on a half-full airplane.

    A. I only
    B. II only
    C. III only
    D. I and II
    E. II and III

12. Which of the following statements about a method's preconditions is true?

A. They must be provided by the writer of the method or the method will not compile.

B. They are translated by the compiler into runtime checks.

C. They provide information to users of the method, specifying what is expected to be true whenever the method is called.

D. They provide information to the writer of the method, specifying how it is to be implemented.

E. They provide information about the class that contains the method.

13. Assume that variable A is an `ArrayList` of `Integers`. Consider the following code segment:

```
boolean flag = false;
Integer zero = new Integer(0);
for (int k = 0; k < A.size(); k++) {
    flag = flag && (A.get(k).compareTo(zero) > 0);
}
```

Which of the following best describes what this code segment does?

A. Always sets `flag` to `true`.

B. Always sets `flag` to `false`.

C. Sets `flag` to `true` if every value in A is positive.

D. Sets `flag` to `true` if any value in A is positive.

E. Sets `flag` to `true` if the last value in A is positive.

14. Consider the following code segment:

```
if (n > 0) n = -n;
if (n < 0) n = 0;
```

This segment is equivalent to which of the following?

A. n = 0;

B. if (n > 0) n = 0;

C. if (n < 0) n = 0;

D. if (n > 0) n = -n; else n = 0;

E. if (n < 0) n = 0; else n = -n;

Questions 15 and 16 refer to the following incomplete definitions of the Person and Child classes (note that Child is a subclass of Person).

```
public class Person {
    private String name;
    private int age;

    // constructor
    public Person(String n, int a) {
        name = n;
        age = a;
    }

    // other methods not shown
}

public class Child extends Person {
    private String school;

    // constructor
    public Child(String n, int a, String s) {
        .
        .   missing code
        .
    }

    public String getSchool() {
        return school;
    }
}
```

15. Which of the following replacements for *missing code* in the Child class constructor would compile without error?

    (A.) `super(n, a);`
        `school = s;`

    B. `school = s;`
       `super(n, a);`

    C. `name = n;`
       `age = a;`
       `school = s;`

    D. `super(n);`
       `age = a;`
       `school = s;`

    E. `super(n, a, s);`

16. Assume that the `Child` constructor has been defined correctly. Consider the following code segment.

```
Person p = new Child("Chris", 10, "Lincoln School");
System.out.println(p.getSchool());
```

Which of the following statements about this code segment is true?

A. It will not compile because the type of p is `Person`, and class `Person` has no `getSchool` method.

B. It will not compile because the type of p is `Person`, and the type of the value assigned to p is `Child`.

C. It will compile, but there will be a runtime error when the first line is executed because the type of p is `Person`, and the type of the value assigned to p is `Child`.

D. It will compile, but there will be a runtime error when the second line is executed because the type of p is `Person`, and class `Person` has no `getSchool` method.

E. It will compile and run without error, and will print `Lincoln School`.

17. Consider the following recursive method:

```
public static void printStars(int k) {
    if (k>0) {
        printStars(k-1);
        for (int j=1; j<=k; j++) System.out.print("*");
        System.out.println();
    }
}
```

What is output as a result of the call `printStars(4)`?

A. ```
****
***
**
*
```

B. ```
*
**
***
****
```

C. ```
***
**
*
```

D. ```
*
**
***
```

E. ```
*
*
*
*
```
```

18. A program is being written by a team of programmers. One programmer is implementing a class called Employee; another programmer is writing code that will use the Employee class. Which of the following aspects of the public methods of the Employee class does *not* need to be known by both programmers?

    A. The methods' names
    B. The methods' return types
    C. What the methods do
    D. How the methods are implemented
    E. The numbers and types of the methods' parameters

19. Consider writing a program to be used by a car dealership to keep track of information about the cars they sell. For each car, they would like to keep track of the model number, the price, and the miles per gallon the car gets in the city and on the highway. Which of the following is the best way to represent the information?

    A. Define one class, Car, with four fields: modelNumber, price, cityMilesPerGallon, and highwayMilesPerGallon.
    B. Define one superclass, Car, with four subclasses: ModelNumber, Price, CityMilesPer-Gallon, and HighwayMilesPerGallon.
    C. Define five unrelated classes: Car, ModelNumber, Price, CityMilesPerGallon, and HighwayMilesPerGallon.
    D. Define five classes: Car, ModelNumber, Price, CityMilesPerGallon, and Highway-MilesPerGallon. Make HighwayMilesPerGallon a subclass of CityMilesPerGallon, make CityMilesPerGallon a subclass of Price, make Price a subclass of ModelNumber, and make ModelNumber a subclass of Car.
    E. Define five classes: Car, ModelNumber, Price, CityMilesPerGallon, and Highway-MilesPerGallon. Make Car a subclass of ModelNumber, make ModelNumber a subclass of Price, make Price a subclass of CityMilesPerGallon, and make CityMilesPer-Gallon a subclass of HighwayMilesPerGallon.

20. Consider using binary search to look for a given value in an array of integers. Which of the following must be true in order for the search to work?

    I.   The values in the array are stored in sorted order.
    II. The array does not contain any duplicate values.
    III. The array does not contain any negative values.

    A. I only
    B. II only
    C. III only
    D. I and II
    E. II and III

Questions 21–24 involve reasoning about the Marine Biology case study.

21. Which of the following classes implements the Locatable interface?

    A. ArrayList
    B. Direction
    C. Location
    D. Color
    E. Fish

22. Assume that variable myFish is a properly initialized Fish. Which of the following method calls could be made from a method that is in a new class that is *not* a subclass of Fish?

    A. myFish.act()
    B. myFish.move()
    C. myFish.breed()
    D. myFish.nextLocation()
    E. myFish.generateChild()

23. Consider implementing a new class called NewFish that extends the Fish class. Assume that a constructor for the NewFish class is written that has four parameters: Environment env, Location loc, Direction dir, Color col. Which of the following could be the body of the NewFish constructor?

    A. The body could be empty (and the default Fish constructor would be called).
    B. super(env, loc, dir, col);
    C. initialize(env, loc, dir, col);
    D. super(env. loc, dir, col);
       initialize(env, loc, dir, col);
    E. initialize(env, loc, dir, col);
       super(env, loc, dir, col);

24. Consider changing the UnboundedEnvironment class so that the Locatable objects in the environment are stored in an array instead of in an ArrayList. Which of the following methods would *not* need to be changed?

    A. numObjects
    B. allObjects
    C. recordMove
    D. isEmpty
    E. objectAt

25. Consider the following code segment. Assume that method `readInt` reads and returns one integer value.

```
int x;
int sumNeg=0;
int sumPos=0;
x = readInt();
while (x != 0) {
    if (x < 0)
        sumNeg += x;
    if (x > 0)
        sumPos += x;
    x = readInt();
}
if (sumNeg < -8)
    System.out.println("negative sum: " + sumNeg);
if (sumPos > 8)
    System.out.println("positive sum: " + sumPos);
```

Which of the following inputs causes every line of code to be executed at least once?

A. 0
B. 2   4   6   8   0
C. 2 -2   4 -4   0
D. 4 -4   6 -6   0
E. -2 -4 -6 -8   0

26. Assume that a program has been run on an input that caused every line of code to be executed at least once. Also assume that there were no runtime errors and that the program produced the correct output. Which of the following is a valid assumption?

A. If the program is changed only by rearranging lines of code, and then run on the same input, there will be no runtime errors, and the program will produce the correct output.

B. If the program is changed only by removing one line of code, and then run on the same input, there will be no runtime errors, and the program will produce the correct output.

C. If the program is run on a different input, there will be no runtime errors, and the program will produce the correct output.

D. If the program is run on a different input, there will be no runtime errors, but the program might produce incorrect output.

E. None of the above assumptions is valid.

Questions 27 and 28 refer to the following incomplete definition of the Time class.

```
public class Time implements Comparable {
    private int hours;    // 0 <= hours
    private int minutes; // 0 <= minutes <= 59

    // constructor not shown

    public int compareTo(Object other) {
        Time oth = (Time)other;
        .
        :   missing code
        .
    }

    // other methods not shown
}
```

27. Which of the following is the best reason for making the Time class implement the Comparable interface?

    (A.) It will allow a Time object to be passed as an argument to any method whose corresponding parameter is of type Comparable.

    B. It will allow a Time object to be stored in an ArrayList.

    C. It will allow a Time object to be printed.

    D. It will allow a Time object to be compared to an int.

    E. It will allow a Time object to be constructed more efficiently.

28. Assume that the hours field is never negative, and the minutes field is always between 0 and 59. Which of the following can be used to replace *missing code* in the body of the compareTo method to correctly complete that method?

    A. `return (hours < oth.hours && minutes < oth.minutes);`

    B. `return (hours < oth.hours || minutes < oth.minutes);`

    C. ```
       if (hours < oth.hours || minutes < oth.minutes) return -1;
       if (hours > oth.hours || minutes > oth.minutes) return 1;
       return 0;
       ```

    (D.) ```
       if (hours < oth.hours) return -1;
       if (hours > oth.hours) return 1;
       if (minutes < oth.minutes) return -1;
       if (minutes == oth.minutes) return 0;
       return 1;
       ```

    E. ```
       if ((hours < oth.hours) && (minutes < oth.minutes)) return -1;
       if ((hours == oth.hours) && (minutes == oth.minutes)) return 0;
       return 1;
       ```
       ```

29. Consider the following code segment:

```
ArrayList L = new ArrayList();
for (int k=1; k<6; k++) {
    if (k%2 == 0) L.add("?");
    else L.add("!");
}
```

Which of the following correctly illustrates the list represented by `ArrayList L` after this code segment executes?

A. `[?, ?, ?, ?, ?]`

B. `[!, !, !, !, !]`

C. `[!, ?, !, ?, !]`

D. `[?, !, ?, !, ?]`

E. `[?, ?, !, ?, ?]`

30. Consider the following data field and method, with line numbers included in the method for reference.

```
String word;
```

```
1 public String oddChars() {
2    String result = "";
3    for (int k=0; k<word.length(); k+=2) {
4        result += word.substring(k, k);
5    }
6    return result;
7 }
```

Method `oddChars` was intended to return a string that contains every other character in `word`, starting with the first character. For example, if `word` is `"abcd"`, `oddChars` should return `"ac"`; and if `word` is `"abcde"`, it should return `"ace"`. However, when the method is tested it is discovered that it always returns an empty string.

Which of the following would fix method `oddChars`?

A. Change the for loop initialization on line 3 from k=0 to k=1

B. Change the for loop stopping condition on line 3 from `k<word.length()` to `k<=word.length()`

C. Change the for loop increment on line 3 from k+=2 to k++

D. Change line 4 to `result += word.substring(k, k+1);`

E. Change line 4 to `result += word.substring(k);`

Questions 31–33 refer to the following Location class.

```java
public class Location {
    private String name;
    private double latitude;
    private double longitude;

    // constructor
    public Location(String n, double lat, double lon) {
        name = n;
        latitude = lat;
        longitude = lon;
    }

    public String getName() {
        return name;
    }

    public void setName(String n) {
        name = n;
    }

    public boolean equals(Object other) {
        return (latitude == ((Location)other).latitude &&
                longitude == ((Location)other).longitude);
    }
}
```

31. Assume that variables L1, L2, and L3 have been declared and initialized as follows:

```java
Location L1 = new Location("Baltimore", 39.18, 76.38);
Location L2 = new Location("Baltimore", 39.18, 76.38);
Location L3 = new Location("Albany",    39.18, 76.38);
```

Which of the following expressions evaluate to true?

I.   L1.equals(L2)

II. L2.equals(L3)

III. L1 == L2

A. I only

B. II only

C. III only

D. I and II

E. I and III

32. Consider the following code segment.

```
Location L1 = new Location("Baltimore", 39.18, 76.38);
Location L2 = L1;
Location L3 = L1;
L1.setName("NewYork");
L2.setName("Chicago");
System.out.print(L1.getName() + " " + L2.getName() +
                " " + L3.getName());
```

What is printed when the code executes?

A. NewYork NewYork NewYork

B. Chicago Chicago Chicago

C. NewYork Chicago Baltimore

D. Chicago Chicago Baltimore

E. NewYork Chicago Baltimore

33. Consider the following data field and incomplete method:

```
Location[] locList;

public boolean locWithName(String name) {
// precondition: neither name nor locList is null
// postcondition: returns true iff there is a location in locList
//                with the given name
   for (int k=0; k<locList.length; k++) {
      if ( condition ) return true;
   }
   return false;
}
```

Which of the following could be used to replace *condition* so that method `locWithName` works as specified by its pre- and postconditions?

A. name.equals(locList[k].getName())

B. name.equals(locList.getName()[k])

C. name == locList.getName[k]

D. name == locList[k].getName()

E. name == locList[k]

34. Consider the following interface definition:

```
public interface Employee {
    public double getSalary();
    public void setSalary( double newSalary );
}
```

Which of the following is a correct implementation of the Employee interface?

A.
```
public class Person implements Employee {
    public double getSalary;
    public void setSalary;
}
```

B.
```
public class Person implements Employee {
    public double getSalary() { return salary; }
    public void setSalary( double newSalary ) {
        salary = newSalary;
    }
}
```

C.
```
public class Person implements Employee {
    private double salary;

    public double getSalary() { return salary; }
}
```

D.
```
public class Person implements Employee {
    private double salary;

    public double getSalary() { return salary; }
    public void setSalary( double newSalary ) {
        salary = newSalary;
    }
}
```

E.
```
public class Person implements Employee {
    private double salary;

    private double getSalary() { return salary; }
    private void setSalary( double newSalary ) {
        salary = newSalary;
    }
}
```

35. Assume that a class includes the following three methods:

```
public static int min(int x, int y) {
    if (x < y) return x;
    else return y;
}

public static int min(String s, String t) {
    if (s.length() < t.length()) return s.length();
    else return t.length();
}

public static void testMin() {
    System.out.println(min(3, "hello"));
}
```

Which of the following best describes what happens when this code is compiled and executed?

(A.) The code will not compile because the types of the arguments used in the call to min do not match the types of the parameters in either version of min.

B. The code will not compile because it includes two methods with the same name and the same return type.

C. The code will not compile because it includes two methods with the same name and the same number of parameters.

D. The code will compile and execute without error; the output will be 3.

E. The code will compile and execute without error; the output will be 5.

36. Which of the following code segments sets variable sum to be the sum of the even numbers between 1 and 99?

A.
```
int k;
int sum = 0;
for (k=1; k<=99; k++) {
    if (k%2 == 0) sum++;
}
```

B.
```
int k;
int sum = 0;
for (k=1; k<=99; k++) {
    if (k%2 == 0) sum += k;
}
```

C.
```
int k = 1;
int sum = 0;
while (k <= 99) {
    sum += k;
    k += 2;
}
```

D.
```
int k = 2;
int sum = 0;
while (k <= 99) {
    sum++;
    k += 2;
}
```

E.
```
int k = 2;
int sum = 0;
while (k <= 99) {
    k += 2;
    sum += k;
}
```

37. Consider the following code segment:

```
String[] myStrings = new String[3];
myStrings[0] = "abc";
myStrings[1] = myStrings[0];
myStrings[0] = "xxx";
myStrings[2] = myStrings[1] + "XYZ";
for (int k=0; k<3; k++) System.out.print(myStrings[k] + " ");
```

abc, abc,
xxx, abc, abcXYZ

What is printed when this code executes?

A. xxx xxx xxxXYZ

B. xxx abc abcXYZ

C. abcxxx abc abcxxxXYZ

D. xxx xxx xxxZYZ

E. abcxxx abcxxx abcxxxXYZ

38. Consider the following (incomplete) method:

```
public void changeOb( Object value ) {
    .
    .
    .
}
```

Assume that variable k is an int, that variable s is a String, and that variable ob is an Object. Which of the following calls to method changeOb will compile without error?

Call I	Call II	Call III
changeOb(k);	changeOb(s);	changeOb(ob);

A. I only

B. II only

C. III only

D. I and II only

E. II and III only

Questions 39 and 40 concern the following recursive method:

```
public int mystery(int k) {
    if (k == 1) return 0;
    else return(1 + mystery(k/2));
}
```

16
8
4
2
1

39. What value is returned by the call `mystery(16)`?

    A. 0

    B. 2

    C. 4

    D. 5

    E. No value is returned because the call causes an infinite recursion.

40. Which of the following best characterizes the values of k for which the call `mystery(k)` leads to an infinite recursion?

    A. No values

    B. All positive values

    C. All nonpositive values

    D. All odd values

    E. All even values

Section II

Time: 1 hour and 45 minutes
Number of questions: 4
Percent of total grade: 50

Question 1

This question involves reasoning about the code from the Marine Biology case study.

Consider implementing a new type of Locatable object as part of the Marine Biology Simulation. This new Locatable will be a Fisherman and will behave as follows during each timestep of the simulation:

- The Fisherman will go home (remove himself from the environment) if he has been fishing for more than 30 timesteps (as recorded by his private steps field) or if he has been fishing for more than 10 timesteps and the number of fish he has caught is less 1/10 times the number of timesteps he has been fishing.

- If the Fisherman does not go home he will move as follows and then increment the number of timesteps he has been fishing.

  - He will check his neighboring locations to determine if there are any Fish around him.
  - If there are Fish around him he will:

      Choose one of the Fish at random.
      Catch that Fish (by asking it to die).
      Increment the number of fish he has caught.
      Move to the location where the Fish was.

  - If there are no Fish around him he will move randomly into a neighboring location.

An incomplete declaration of the Fisherman class is shown below.

```
public class Fisherman implements Locatable {

    private int steps;
    private int fishCaught;
    // other private fields not shown

    public Location location() { /* not shown */ }
    public Environment environment() { /* not shown */ }

    //
    // Finds all neighboring locations that contain a fish object
    // postcondition: Returns an ArrayList containing the Locations of
    //                any fish in the neighbors of the fisherman's
    //                current location. If there are no fish adjacent
    //                to the fisherman, an empty ArrayList is returned.
    //
    private ArrayList fishNeighbors() { /* part (a) */ }
```

```
//
// Moves this Fisherman in its environment
//
protected void move() { /* part (b) */ }


//
// Acts for one step in the simulation
//
public void act() { /* part (c) */ }


//
// Modifies the fisherman's location and notifies the environment.
//
protected void changeLocation(Location newLoc) { /* not shown */ }


    // other methods not shown
}
```

Assume that, in order to allow the Fisherman to catch a fish, the die method in the Fish class has been changed from a protected method to a public method.

Also assume that in the Environment being used by this simulation the neighborsOf method returns all eight neighbors, including diagonals, of the given location.

Part (a)

Write the helper method `fishNeighbors`, which returns an `ArrayList` containing the `Locations` of the `Fish` adjacent to the `Fisherman`. Below are some examples illustrating how the method should work.

Environment   Result of Calling `fishNeighbors`

	0	1	2	3
0	Fish		Fish	
1		Fisherman		
2	Fish			Fish
3				

[(0,0) (0,2) (2,0)]

	0	1	2	3
0	Fish	Fish	Fish	
1		Fisherman	Fish	
2	Fish	Fish		Fish
3		Fish		

[(0,0) (0,1) (0,2) (1,2) (2,0) (2,1)]

	0	1	2	3
0				Fish
1		Fisherman		
2				Fish
3		Fish	Fish	

[ ]

Assume that the `Fisherman`'s neighboring locations are either empty or contain `Fish` (i.e., there are no other objects in the environment). Complete method `fishNeighbors` below.

```
//
// Finds all neighboring locations that contain a fish object
// postcondition: Returns an ArrayList containing the Locations of
//                any fish in the neighbors of the fisherman's
//                current location.  If there are no fish adjacent
//                to the fisherman, an empty ArrayList is returned.
//
private ArrayList fishNeighbors() {
```

Part (b)

Write the `move` method for the `Fisherman` class. The `Fisherman` moves as follows:

- He will check his neighboring locations to determine if there are any `Fish` around him.
- If there are `Fish` around him he will:
  - Choose one of the `Fish` at random.
  - Catch that `Fish` (by asking it to die).
  - Increment the number of fish he has caught.
  - Move to the location where the `Fish` was.
- If there are no `Fish` around him he will move randomly into a neighboring location.

In writing the `move` method you must use the `changeLocation` method specified in the class declaration. You may also call `fishNeighbors`; assume that `fishNeighbors` works as specified regardless of what you wrote in part (a).

Complete method `move` below.

```
//
// Moves this Fisherman in its environment
//
protected void move() {
```

Part (c)

Write the `act` method for the `Fisherman` class. The `Fisherman` will act as follows:

- The `Fisherman` will go home (remove himself from the environment) if he has been fishing for more than 30 timesteps (as recorded by his private `steps` field), or if he has been fishing for more than 10 timesteps and the number of fish he has caught is less than 1/10 times the number of timesteps he has been fishing.
- If the `Fisherman` does not go home he will move and then increment the number of timesteps he has been fishing.

In writing the `act` method you may call `move`; assume that `move` works as specified regardless of what you wrote in part (b).

Complete method `act` below.

```
//
// Acts for one step in the simulation
//
public void act() {
```

Question 2

Assume that a class called `BankAccount` has been implemented to represent one person's bank account. A partial declaration of the `BankAccount` class is given below.

```
public class BankAccount {

    private int accountNum;
    private double balance;

    // constructor not shown

    // returns the account number
    public int getAccountNum() { return accountNum; }

    // returns the current balance (how much money is in the account)
    public double getBalance() { return balance; }

    // adds the given amount to the current balance
    public void doDeposit(double amount) { balance += amount; }

    // subtracts the given amount from the current balance
    public void doWithdrawal(double amount) { balance -= amount; }
}
```

Part (a)

In order to process the various transactions performed at the bank (either by ATM or bank teller) a `Transaction` class is needed: A `Transaction` includes an account number (an integer), the transaction type (a string with a single character "d" for deposit or "w" for withdrawal), and the amount of the transaction (a double value for the amount to be deposited or withdrawn). Those values are assigned when the `Transaction` is created, and can be accessed but not modified.

Write the complete class declaration for class `Transaction`. Include all necessary instance variables and implementations of its constructor and methods.

Part (b)

An `ATMTransaction` class (a subclass of `Transaction`) is also needed to represent one ATM transaction. In addition to the information in a `Transaction`, an `ATMTransaction` contains a string that represents the location of the ATM that was used. The value of that location is assigned when the `ATMTransaction` is created, and can be accessed but not modified. Write a complete class declaration for the `ATMTransaction` class. Include all necessary instance variables and implementations of its constructor and methods.

Part (c)

A class Bank will be used to store information about all of the accounts in one bank, and to perform transactions on those accounts. An incomplete declaration of the Bank class is given below.

```
public class Bank {

    private BankAccount [] accounts;

    // precondition: accountNum is the number of an account in the
    //                accounts array.
    // postcondition: returns the index in the accounts array of
    //                the given account number.
    private int getIndex(int accountNum) { /* not shown */ }

    // precondition: trans is a transaction for an account in the
    //                accounts array.
    // postcondition: the account for trans has been modified to
    //                reflect the change specified by the transaction
    public void doOneTransaction(Transaction trans) { /* part (c) */ }
}
```

Write the doOneTransaction method of the Bank class, which has one Transaction parameter. Method doOneTransaction should find the BankAccount with the account number in the given Transaction, and it should deposit or withdraw the amount in the given Transaction from that account as appropriate.

For example, assume that accounts.length is 4 and that the elements in the array have the account numbers and balances shown below.

```
              [0]       [1]       [2]       [3]
account #:    100       107       102       105
balance:      100.27    57.30     150.00    5.25
```

Here are some examples to illustrate what the call oneTransaction(trans) should do.

Value of trans		Modified element of accounts array
accountNum:	107	[1]
transactionType:	"d"	107
amount:	10.50	67.80
accountNum:	100	[0]
transactionType:	"w"	100
amount:	100.27	0.0
accountNum:	105	[3]
transactionType:	"w"	105
amount:	6.00	-.75

In writing method doOneTransaction, you may include calls to method getIndex specified above in the declaration of the Bank class. You may also call the methods of the BankAccount and Transaction classes.

Complete method doOneTransaction below.

```
// precondition: trans is a transaction for an account in the
//               accounts array
// postcondition: the account for trans has been modified to
//                reflect the change specified by the transaction
public void doOneTransaction(Transaction trans) {
```

Question 3

Part (a)

Write method `numInArray`, as started below. `numInArray` should return the number of times the string `s` occurs in array `A`.

For example, assume that array `A` is as shown below.

[0]	[1]	[2]	[3]	[4]	[5]	[6]
"java"	"is"	"nice"	"so"	"nice"	"it"	"is"

Here are some examples of calls to method `numInArray`.

Method call	Returned value
`numInArray(A, "java")`	1
`numInArray(A, "is")`	2
`numInArray(A, "nice")`	2
`numInArray(A, "ja")`	0

Complete method `numInArray` below.

```
// postcondition: returns the number of times s occurs in A
public static int numInArray(String[] A, String s) {
```

Part (b)

Write method `printAllNums`, as started below. For every string s in array A, `printAllNums` should write (using `System.out.println`) the string s, followed by a colon and a space, then followed by the number of times that string occurs in array B.

For example, assume that arrays A and B are as shown below.

```
          [0]      [1]      [2]     [3]
   A:     "ice"   "cream"   "is"   "nice"


          [0]      [1]      [2]     [3]     [4]      [5]      [6]
   B:     "java"   "is"    "nice"  "so"   "nice"   "it"     "is"
```

The call `printAllNums(A, B)` should produce the following output:

```
ice: 0
cream: 0
is: 2
nice: 2
```

In writing `printAllNums`, you may include calls to method `numInArray`. Assume that `numInArray` works as specified, regardless of what you wrote in part (a).

Complete method `printAllNums` below.

```
// postcondition: for all k such that 0 <= k < A.length,
//                prints the string in A[k] followed by a colon
//                and a space and the number of times that string
//                occurs in B
public static void printAllNums( String[] A, String[] B ) {
```

Question 4

Assume that the `Name` class, which is partially defined below, is used to represent people's first names.

```java
public class Name {
    private String myName;

    public Name( String S ) { myName = S; }  // constructor
    public int length() { return myName.length(); }
    public String prefix( int k ) { /* part (a) */ }
    public String suffix( int k ) { /* part (b) */ }
    public boolean isNickname( Name n ) { /* part (c) */ }
}
```

Part (a)

Write the `prefix` method of the `Name` class. The `prefix` method should return a string containing the first k characters in the name. If the name has fewer than k characters, the `prefix` method should return the entire string.

For example, assume that name N represents the name `"Sandy"`. Below are some examples of calls to N's `prefix` method.

k	Result of the call `N.prefix( k )`
0	`""`
1	`"S"`
2	`"Sa"`
3	`"San"`
5	`"Sandy"`
6	`"Sandy"`

Complete method `prefix` below.

```java
// precondition: k >= 0
// postcondition: returns a string containing the first k letters
//                in this name; if this name has fewer than k
//                letters, returns the whole name
public String prefix( int k ) {
```

Part (b)

Write the `suffix` method of the `Name` class. The `suffix` method should return a string containing the last `k` characters in the name. If the name has fewer than `k` characters, the `suffix` method should return the entire string.

For example, assume that name `N` represents the name `"Sandy"`. Below are some examples of calls to `N`'s `suffix` method.

k	Result of the call `N.suffix( k )`
0	`""`
1	`"y"`
2	`"dy"`
3	`"ndy"`
5	`"Sandy"`
6	`"Sandy"`

Complete method `suffix` below.

```
// precondition: k >= 0
// postcondition: returns a string containing the last k letters in
//                this name; if this name has fewer than k letters,
//                returns the whole name
public String suffix( int k ) {
```

Part (c)

Write the `isNickname` method of the `Name` class. The `isNickname` method should return `true` if and only if its parameter `nick` is made up of two parts:

1. A nonempty string that is a prefix of this name

2. The suffix `"ie"`

Below are some examples.

Name represented by N	Name represented by `nick`	Value returned by the call `N.isNickname( nick )`
Susan	Susie	true
David	Davie	true
Ann	Annie	true
Susan	Sus	false
Ann	Robbie	false
David	Davy	false

In writing method `isNickname`, you may include calls to methods `prefix` and `suffix`. Assume that both methods work as specified, regardless of what you wrote in parts (a) and (b).

Complete method `isNickname` below.

```
// precondition: nick is not null
public boolean isNickname( Name nick ) {
```

Answers to Section I

1.	C	21.	E
2.	A	22.	A
3.	E	23.	B
4.	D	24.	D
5.	E	25.	D
6.	A	26.	E
7.	A	27.	A
8.	D	28.	D
9.	B	29.	C
10.	B	30.	D
11.	E	31.	D
12.	C	32.	B
13.	B	33.	A
14.	A	34.	D
15.	A	35.	A
16.	A	36.	B
17.	B	37.	B
18.	D	38.	E
19.	A	39.	C
20.	A	40.	C

Answers to Section II

Question 1
Part (a)

```
private ArrayList fishNeighbors() {
    ArrayList nbrs = environment().neighborsOf(location());
    ArrayList fsh = new ArrayList();

    for(int i=0; i<nbrs.size(); i++) {
        Location loc = (Location)nbrs.get(i);
        if(!environment().isEmpty(loc)) fsh.add(loc);
    }
    return fsh;
}
```

Part (b)

```
protected void move() {
    Random r = RandNumGenerator.getInstance();
    ArrayList fshLocations = fishNeighbors();

    if (fshLocations.size() > 0) {
        int x = r.nextInt(fshLocations.size());
        Location loc = (Location)fshLocations.get(x));
        Fish f = (Fish)(environment().objectAt(loc));
        f.die();
        fishCaught++;
        changeLocation(loc);
    } else {
        ArrayList nbrs = environment().neighborsOf(location());
        int x = r.nextInt(nbrs.size());
        changeLocation((Location)nbrs.get(x));
    }
}
```

Part (c)

```
public void act() {
    if ( steps > 30 || ( steps > 10 && steps/10 > fishCaught) )
        environment().remove(this);
    else {
        move();
        steps++;
    }
}
```

Grading Guide

Part (a) `fishNeighbors`   3 Points

+ $\frac{1}{2}$ Retrieve the neighbors of the current location

+1 Loop over the neighbors
    + $\frac{1}{2}$ attempt (must reference list in loop)
    + $\frac{1}{2}$ correct

+1 Determine and store locations of objects
    + $\frac{1}{2}$ attempt to check location in environment to see if it is empty
    + $\frac{1}{2}$ correctly check location and add it to result list

+ $\frac{1}{2}$ Correctly initialize result list and return it (must add to it during method)

Part (b) `move`   4 Points

+ $\frac{1}{2}$ Create and use an instance of `RandomNumGenerator`

+ $\frac{1}{2}$ Call `fishNeighbors`

+2 Fish around the `Fisherman` (all pieces must be contained within a decision structure)
    + $\frac{1}{2}$ choose an appropriate index from available list
    + $\frac{1}{2}$ retrieve the object at the chosen location and ask it to die
    + $\frac{1}{2}$ increment `fishCaught`
    + $\frac{1}{2}$ appropriately call `changeLocation`

+1 No Fish around the `Fisherman`
    + $\frac{1}{2}$ retrieve neighboring locations and choose one at random
    + $\frac{1}{2}$ appropriately call `changeLocation`

Part (c) `act`   2 Points

+1 Decision
    + $\frac{1}{2}$ attempt at decision (must have at least one part of the condition correct for attempt)
    + $\frac{1}{2}$ correct decision

+1 Actions (need to be in correct place with respect to condition)
    + $\frac{1}{2}$ remove the current object from the environment
    + $\frac{1}{2}$ call `move` and increment the step count

Question 2
Part (a)

```
public class Transaction {

    private int accountNum;
    private String type;
    private double amount;

    public Transaction(int an, String t, double amt) {
        accountNum = an;
        type = t;
        amount = amt;
    }

    public int getAccountNum() { return accountNum; }
    public String getType() { return type; }
    public double getAmount() { return amount; }
}
```

Note: Points will be deducted if modifier methods (e.g., setAmount) are written.

Part (b)

```
public class ATMTransaction extends Transaction {

    private String location;

    public ATMTransaction(int an, String t, double amt, String loc) {
        super(an, t, amt);
        location = loc;
    }

    public String getLocation() { return location; }
}
```

Part (c)

```
public void doOneTransaction(Transaction trans) {
    int index = getIndex(trans.getAccountNum());
    if (trans.getType().equals("w"))
        accounts[index].doWithdrawal(trans.getAmount());
    else
        accounts[index].doDeposit(trans.getAmount());
}
```

Grading Guide

Part (a) The Transaction class   4 Points

   +1 Private field declarations

   +1 Constructor

      + 1/2 attempt (must include some parameters)

      + 1/2 correct

   +1 1/2 Accessor methods

      + 1/2 attempt (must contain an attempt at methods for each variable)

      +1 correct

   + 1/2 Absence of mutator methods

Part (b) The ATMTransactions class   3 Points

   + 1/2 Class header

   + 1/2 Private fields

   +1 Constructor

      + 1/2 attempt (must include some parameters and a call to super)

      + 1/2 correct

   +1 Accessor method for location

Part (c) doOneTransaction   2 Points

   + 1/2 Call to getIndex

   +1 Determine transaction type

      + 1/2 attempt (must include a call to accessor method from part (a))

      + 1/2 correct

   + 1/2 Appropriate call to BankAccount method to perform the transaction

Question 3
Part (a)

```java
public static int numInArray(String[] A, String s) {
   int count = 0;

   for (int k=0; k<A.length; k++) {
      if (A[k].equals(s)) count++;
   }
   return count;
}
```

Part (b)

```java
public static void printAllNums( String[] A, String[] B ) {
   for (int k=0; k<A.length; k++) {
      System.out.println(A[k] + ": " + numInArray(B, A[k]));
   }
}
```

Grading Guide

Part (a) numInArray   5 Points

+1 Initialize counter

+1 Loop over values in array
   + 1/2 attempt
   + 1/2 correct

+1 Compare against parameter
   + 1/2 attempt
   + 1/2 correct

+1 Increment counter in appropriate place

+1 Return counter

Part (b) printAllNums   4 Points

+1 Loop over values in A
   + 1/2 attempt
   + 1/2 correct

+1 Retrieve each individual value from A

+1 Call numInArray to check for number of occurrences

+1 Use System.out.println with value from A and count

Question 4
Part (a)

```
public String prefix( int k ) {
    if (myName.length() < k) return myName;
    else return myName.substring(0,k);
}
```

Part (b)

```
public String suffix( int k ) {
    int from;
    if (k > myName.length()) from = 0;
    else from = myName.length() - k;
    return myName.substring(from);
}
```

Part (c)

```
public boolean isNickname( Name n ) {
    if (!n.suffix(2).equals("ie")) return false;
    String pre1 = prefix(n.length() - 2);
    String pre2 = n.prefix(n.length() - 2);
    if (!pre1.equals(pre2)) return false;
    return true;
}
```

Grading Guide

Part (a) prefix   2 Points

   + 1/2 Check the length of the name

   + 1/2 Return the entire string when appropriate

   +1 Return the appropriate substring
       + 1/2 attempt
       + 1/2 correct

Part (b) suffix   3 Points

   + 1/2 Check the length of the name

   + 1/2 Return the entire string when appropriate

   +1 Return a string of the correct length

   +1 Return the correct substring

Part (c) `isNickname`   4 Points

+2 Check for "ie" ending
   + 1/2 retrieve suffix
   + 1/2 attempt comparison (== ok for attempt)
   + 1/2 correct comparison
   + 1/2 return `false`

+ 1/2 Retrieve prefix of current name

+ 1/2 Retrieve prefix of parameter name

+ 1/2 Compare and return `true` if equal

+ 1/2 Return `false` otherwise

Practice Examination A-2

Section I

Time: 1 hour and 15 minutes
Number of questions: 40
Percent of total grade: 50

1. If addition had higher precedence than multiplication, then the value of the expression

   ```
   2 * 3 + 4 * 5
   ```

   would be which of the following?

   A. 14
   B. 26
   C. 50
   D. 70
   E. 120

2. Assume that x, y, and z are all `int` variables. Consider the following code segment:

   ```
   if (x == 0) {
       if (y == 1) z += 2;
   }
   else {
       z += 4;
   }
   System.out.print(z);
   ```

   What is printed if x, y, and z are all equal to zero before the code segment executes?

   A. 0
   B. 1
   C. 2
   D. 4
   E. 6

3. Consider the following incomplete code segment:

```
int sum=0;
for ( int k=0; condition; k++ ) {
    statement1;
}
statement2;
```

Assume that variable A is an array of ints. Which of the following can be used to replace the placeholders *condition*, *statement1*, and *statement2* so that the code segment computes and returns the sum of the values in A?

condition	*statement1*	*statement2*
A. k < A.length	sum++	System.out.println(sum)
B. k < A.length	sum += A[k]	return sum
C. k <= A.length	sum += A[k]	return sum
D. k <= A.length	sum++	return sum
E. k <= A.length	sum += A[k]	System.out.println(sum)

4. Assume that arrays A and B both contain int values. Which of the following code segments returns true if and only if the kth elements of the two arrays are the same?

```
I.   return(A[k] == B[k]);
II.  if (A[k] == B[k]) {
        return true;
     }
     else return false;
III. if (A[k] == B[k]) {
        return true;
     }
     return false;
```

A. I only

B. II only

C. III only

D. II and III only

E. I, II, and III

5. Which of the following best describes what a class's constructor should do?

A. Test all of the class's methods.

B. Initialize the fields of this instance of the class.

C. Determine and return the amount of storage needed by the fields of the class.

D. Return to free storage all memory used by this instance of the class.

E. Print a message informing the user that a new instance of this class has been created.

6. Consider designing an `Employee` interface that includes the following operations:

-   Return the number of hours worked this month.
-   Return the amount earned this month.
-   Raise the salary by a given amount.

Which of the following is the best definition of the `Employee` interface?

A.
```
public interface Employee {
    private double hours;
    private double salary;
    double hoursWorked();
    double monthlyEarnings();
    void raiseSalary(double raise);
}
```

B.
```
public interface Employee {
    private double hours;
    private double salary;
    double hoursWorked() { return hours; }
    double monthlyEarnings() { return hours * salary; }
    void raiseSalary(double raise) { salary += raise; }
}
```

C.
```
public interface Employee {
    double hoursWorked();
    double monthlyEarnings();
    void raiseSalary( double raise );
}
```

D.
```
public interface Employee {
    void hoursWorked();
    void monthlyEarnings();
    double raiseSalary(double raise);
}
```

E.
```
public interface Employee {
    void hoursWorked() { hours = 40; }
    void monthlyEarnings() { earnings = 40 * salary; }
    double raiseSalary(double raise) { return salary+raise;}
}
```

7.   Assume that variable A is an array of ints. Consider the following code segment:

```
// precondition: A.length > 0
   int x = 0;
   for (int k = 1; k < A.length; k++) {
      if (A[k] < A[x]) x = k;
   }
   return x;
```

Which of the following best describes what the code segment does?

A.   It returns the value of the smallest element of A.

B.   It returns the value of the largest element of A.

C.   It returns the index of the smallest element of A.

D.   It returns the index of the largest element of A.

E.   It is not possible to determine what the code segment does without knowing how A is initialized.

8.   Consider the following data field and method:

```
Comparable[] myList;

public boolean testList(Comparable val) {
   for (int k=0; k<myList.length; k++) {
      if (myList[k].compareTo(val) > 0) return false;
   }
   return true;
}
```

Which of the following best describes the circumstances under which method testList returns true?

A.   When no item in myList is greater than val.

B.   When no item in myList is less than val.

C.   When no item in myList is equal to val.

D.   When all items in myList are equal to val.

E.   When all items in myList are less than val.

Questions 9–11 rely on the following (incomplete) definition of the Book class:

```
public class Book {
    private double price;                // the price of this book

    public double getPrice() { ... } // returns the price of this book

    public static double totalPrice( Book[] inventory ) {
    // postcondition: returns the sum of the prices of the books in
    //                 the inventory array
        double sum = 0.0;
        for (int k=0; k<inventory.length; k++) {
            .
            .  missing code
            .
        }
        return sum;
    }
}
```

9. Consider changing the Book class so that the price of a book can be set when a Book object is created. For example:

    ```
    Book b1 = new Book(10.50);   // price of b1 is $10.50
    Book b2 = new Book(25.00);   // price of b2 is $25.00
    ```

    Which of the following best describes the change that should be made?

    A. Define a constructor with no arguments.
    B. Define a constructor with one argument.
    C. Define a constructor with two arguments.
    D. Define a method named setPrice.
    E. It is not possible to change the Book class as specified.

10. Which of the following code segments could be used to replace *missing code* in method totalPrice so that it works as specified by its postcondition?

    A. `sum += inventory.price[k];`
    B. `sum += inventory.getPrice(k);`
    C. `sum += inventory.Book[k];`
    D. `sum += inventory[k].Book();`
    E. `sum += inventory[k].getPrice();`

11. Consider adding another method to the Book class with the following header:

    ```
    public static double totalPrice( ArrayList inventory )
    ```

    The new method would be the same as the existing totalPrice method except that its parameter, inventory, is an ArrayList of Books instead of an array of Books.

    Which of the following statements about the proposed new method is true?

    A. It is an example of inheritance.
    B. It is an example of an interface.
    C. It is an example of overloading.
    D. It is an example of an abstract method.
    E. It is an example of casting.

12. Consider the following code segment:

    ```
    for (int j=0; j<M; j++) {
        for (int k=0; k<N; k++) {
            System.out.print("*");
        }
        System.out.println();
    }
    ```

    Assume that M and N are int variables, initialized to 2 and 3, respectively.

    What is printed when the code segment executes?

    A. ******

    B. ***
       ***

    C. **
       **
       **

    D. ***
       **

    E. **
       ***

13. Consider the incomplete method shown below.

```
public static int doSum(int start, int finish) {
// precondition: start <= finish
// postcondition returns the sum of the numbers from start to finish
    if ( start == finish ) return expression1;
    return expression2;
}
```

Which of the following could be used to replace *expression1* and *expression2* so that the method works as specified by its pre- and postconditions?

	expression1	*expression2*
A.	0	doSum(start+1, finish)
B.	0	doSum(start, finish-1)
C.	1	start + doSum(start, finish-1)
D.	start	doSum(start+1, finish)
E.	start	start + doSum(start+1, finish)

Questions 14 and 15 refer to the following information:

Assume that N and k are int variables and that A is an array of ints. Consider the following expression:

```
((k <= N) && (A[k] < 0)) || (A[k] == 0)
```

14. Under which of the following conditions must the expression evaluate to true?

   A. A[k] is not equal to zero.

   B. A[k] is equal to zero.

   C. k is less than N.

   D. k is less than or equal to N.

   E. k is less than N, and A[k] is not equal to zero.

15. Assume that A contains N+1 values. Recall that an out-of-bounds array index causes a runtime error. Which of the following statements is true?

   A. Evaluating the expression will never cause a runtime error.

   B. Evaluating the expression will cause a runtime error whenever A[k] is zero.

   C. Evaluating the expression will cause a runtime error whenever A[k] is not zero.

   D. Evaluating the expression will cause a runtime error whenever k is equal to N.

   E. Evaluating the expression will cause a runtime error whenever k is greater than N.

Questions 16 and 17 refer to the following (incorrect) definitions of the `Car` and `SportsCar` classes (note that `SportsCar` is a subclass of `Car`).

```
public class Car {
    private double price;
    private double milesPerGallon;
    private int daysSinceOilchange;

    // constructor
    public Car( double p, double mpg ) {
        price = p;
        milesPerGallon = mpg;
        daysSinceOilchange = 0;
    }

    public boolean needsOilchange() {
        return (daysSinceOilchange >= 90);
    }

    public void setDaysSinceOilchange(int days) {
        daysSinceOilchange = days;
    }

    public int getDaysSinceOilchange( ) {
        return daysSinceOilchange;
    }
}

public class SportsCar extends Car {
    private int maxSpeed;

    // constructor
    public SportsCar(double p, double mpg, int max) {
        maxSpeed = max;
    }

    // override the needsOilchange method
    public boolean needsOilchange() {
        return (getDaysSinceOilchange() >= 30);
    }
}
```

16. The `SportsCar` constructor shown above does not compile. Which of the following correctly explains the error?

    A. Parameters p and mpg are not used.

    B. The order of the parameters is not correct.

    C. The types of the left- and right-hand sides in the assignment to maxSpeed do not match.

    D. The price, milesPerGallon, and daysSinceOilchange fields are not initialized.

    E. There is no explicit call to the superclass constructor, and the superclass has no default (no-argument) constructor.

17. Assume that the `SportsCar` constructor has been defined correctly. Consider the following code segment:

    ```
    Car myCar = new SportsCar(30000, 14.5, 120);
    myCar.setDaysSinceOilchange(40);
    if (myCar.needsOilchange()) System.out.println("Change oil");
    else System.out.println("Do not change oil");
    ```

    Which of the following statements about this code segment is true?

    A. It will compile and run without error and will print Change oil.

    B. It will compile and run without error and will print Do not change oil.

    C. It will not compile because the type of myCar is Car, and the type of the value assigned to myCar is SportsCar.

    D. It will not compile because myCar points to a SportsCar, and SportsCar has no setDaysSinceOilchange method.

    E. It will compile, but there will be a runtime error when the second line is executed because myCar points to a SportsCar, and SportsCar has no setDaysSinceOilchange method.

18. Assume that A and B are arrays of ints, both of the same length. Which of the following code segments returns true if and only if the two arrays contain the same sequence of values?

    A. `return (A == B);`

    B. `return (A.equals(B));`

    C.
    ```
    for (int k=0; k < A.length; k++) {
        if (A[k] != B[k]) return false;
    }
    return true;
    ```

    D.
    ```
    for (int k=0; k < A.length; k++) {
        if (A[k] == B[k]) return true;
    }
    return false;
    ```

    E.
    ```
    boolean match;
    for (int k=0; k < A.length; k++) {
        match = (A[k] == B[k]);
    }
    return match;
    ```

19. Consider the following code segment:

```
String[] firstArray, secondArray;
String s1, s2;
s1 = "cat";
s2 = "s" + s1;
firstArray = new String[3];
secondArray = firstArray;
firstArray[0] = s1;
firstArray[1] = s1;
firstArray[2] = s1;
secondArray[2] = s2;
s1 = "pig";
for (int k=0; k<3; k++) System.out.print(firstArray[k] + " ");
```

What happens when this code executes?

A. "cat cat cat" is printed.

B. "cat cat scat" is printed.

C. "pig pig pig" is printed.

D. Nothing is printed because the assignment to secondArray[2] causes an IndexOutOf-BoundsException.

E. Nothing is printed because the assignment to secondArray[2] causes a NullPointer-Exception.

20. Assume that variable A is an array of ints. Consider the following incomplete code segment:

```
// postcondition: returns true if some value occurs more than
//                 once in A, false otherwise
    for (int j=0; j<A.length-1; j++) {
        statement
    }
    return false;
```

Which of the following can be used to replace the placeholder *statement* so that the code segment works as specified by its postcondition?

A. `if (A[j] == A[j+1]) return true;`

B. `if (A[j] == A[A.length]) return true;`

C. ```
for (int k=0; k<A.length; k++) {
    if (A[j] == A[k]) return true;
}
```

D. ```
for (int k=j; k<A.length; k++) {
    if (A[j] == A[k]) return true;
}
```

E. ```
for (int k=j+1; k<A.length; k++) {
    if (A[j] == A[k]) return true;
}
```
```

Questions 21–24 involve reasoning about the Marine Biology case study.

21. Which of the following methods returns a data structure that might contain Fish objects?

    I.   The neighborsOf method of the Environment interface
    II. The emptyNeighbors method of the Fish class
    III. The allObjects method of the Environment interface

    A. I only

    B. II only

    C. III only

    D. I and II only

    E. I, II, and III

22. Which of the following statements about the inheritance structure of Fish, DarterFish and SlowFish is true?

    A. DarterFish and SlowFish are both subclasses of Fish

    B. DarterFish is a subclass of SlowFish

    C. SlowFish is a subclass of DarterFish

    D. Fish is a subclass of both DarterFish and SlowFish

    E. Fish is a subclass of DarterFish only

23. Which of the following Fish methods could *not* be called from a method in the DarterFish class?

    A. initialize

    B. generateChild

    C. act

    D. move

    E. There are no methods of Fish that cannot be called from a DarterFish method.

24. A new type of fish, BlueFish, is being defined. The BlueFish constructor should create a blue fish facing in a random direction. An incomplete version of the constructor is given below.

```
public BlueFish(Environment env, Location loc) {
    .
    .   missing statements
    .
}
```

Which of the following could be used to replace *missing statements* to correctly complete the constructor?

A. ```
   theEnv = env;
   myLoc = loc;
   myDir = env.randomDirection();
   myColor = blue;
   ```

B. ```
   myColor = Color.blue;
   super(env, loc, env.randomDirection());
   ```

C. ```
   super(env, loc, env.randomDirection());
   myColor = Color.blue;
   ```

D. ```
   super(env, loc, env.randomDirection(), Color.blue);
   ```

E. ```
   initialize(env, loc, env.randomDirection(), Color.blue);
   ```

25. Consider writing a program to be used to manage a collection of movies. There are three kinds of movies in the collection: dramas, comedies, and documentaries. The collector would like to keep track, for each movie, of its name, the name of the director, and the date when it was made. Some operations are to be implemented for all movies, and there will also be special operations for each of the three different kinds of movies. Which of the following is the best design?

A. Define one class, Movie, with six fields: drama, comedy, documentary, name, director, and date.

B. Define one superclass, Movie, with six subclasses: Drama, Comedy, Documentary, Name, Director, and Date.

C. Define one superclass, Movie, with three fields: name, director, and date; and with three subclasses: Drama, Comedy, and Documentary.

D. Define six unrelated classes: Drama, Comedy, Documentary, Name, Director, and Date.

E. Define six classes: Drama, Comedy, Documentary, Name, Director, and Date. Make Date and Director subclasses of Name, and make Documentary and Comedy subclasses of Drama.
   ```

26. Assume that a method called `checkStr` has been written to determine whether a string is the same forwards and backwards. The following two sets of data are being considered to be used to test method `checkStr`:

Data Set 1	Data Set 2
"aba"	"abba"
"?"	"abab"
"z&*&z"	
"##"	

Which of the following is an advantage of Data Set 2 over Data Set 1?

A. All strings in Data Set 2 have the same number of characters.

B. Data Set 2 contains a string for which method `checkStr` should return `false`, as well as a string for which method `checkStr` should return `true`.

C. The strings in Data Set 2 contain only lowercase letters.

D. Data Set 2 contains fewer values than Data Set 1.

E. Data Set 2 has no advantage over Data Set 1.

Questions 27 and 28 refer to the following recursive method:

```
public static int compute(int x, int y) {
    if (x == y) return x;
    else return( compute(x+1, y-1) );
}
```

27. What is returned by the call `compute(1, 5)`?

A. 1

B. 2

C. 3

D. 4

E. No value is returned because an infinite recursion occurs.

28. Which of the following calls leads to an infinite recursion?

I.   `compute(2, 8)`
II. `compute(8, 2)`
III. `compute(2, 5)`

A. I only

B. II only

C. III only

D. I and II

E. II and III

29. Three algorithms are being considered to look for a given value in an *unsorted* array of integers.

    Algorithm 1: Use binary search.
    Algorithm 2: Use sequential search.
    Algorithm 3: Sort the array, then use binary search.

    Which of the following statements about the three algorithms is true?

    A. All three will work; Algorithm 1 will be most efficient.

    B. Only Algorithms 1 and 2 will work; Algorithm 1 will be most efficient.

    C. Only Algorithms 1 and 3 will work; Algorithm 1 will be most efficient.

    D. Only Algorithms 2 and 3 will work; Algorithm 2 will be most efficient.

    E. Only Algorithms 2 and 3 will work; Algorithm 3 will be most efficient.

30. Assume that the following interface and class have been defined:

    ```java
    public interface Person {
        public String getName();
        public int getAge();
    }

    public class Student implements Person {
        private String name;
        private int age;

        //constructor
        public Student( String n, int a ) {
            name = n;
            age = a;
        }
        public String getName() { return name; }
        public int getAge() { return age; }
    }
    ```

    Which of the following will cause a compile-time error?

    A. An attempt to create an instance of a `Person`

    B. An attempt to create an instance of a `Student`

    C. An attempt to define a method with a parameter of type `Person`

    D. An attempt to define a method with a parameter of type `Student`

    E. An attempt to define a subclass of the `Student` class

31. Which of the following best explains why a method might have the precondition N > 0?

    A. Every method must have a precondition or it will not compile.

    B. Including a precondition makes a method more efficient.

    C. Including the precondition ensures that if, when the method is called, variable N is *not* greater than 0, it will be set to 1 so that the precondition is satisfied.

    D. Including the precondition provides information to users of the method, specifying what is expected to be true whenever the method is called.

    E. This is an example of bottom-up design. The precondition is included to permit the method to be tested and debugged in isolation from the rest of the program. The precondition should be removed as soon as that phase of program development is complete.

Questions 32 and 33 concern the code segment shown below. The code segment was intended to count and return the number of values in *sorted* array A (which contains ints) that are smaller than the value in int variable x. However, the code segment sometimes causes an IndexOutOfBounds-Exception.

```
// precondition: A is sorted in ascending order.
    int k = 0;
    while ((A[k] < x) && (k < A.length)) k++;
    return k;
```

32. Under what conditions does the code segment cause an IndexOutOfBoundsException?

    A. Always

    B. Whenever *no* values in array A are smaller than x

    C. Whenever *all* values in array A are smaller than x

    D. Whenever *some* value in array A is smaller than x

    E. Whenever *most* values in array A are smaller than x

33. Which of the following replacements for the while-loop condition would fix the code segment so that it works as intended?

    A. (A[k] < x) || (k < A.length)

    B. (A[k] < x) && (k <= A.length)

    C. (A[k] <= x) && (k < A.length)

    D. (k < A.length) || (A[k] < x)

    E. (k < A.length) && (A[k] < x)

34. Under which of the following conditions can a method be *overloaded;* that is, when can two methods with the same name be included in the same class?

  A. The methods do different things.

  B. The methods have different numbers or types of parameters.

  C. The methods have different parameter names.

  D. The methods have different preconditions.

  E. Two methods with the same name can never be included in the same class.

Questions 35 and 36 concern the following two ways to represent a set of integers (with no duplicates) with values in the range 0 to N:

  Method 1: Use an array of booleans of size $N+1$. The kth element of the array is `true` if k is in the set; otherwise, it is `false`.

  Method 2: Use an array of integers. The size of the array is the same as the current size of the set. Each element of the array holds one of the values that is in the set. The values are stored in the array in sorted order.

35. Which of the following statements about the storage requirements of the two methods is true?

  A. Method 1 requires less storage than Method 2 to represent an empty set.

  B. The amount of storage required for Method 1 is independent of the number of values in the set, whereas the amount of storage required for Method 2 varies depending on the number of values in the set.

  C. The amount of storage required for Method 2 is independent of the number of values in the set, whereas the amount of storage required for Method 1 varies depending on the number of values in the set.

  D. The amount of storage required for both Method 1 and Method 2 is independent of the number of values in the set.

  E. The amount of storage required for both Method 1 and Method 2 varies depending on the number of values in the set.

36. Which of the following operations can be implemented more efficiently using Method 1 rather than using Method 2?

  I.   Determine whether a given value is in the set.
  II. Remove a given value from the set.
  III. Print all of the values in the set.

  A. I only

  B. II only

  C. III only

  D. I and II only

  E. I, II, and III

37. Two programmers are working together to write a program. One is implementing a `List` class, and the other is writing code that includes variables of type `List`. The programmers have decided that the `List` class will include a public method named `search`. Which of the following facts about the `search` method does *not* need to be agreed on by both programmers?

   A. The names of the parameters

   B. The number of parameters

   C. The pre- and postconditions

   D. The type of each parameter

   E. The return type

38. Consider the following recursive method. (Assume that method `readInt` reads one integer value typed in by the user.)

```
public static void print(int n) {
    int x;
    if (n > 0) {
        x = readInt();
        if (x > 0) {
            print(n-1);
            System.out.println(x);
        }
        else print(n);
    }
}
```

   Which of the following best describes what happens as a result of the call `print(5)`?

   A. The first five numbers typed by the user are printed in the order in which they are typed.

   B. The first five numbers typed by the user are printed in the opposite order to that in which they are typed.

   C. The first five positive numbers typed by the user are printed in the order in which they are typed.

   D. The first five positive numbers typed by the user are printed in the opposite order to that in which they are typed.

   E. Nothing is printed because the call causes an infinite recursion.

39. Consider the following code segment:

```
x = y;
y = !x;
x = !y;
```

Assume that x and y are initialized boolean variables. Which of the following statements is true?

A. The final value of x is the same as the initial value of x.

B. The final value of x is the same as the initial value of y.

C. The final value of y is the same as the initial value of y.

D. The final value of y is the same as the initial value of x.

E. It is not possible to say anything about the final values of x and y without knowing their initial values.

40. Assume that a class includes the following data fields and methods:

```
private double[] dblList;
private int[] intList;

public boolean search(double d) {
// search version 1
    for (int k=0; k<dblList.length; k++) {
        if (d == dblList[k]) return true;
    }
    return false;
}

public boolean search(int n) {
// search version 2
    for (int k=0; k<intList.length; k++) {
        if (n == intList[k]) return true;
    }
    return false;
}

public void test() {
    if (search(5.5)) System.out.println("found!");
}
```

Which of the following statements about this code is true?

A. It will not compile because the class includes two methods named `search`.

B. It will not compile because the class does not include a version of the `search` method that matches the call in method `test`.

C. It will compile. When method `test` is called, if `dblList` is not null, version 1 of the `search` method will be called; if `dblList` is null, version 2 of the `search` method will be called.

D. It will compile. When method `test` is called, version 1 of the `search` method will be called.

E. It will compile. When method `test` is called, version 2 of the `search` method will be called.

Section II

Time: 1 hour and 45 minutes
Number of questions: 4
Percent of total grade: 50

Question 1

This question involves reasoning about the code from the Marine Biology case study.

Consider modifying the Marine Biology Simulation to implement a new simulation: a simulation of racing fish. Racing fish move horizontally across the environment (their rows stay the same and their columns change as they move). The fish that arrive at the other side of the environment first win the race.

Two new classes will be used in the Racing Fish simulation:

1. A RacingFish class, which extends the Fish class and has a new nextLocation method.
2. A RaceEnvironment class, which extends the BoundedEnvironment class, and has a new winners method that determines the winners of a race.

Partial declarations for the two classes are given below.

```
public class RacingFish extends Fish {
    protected Location nextLocation() { /* part (a) */ }
}


public class RaceEnvironment extends BoundedEnvironment {
    // constructs the environment with the given number of rows
    // and columns
    public RaceEnvironment(int r, int c) { /* part (b) */ }

    // postcondition: returns an ArrayList containing all of the objects
    //                that are in the last column of the environment;
    //                if there are no objects in the last column,
    //                an empty ArrayList is returned
    public ArrayList winners() { /* part (c) */ }
}
```

Part (a)

Write the `RacingFish` method `nextLocation`. The `nextLocation` method returns the next location in the environment where the fish will move. A `RacingFish` will move according to the following rules:

- If the fish is within 3 spaces of the end of the race (the last column of the environment) the fish will move forward a random number of spaces between 1 and the number of spaces remaining to the end of the environment.
- Otherwise the fish will move forward a random number of spaces between 1 and 4.

Complete method `nextLocation` below.

```
// precondition: The fish is in an environment and is not at the
//               end of its row.
// postcondition: returns a location in the same row and a different
//                column based on the rules given above
//
protected Location nextLocation() {
```

Part (b)

Write the constructor for the `RaceEnvironment` class. The constructor should create an environment with the given number of rows and columns.

Complete the constructor below.

```
// constructs the environment with the given number of rows and columns
public RaceEnvironment(int r, int c) {
```

Part (c)

Write the `RaceEnvironment` method `winners`, which returns an `ArrayList` containing all of the objects currently in the last column of the environment, or an empty `ArrayList` if there are no objects in the last column.

Complete method `winners` below.

```
// postcondition: returns an ArrayList containing all of the objects
//                that are in the last column of the environment;
//                if there are no objects in the last column,
//                an empty ArrayList is returned
public ArrayList winners() {
```

Question 2

Consider a hierarchy of classes used by a power company to keep track of the buildings where they supply electricity. The hierarchy is represented by the following diagram:

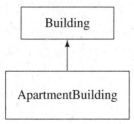

Note that an `ApartmentBuilding` is a subclass of `Building`.

A building is represented by the class defined below.

```
public class Building {
    public static final double RATE = 3.25;
    private String address;
    private double wattHours;   // units of electricity used in 1 month

    public Building(String ad) {
        address = ad;
        wattHours = 0;
    }

    // returns the amount owed by this building
    public double amtOwed( ) { /* not shown */ }

    // other methods not shown
}
```

Part (a)

An `ApartmentBuilding` is different from a regular building because instead of keeping track of the watt hours used for the whole building, it needs to keep track of the watt hours used by each of the individual apartments in the building.

Write a complete declaration of class `ApartmentBuilding` including the following:

- A private instance variable (an array) to be used to store the apartments' watt hours.
- A constructor with two parameters: the address of the apartment building, and the number of apartments. The constructor should initialize the building's address field as well as initializing the array to be big enough to store watt hours for each apartment in the building.
- An implementation of `amtOwed` that returns the amount of money owed by the entire building for the electricity used (calculated by multiplying the sum of the `wattHours` for the entire building by the `RATE`).

Write the complete `ApartmentBuilding` class declaration.

Part (b)

Consider the following partial declaration for the ServiceArea class. A ServiceArea represents an entire area being served by this power company.

```
public class ServiceArea {

    private ArrayList allBuildings;  // a list of Buildings

    public ServiceArea() { /* constructor not shown */ }

    public double totalSales() { /* part (b) */ }

    // other methods not shown
}
```

Write the totalSales method of class ServiceArea. The method should return the total amount of money owed by all of the buildings in the allBuildings list. Assume that the buildings' amtOwed methods work correctly regardless of what you wrote for part (a).

Complete method totalSales below.

```
public double totalSales() {
```

Question 3

This question concerns the two classes, Product and GroceryStore, partially defined below.

```java
public class Product {
    private String name;
    private int numInStock;

    // constructor not shown
    public String getName() { return name; }
    public int getNumInStock() { return numInStock; }
    public void sellOne() { numInStock--; }
}

public class GroceryStore {
    private Product[] stock;

    // constructor not shown

    // precondition: no two Products in the stock array have the
    //               same name
    // postcondition: carries out the sale of the named product if
    //                possible and returns true or false depending
    //                on whether the sale is successful
    public boolean oneSale(String name) {
        /* part (b) */
    }

    // precondition: no two Products in the stock array have the
    //               same name
    // postcondition: attempts to carry out a sale for each name
    //                in the orders array, creating and returning
    //                an ArrayList containing the names of all
    //                products for which a sale is not successful
    public ArrayList allSales(String[] orders) {
        /* part (c) */
    }

    // precondition: no two Products in the stock array have the
    //               same name
    // postcondition: returns the index of the Product in the stock
    //                array with the given name, or -1 if there is
    //                no such Product in the array
    private int findItem(String name) {
        /* part (a) */
    }
}
```

Part (a)

Write the findItem method of the GroceryStore class. As specified by its postcondition, find-Item should return the index of the Product in the stock array with the given name, or it should return −1 if there is no such Product in the array.

Complete method findItem below.

```
// precondition: no two Products in the stock array have the
//               same name
// postcondition: returns the index of the Product in the stock array
//                with the given name, or returns -1 if there is no
//                such Product in the array
private int findItem(String name) {
```

Part (b)

Write the oneSale method of the GroceryStore class. Method oneSale has one parameter: the name of one product (that a customer would like to buy). Method oneSale should attempt to carry out the sale of the named product, and it should return true or false depending on whether the sale is successful. The sale is successful if there is a product in the stock array with the given name and if the number of items in stock of that product is greater than zero. In that case, oneSale should subtract one from the number of items in stock and return true. If there is no product in the stock array with the given name or if the number of items in stock for that product is less than or equal to zero, oneSale should return false.

For example, assume that stock.length is 4 and that the elements in the array are as shown below.

	[0]	[1]	[2]	[3]
name:	"milk"	"eggs"	"butter"	"coffee"
numInStock:	20	3	0	1

If oneSale is called with the name "eggs", it should subtract one from the number of eggs in stock and return true. If oneSale is called with the name "juice", it should return false (because there is no juice in the stock array). If oneSale is called with the name "butter", it should return false (because there are no butter items currently in stock).

In writing method oneSale, you may include calls to method findItem. Assume that findItem works correctly, regardless of what you wrote for part (a).

Complete method oneSale below.

```
// precondition: no two Products in the stock array have the
//               same name
// postcondition: carries out the sale of the named product if
//                possible and returns true or false depending
//                on whether the sale is successful
public boolean oneSale(String name) {
```

Part (c)

Write the allSales method of the GroceryStore class. Method allSales has one parameter: an array of product names called orders. For each name in the orders array, allSales should attempt to carry out the sale of the named product. It should create a new ArrayList containing the names of all products for which a sale is not successful (a product name should appear more than once in the new ArrayList if there is more than one failing sale of that product). Finally, it should return the new ArrayList.

For example, assume that the stock array is initially as shown in part (b). Also assume that allSales is called with the array of names:

```
    [0]       [1]       [2]       [3]       [4]      [5]      [6]       [7]       [8]
  "eggs"    "milk"    "milk"   "butter"  "coffee"  "tea"  "coffee"  "milk"   "coffee"
```

Method allSales should carry out five successful sales (eggs, milk, milk, coffee, milk), changing the appropriate Products in the stock array. It should create and return a new ArrayList containing the strings

```
"butter" "tea" "coffee" "coffee"
```

because the number of butter items is initially zero, there is no tea product, and the number of coffee items is zero when the second and third attempts to sell one coffee item are made.

In writing method allSales, you may include calls to method oneSale. Assume that oneSale works correctly, regardless of what you wrote for part (b).

Complete method allSales below.

```
// precondition: no two Products in the stock array have the
//               same name
// postcondition: attempts to carry out a sale for each name in the
//                orders array, creating and returning an ArrayList
//                containing the names of all products for which a
//                sale is not successful
public ArrayList allSales(String[] orders) {
```

Question 4

A restaurant uses a class called Table to keep track of the orders placed by the diners at one table. An order includes a String (the food being ordered) and a Double (the price of the order). A declaration of the Table class is given below.

```
public class Table {
    private ArrayList foods;   // a list of Strings, one for each person
                               // at this table
    private ArrayList prices;  // a list of Doubles, one for each
                               // person at this table


    // constructor
    public Table() {
        foods = new ArrayList();
        prices = new ArrayList();
    }


    public void placeOrder(String food, Double price) {
        foods.add(order);
        prices.add(price);
    }


    public void getFoods() { return foods; }


    public void getPrices() { return prices; }
}
```

A RestaurantTables class is used to represent all of the tables in the restaurant, and to place orders and compute bills and tips for each table. A partial declaration of the RestaurantTables class is given below.

```
public class RestaurantTables {

    private Table[] allTables;  // one element in the array for each
                                // table in the restaurant

    // constructor not shown

    // precondition: 0 <= tableNum < allTables.length, and
    //                    foods.length == prices.length
    // postcondition: all of the foods and prices in the two parameters
    //                    have been added to the orders for allTables[tableNum]
    public void placeTableOrders(int tableNum, String[] foods,
                                 double[] prices) {
        /* part (a) */
    }
}
```

```
// precondition: 0 <= tableNum < allTables.length
// postcondition: returns an ArrayList of Double values: the prices
//                for the orders at the given table
private ArrayList tableOrderPrices(int table) {
    return allTables[tableNum].getPrices();
}


// precondition: 0 <= tableNum < allTables.length
// postcondition: returns the total bill for table tableNum
//                (the sum of the prices of the orders)
public double totalBill(int tableNum) { /* part (b) */ }


// precondition: 0 <= tableNum < allTables.length
// postcondition: returns the tip for table tableNum: 15% of the total
//                bill if there are 6 or more orders for table tableNum;
//                0 otherwise.
public double computeTip(int tableNum) { /* part (c) */ }
}
```

Part (a)

Write method `placeTableOrders`. Method `placeTableOrders` should place the orders represented by its two array parameters for table `tableNum`.

Complete method `placeTableOrders` below.

```
// precondition: 0 <= tableNum < allTables.length, and
//                foods.length == prices.length
// postcondition: all of the foods and prices in the two parameters
//                have been added to the orders for allTables[tableNum]
public void placeTableOrders(int tableNum, String[] foods,
                             double[] prices) {
```

Part (b)

Write method `totalBill`. Method `totalBill` should compute and return the bill for table `tableNum` (the sum of the prices for the orders placed by that table).

Complete method `totalBill` below.

```
// precondition: 0 <= tableNum < allTables.length
// postcondition: returns the total bill for table tableNum
//                (the sum of the prices of the orders)
public double totalBill(int tableNum) {
```

Part (c)

Write method `computeTip`. Method `computeTip` should return 15% of the total bill if there are 6 or more orders from the table; otherwise, it should return 0.

Complete method `computeTip` below.

```
// precondition: 0 <= tableNum < allTables.length
// postcondition: returns the tip for table tableNum: 15% of the total
//                bill if there are 6 or more orders for table tableNum;
//                0.0 otherwise.
public double computeTip(int tableNum) {
```

Answers to Section I

1.	D	21.	C
2.	A	22.	A
3.	B	23.	A
4.	E	24.	D
5.	B	25.	C
6.	C	26.	B
7.	C	27.	C
8.	A	28.	E
9.	B	29.	D
10.	E	30.	A
11.	C	31.	D
12.	B	32.	C
13.	E	33.	E
14.	B	34.	B
15.	E	35.	B
16.	E	36.	D
17.	A	37.	A
18.	C	38.	D
19.	B	39.	B
20.	E	40.	D

Answers to Section II

Question 1
Part (a)

```
protected Location nextLocation() {
    Random r = RandNumGenerator.getInstance();
    int spacesLeft = environment().numCols() - location().col();
    int move;
    if (spacesLeft <= 3) move = r.nextInt(spacesLeft) + 1;
    else move = r.nextInt(4) + 1;
    return new Location(location().row(), location().col() + move);
}
```

Part (b)

```
public RaceEnvironment(int r, int c) {
    super(r, c);
}
```

Part (c)

Version 1: Iterate over the locations in the last column.

```
public ArrayList winners() {
    ArrayList win = new ArrayList();
    for (int i=0; i<numRows(); i++) {
        Location loc = new Location(i, numCols() - 1);
        if (!isEmpty(loc)) win.add(objectAt(loc));
    }
    return win;
}
```

Version 2: Iterate over the objects in the environment.

```
public ArrayList winners() {
    ArrayList win = new ArrayList();
    Locatable [] objs = allObjects();

    for (int i=0; i<objs.length; i++) {
        if (objs[i].location().col() == numCols()-1) {
            win.add(objs[i]);
        }
    }
    return win;
}
```

Grading Guide

Part (a) `nextLocation`   4 Points

+1 Determine the number of spaces left in the row

   $+\frac{1}{2}$ attempt (must include a calculation with `numCols` − current column)

   $+\frac{1}{2}$ correct (must include calls to the `environment` and `location` methods)

+2 Calculate the number of spaces to move

   +1 condition (comparison of number of spaces to 3)

   +1 creation and correct use of `RandNumGenerator` instance

+1 Create and return appropriate `location` object

Part (b) `RaceEnvironment`   1 Point

$+\frac{1}{2}$ Attempt to call `super`

$+\frac{1}{2}$ Correct call with parameters (any extraneous code will lose the $\frac{1}{2}$ correct point)

Part (c) `winners`   4 Points

$+\frac{1}{2}$ Correct creation and instantiation of new `ArrayList`

+1 Loop over objects in environment (check every object in the environment, or every space in the last column)

   $+\frac{1}{2}$ attempt (must access data within the loop)

   $+\frac{1}{2}$ correct (correct iteration)

+1 Check every object in the iteration

   $+\frac{1}{2}$ attempt (must have some conditional that checks for location or not empty)

   $+\frac{1}{2}$ correct (within context of student's solution)

+1 Add objects to the created `ArrayList`

$+\frac{1}{2}$ Return the `ArrayList` created

Question 2
Part (a)

```
public class ApartmentBuilding extends Building {

    private double [] wattHours;

    public ApartmentBuilding(String ad, int numUnits) {
        super(ad);
        wattHours = new double[numUnits];
    }

    public double amtOwed() {
        double sum = 0;
        for (int i=0; i<wattHours.length; i++) {
            sum += wattHours[i];
        }
        return sum*RATE;
    }
}
```

Part (b)

```
public double totalSales() {
    double sum = 0;
    for (int i=0; i<allBuildings.size(); i++) {
        sum += ((Building)allBuildings.get(i)).amtOwed();
    }
    return sum;
}
```

Grading Guide

Part (a) The `ApartmentBuilding` class   6 Points

    +1 Class declaration (must extend `Building`)

    +1 Private field declaration (array should not be initialized)

    +2 Constructor

        + $\frac{1}{2}$ method header attempt

        + $\frac{1}{2}$ call to super attempt

        + $\frac{1}{2}$ initialization of array attempt (must include passed parameter)

        + $\frac{1}{2}$ correct

    +2 amtOwed

        + $\frac{1}{2}$ initialize sum

        + $\frac{1}{2}$ loop

        + $\frac{1}{2}$ update of sum

        + $\frac{1}{2}$ return sum

Part (b) `totalSales`   3 Points

    + $\frac{1}{2}$ Initialization of sum

    +1 Loop (correct point only)

    +1 Update of sum

        + $\frac{1}{2}$ attempt (must reference `allBuildings`)

        + $\frac{1}{2}$ correct (must include correct call to `amtOwed`)

    + $\frac{1}{2}$ Return sum

Question 3
Part (a)

```
private int findItem(String name) {
    for (int k=0; k<stock.length; k++) {
        if (stock[k].getName().equals(name)) return k;
    }
    return -1;
}
```

Part (b)

```
public boolean oneSale(String name) {
    int k = findItem(name);
    if (k == -1) return false;
    if (stock[k].getNumInStock() <= 0) return false;
    stock[k].sellOne();
    return true;
}
```

Part (c)

```
public ArrayList allSales(String[] orders) {
    ArrayList L = new ArrayList();
    for (int k=0; k<orders.length; k++) {
        if (!oneSale(orders[k])) {
            L.add(orders[k]);
        }
    }
    return L;
}
```

Grading Guide

Part (a) findItem   3 Points

 +1 Loop over stock array

  + 1/2 attempt (must reference stock within the loop)

  + 1/2 correct

 +1 Compare the name in the array to parameter

  + 1/2 attempt

  + 1/2 correct

 +1 Return appropriate values

  + 1/2 return index from loop

  + 1/2 return -1

Part (b) oneSale   3 Points

 +1 Call findItem

 +1 Comparison for appropriate stock

  + 1/2 attempt (must include either check for not found (-1) or numInStock < 0)

  + 1/2 correct

 + 1/2 Sell one

 + 1/2 Appropriate return

Part (c) allSales   3 Points

 +1 ArrayList

  + 1/2 creation of ArrayList

  + 1/2 return of ArrayList

 +1 Loop over orders array

  + 1/2 attempt (must reference orders within loop)

  + 1/2 correct

 + 1/2 Call to oneSale with test for success

 + 1/2 Add value to the ArrayList

Question 4
Part (a)

```
public void placeTableOrders(int tableNum, String[] foods,
                             double[] prices) {
   for (int i=0; i<orders.length; i++) {
      allTables[tableNum].placeOrder(foods[i], prices[i]);
   }
}
```

Part (b)

```
public double totalBill(int tableNum) {
   ArrayList prices = allTables[tableNum].getPrices();
   double total = 0;

   for (int i=0; i<prices.size(); i++) {
      total += ((Double)prices.get(i)).doubleValue();
   }

   return total;
}
```

Part (c)

```
public double computeTip(int tableNum) {
   ArrayList prices = allTables[tableNum].getPrices();
   if (prices.size() < 6) return 0;
   return .015 * totalBill(tableNum);
}
```

Grading Guide

Part (a) `placeTableOrders`   2 Points

> +1 Loop over foods or prices
>> + 1/2 attempt (must reference foods and prices in body)
>> + 1/2 correct
>
> +1 Correctly add orders
>> + 1/2 attempt (must call `placeOrder`)
>> + 1/2 correct

Part (b) `totalBill`   4 Points

> +1 Get list of prices for table `tableNum`
>> + 1/2 attempt
>> + 1/2 correct
>
> +1 Loop over prices
>> + 1/2 attempt
>> + 1/2 correct (must reference `ArrayList` in body)
>
> +1 Add the values of prices to the total
>
> +1 Create and return the sum
>> + 1/2 create variable to store the sum
>> + 1/2 return calculated value

Part (c) `computeTip`   3 Points

> +1 1/2 Determine number of orders
>> + 1/2 attempt
>> +1 correct
>
> +1 Return tip if >= 6 orders
>> + 1/2 attempt (must include call to `totalBill`)
>> + 1/2 correct
>
> + 1/2 Return 0 if < 6 orders

Practice Examination A-3

Section I

Time: 1 hour and 15 minutes
Number of questions: 40
Percent of total grade: 50

1. Which of the following statements about Java variables and parameters is true?

    A. A variable must be declared before it is used.

    B. The same variable name cannot be used in two different methods.

    C. Variables used as indexes in *for-loops* must be named i, j, or k.

    D. It is good programming practice to use single letters as the names of all variables.

    E. It is good programming practice to name formal parameters param1, param2, and so on, so that it is clear where they appear in the method's list of parameters.

2. The expression

    (x && !y)

    is equivalent to which of the following expressions?

    A. (x || !y)

    B. (!x || y)

    C. !(!x || y)

    D. (!x && y)

    E. !(!x && y)

3. Which of the following is *not* an example of a good use of comments?

    A. Comments included at the beginning of a method to specify the method's pre- and post-conditions

    B. Comments included at the end of every line of a method to explain what that line of code does

    C. Comments included at the beginning of a method to say which of the class's fields are modified by that method

    D. Comments included in a class's constructor to explain how the class object is initialized

    E. Comments included before a loop to say what is true each time the loop is executed

4. Assume that variable A is an array of Objects and variable ob is an Object. Consider the following two expressions:

   Expression 1: `(A[k].equals(ob)) && (A[k] != null)`
   Expression 2: `(A[k] != null) && (A[k].equals(ob))`

   Which of the following statements about these two expressions is true?

   A. If ob is null, Expression 1 will cause a NullPointerException and Expression 2 will not cause that exception.

   B. If ob is null, both Expression 1 and Expression 2 will cause a NullPointerException.

   C. If A[k] is null, Expression 1 will cause a NullPointerException and Expression 2 will not cause that exception.

   D. If A[k] is null, Expression 2 will cause a NullPointerException and Expression 1 will not cause that exception.

   E. If A[k] is null, both Expression 1 and Expression 2 will cause a NullPointerException.

5. Consider the following code segment; assume that A is an array of doubles, and that val is a double.

```
boolean tmp=false;
for (int k=0; k<A.length; k++) {
    tmp = (A[k] == val);
}
return tmp;
```

   Which of the following best characterizes the conditions under which this code segment returns true?

   A. Whenever array A contains value val

   B. Whenever the first element of array A has value val

   C. Whenever the last element of array A has value val

   D. Whenever more than one element of array A has value val

   E. Whenever exactly one element of array A has value val

6. Consider the following data field and methods. Assume that method `myListContains` is implemented correctly.

```
private ArrayList myList;

public ArrayList combine(ArrayList A) {
    ArrayList result = new ArrayList();

    // copy all items from myList into result
    for (int j=0; j<myList.size(); j++) {
        result.add(myList.get(j));
    }

    // now add items in list A that are not already in result
    for (int j=0; j<A.size(); j++) {
        Object ob = A.get(j);
        if (! myListContains(ob)) result.add(ob);
    }
    return result;
}

private boolean myListContains(Object ob) {
    // returns true iff ob is in myList
        :
        .  code not shown
        :
}
```

Method `combine` was intended to create and return a list containing all items that are in either `myList` or `A`. If an item occurs more than once in one or both of those lists, the number of those items in the returned list should be the *maximum* of the number in `myList` and the number in list `A`.

For which of the following pairs of lists does method `combine` fail to work correctly?

	myList	A
A.	[0, 1, 2]	[0, 1, 2, 2]
B.	[0, 1, 2, 2]	[0, 1, 2]
C.	[0, 1, 2, 2]	[0, 1]
D.	[0, 1, 2, 2]	[0, 1, 2, 2]
E.	[0, 1]	[0, 2]

Questions 7–9 refer to the following incomplete definitions of the Book and TextBook classes (note that TextBook is a subclass of Book).

```
public class Book {
    private String name;
    private double price;

    // constructor
    public Book( String n, double p ) {
        name = n;
        price = p;
        System.out.println("created a book");
    }

    public static Book cheapestBook( Book[] bookList ) {
    // precondition: bookList.length > 0
    // return the book with the lowest price
        :    missing code

    }
}


public class TextBook extends Book {
    private String classUsedIn;

    // constructor
    public TextBook( String n, double p, String class ) {
        super(n, p);
        classUsedIn = class;
        System.out.println("created a textbook");
    }

    public static TextBook getBookForClass(String className,
                                    TextBook[] textbookList) {
    // return the first textbook in textbookList that is used in the given
    // class (or null if there is no such textbook)
        :    missing code

    }
}
```

7. Assume that the following declarations have been made:

    ```
    Book b;
    Book[] B;
    TextBook tb;
    TextBook[] TB;
    ```

    and that all four variables have been properly initialized. Which of the following statements will *not* compile?

    A. `b = Book.cheapestBook(B);`

    B. `b = Book.cheapestBook(TB);`

    C. `b = TextBook.getBookForClass("Intro to Java", TB);`

    D. `tb = TextBook.getBookForClass("Intro to Java", B);`

    E. `tb = TextBook.getBookForClass("Intro to Java", TB);`

8. Note that methods `cheapestBook` and `getBookForClass` are declared *static*. Which of the following statements is true?

    A. It is appropriate for the two methods to be static because they both operate on arrays passed as parameters rather than on fields of the two classes.

    B. Although the code works as is, because the two methods return single objects rather than arrays, they really shouldn't be declared static.

    C. It is appropriate for the `cheapestBook` method to be either static or non-static, but because `TextBook` is a subclass of `Book`, the `getBookForClass` method must be static if the `cheapestBook` method is static.

    D. Because the two methods are static, the *missing code* for the method bodies cannot contain any recursive calls.

    E. It is appropriate for the two methods to be static but if they had return type `void` they could not be static.

9. Consider the following declaration and initialization:

    ```
    Book oneBook = new TextBook("ABC", 10.50, "kindergarten");
    ```

    Which of the following statements about this code is true?

    A. The code will not compile because the type of the left-hand side of the assignment is `Book`, and the type of the right-hand side is `TextBook`.

    B. The code will compile, but there will be a runtime error when it is executed because the type of the left-hand side of the assignment is `Book`, and the type of the right-hand side is `TextBook`.

    C. The code will compile and execute without error; only `created a book` will be printed.

    D. The code will compile and execute without error; only `created a textbook` will be printed.

    E. The code will compile and execute without error, and both `created a book` and `created a textbook` will be printed.

10. Consider the following definitions of the `Baseclass` and `Subclass` classes.

```
public class Baseclass {
    private int myInt;
    private String myString;

    // constructor
    public Baseclass( ) {
        myInt = 0;
        myString = "";
    }

    // other methods not shown
}

public class Subclass extends Baseclass {
    private double myDouble;

    // constructor
    public Subclass(int anInt, String aString, double aDouble) {
        myInt = anInt;
        myString = aString;
    }

    // other methods not shown
}
```

The `Subclass` constructor shown above does not compile. Which of the following correctly explains the error?

A. The superclass constructor has no arguments, so the `Subclass` constructor cannot have any arguments, either.

B. Fields `myInt` and `myString` are *private* fields of `Baseclass`, so they cannot be assigned to in the `Subclass` constructor.

C. There is no call to the superclass constructor.

D. Parameter `aDouble` is not used.

E. The `myDouble` field is not initialized.

11. Consider the following two code segments:

Segment 1

```
while (k > 0) {
  System.out.println(k);
  k--;
}
```

Segment 2

```
while (k > 0) {
  System.out.println(k);
  k--;
}
while (k > 0) {
  System.out.println(k);
  k--;
}
```

Assume that in both cases variable k has the *same* initial value. Under which of the following conditions will the two code segments produce identical output?

I.   The initial value of k is greater than zero.
II. The initial value of k is zero.
III. The initial value of k is less than zero.

A. I only

B. II only

C. III only

D. I and III only

E. I, II, and III

12. Consider the following code segment:

```
ArrayList L = new ArrayList();
int k = 0;
while (k<11) {
    L.add(new Integer(k));
    k++;
}
k = 0;
while (k<L.size()) {
    L.remove(k);
    k++;
}
for (k=0; k<L.size(); k++) {
    System.out.print(L.get(k) + " ");
}
```

What happens when this code executes?

A. The second *while-loop* causes an IndexOutOfBoundsException.

B. The *for-loop* causes an IndexOutOfBoundsException.

C. There is no exception, but nothing is printed because the list is empty after the second *while-loop*.

D. There is no exception; 1 3 5 7 9 is printed.

E. There is no exception; 6 7 8 9 10 is printed.

13. Assume that variable A is an array of *N* integers and that the following assertion is true:

    ```
    A[0] != A[k] for all k such that 1 <= k < N
    ```

    Which of the following is a valid conclusion?

    A. Array A is sorted.

    B. Array A is not sorted.

    C. Array A contains no duplicates.

    D. The value in A[0] is the smallest value in the array.

    E. The value in A[0] does not occur anywhere else in the array.

14. Assume that variable A is an `ArrayList` of size five. Consider the following code segment:

    ```
    int N = A.size();
    for (int k=0; k<=N/2; k++) {
        A.set(k, "X");
        A.set(N-k-1, "O");
    }
    ```

    Which of the following correctly illustrates A after the code segment executes?

    A. X X O O O

    B. X X X O O

    C. O O O O O

    D. X X X X X

    E. It is not possible to determine the values in A after the code segment executes without knowing what values are in A before the code segment executes.

15. Consider the following code segment:

    ```
    x = !y;
    y = !x;
    x = !y;
    ```

    Assume that x and y are initialized boolean variables. Which of the following statements is true?

    A. The final value of y is the same as the initial value of y.

    B. The final value of x is the same as the initial value of x.

    C. The final value of x is the same as the initial value of y.

    D. The final value of y is the same as the initial value of x.

    E. It is not possible to say anything about the final values of x and y without knowing their initial values.

Questions 16 and 17 refer to the following code segment (line numbers are included for reference). Assume that method `readInt` reads and returns one integer value.

```
1  int x, sum;
2  x = -1;
3  sum = 1;
4  x = readInt();
5  while (x >= 0) {
6     if (x > 0) {
7         sum += x;
8     }
9     x = readInt();
10 }
11 System.out.println(sum);
```

16. For the purposes of this question, two code segments are considered to be *equivalent* if, when they are run using the same input, they produce the same output. Which line could be removed from the code segment given above so that the resulting code segment is equivalent to the original one?

   A. Line 2
   B. Line 3
   C. Line 4
   D. Line 7
   E. Line 9

17. The code segment given above was intended to read values until a negative value was read and then to print the sum of the positive values read. However, the code does not work as intended. Which of the following best describes the error?

   A. Variable x is not initialized correctly.
   B. Variable sum is not initialized correctly.
   C. Variable x is used before being initialized.
   D. Variable sum is used before being initialized.
   E. The negative value intended to signal end of input is included in the sum.

Questions 18 and 19 rely on the following information:

A dairy farm has 100 cows, kept in 5 fields, with 20 cows per field. The farmer needs a data structure to record the amount of milk given by each cow in one day.

Two different data structures are being considered:

Structure 1: An array of `doubles` of length 100. Each array entry is the amount of milk given by one cow on one day. The first 20 entries will be used for the cows in field 1, the next 20 entries will be used for the cows in field 2, and so on.

Structure 2: Five arrays of `doubles`, each of length 20. Each array entry is the amount of milk given by one cow on one day. The first array will be used for the cows in field 1, the second array will be used for the cows in field 2, and so on.

18. The following operations are to be performed on the data structure:

    Operation 1: Compute, for each of the five fields, the total amount of milk produced by the cows in that field.

    Operation 2: Compute the total amount of milk produced by all of the cows.

    Which of the following statements about these operations is true?

    A. Both operations can be implemented using either of the two data structures.

    B. Operation 1 can be implemented using either of the two data structures, but Operation 2 can only be implemented using Structure 1.

    C. Operation 2 can be implemented using either of the two data structures, but Operation 1 can only be implemented using Structure 1.

    D. Operation 1 can be implemented using either of the two data structures, but Operation 2 can only be implemented using Structure 2.

    E. Operation 2 can be implemented using either of the two data structures, but Operation 1 can only be implemented using Structure 2.

19. Under which of the following conditions does Data Structure 1 require more storage than Data Structure 2?

    A. When the total amount of milk produced is the same for all five fields

    B. When the total amount of milk produced is different for each of the five fields

    C. When the cows in the first field produce the most milk, then the cows in the second field, then the cows in the third field, and so on.

    D. When the cows in the fifth field produce the most milk, then the cows in the fourth field, then the cows in the third field, and so on.

    E. Data Structure 1 never requires more storage than Data Structure 2.

20. Assume that variables s1 and s2 are both of type String. Consider the following three code segments:

Segment I	**Segment II**	**Segment III**
s1 = "hello";	s1 = "hello";	s1 = "hello";
s2 = s1;	s2 = s1;	s2 = s1 + "!";
	s1 = "bye";	

After executing which of the three segments will the expression s1 == s2 evaluate to true?

A. I only

B. II only

C. III only

D. I and II only

E. I, II, and III

21. Consider the following code segment:

```
int[] A = new int[3];
int[] B;

for (int j=0; j<A.length; j++) A[j] = j;
B = A;
for (int j=0; j<A.length; j++) A[j]++;
for (int j=0; j<A.length; j++) {
    System.out.print(A[j] + " " + B[j] + " ");
}
System.out.println();
}
```

What is printed when this code segment executes?

A. 0 0 1 1 2 2

B. 1 0 2 1 3 2

C. 1 1 2 2 3 3

D. 0 1 1 2 2 3

E. Nothing is printed because the use of B[j] in the print statement causes an ArrayIndex-OutOfBoundsException.

Questions 22–25 involve reasoning about the Marine Biology case study.

22. Which of the following methods could *not* be called from a method in the SlowFish class?

    A. act

    B. move

    C. location

    D. initialize

    E. nextLocation

23. Assume that variable env is a properly initialized Environment. Which of the following expressions evaluate(s) to the number of objects in the environment represented by env?

    I.   env.numObjects()
    II. env.allObjects().length
    III. env.neighborsOf().size()

    A. I only

    B. II only

    C. I and II only

    D. I and III only

    E. I, II, and III

24. Assume that a new class called newLocatable that implements the Locatable interface is defined. Which of the following methods must be provided by both a newLocatable object and a Fish object?

    I.   act
    II. location
    III. initialize

    A. I only

    B. II only

    C. I and II only

    D. I and III only

    E. I, II, and III

25. Consider defining a new kind of fish called a `JumpingDarterFish` that extends the `Darter-Fish` class. The `JumpingDarterFish`'s `nextLocation` method is given below.

```
protected Location nextLocation() {
    Environment env = environment();
    Location oneInFront = env.getNeighbor(location(), direction());
    Location twoInFront = env.getNeighbor(oneInFront, direction());

    if ( env.isEmpty(twoInFront) ) return twoInFront;
    else return location();
}
```

Which of the following statements is true?

A. A `JumpingDarterFish` will move forward two spaces if both that space and the space directly in front of it are empty.

B. A `JumpingDarterFish` will move forward two spaces if that space is empty, regardless of whether the space directly in front of it is empty.

C. A `JumpingDarterFish` may move outside of its environment because it does not check for the bounds of the environment, it just moves forward.

D. The `JumpingDarterFish`'s `nextLocation` method may cause a runtime error because it checks to see if a `Location` is empty without determining if it is contained in the environment.

E. The `JumpingDarterFish`'s `nextLocation` method may cause a runtime error because it does not check whether `twoInFront` is null before checking whether it is empty.

Questions 26 and 27 refer to the following Horse, WorkHorse, and RaceHorse classes (note that WorkHorse and RaceHorse are subclasses of Horse).

```java
public class Horse {
    private int age;
    private double price;

    // constructor
    public Horse(int a, double p) {
        age = a;
        price = p;
    }

    public int getAge() { return age; }

    public double getPrice() { return price; }

    public void setAge(int newAge) { age = newAge; }

    public void setPrice(double newPrice) { price = newPrice; }

    public void haveBirthday() {
        age++;
        price = price - .1*price;
    }
}

public class WorkHorse extends Horse {
    private double weight;

    // constructor
    public WorkHorse(int a, double p, double w) {
        super(a, p);
        weight = w;
    }
}

public class RaceHorse extends Horse {
    // constructor
    public RaceHorse(int a, double p) {
        super(a, p);
    }

    public void haveBirthday() {
        setAge( getAge()+1 );
        setPrice( getPrice() - .2*getPrice() );
    }
}
```

26. Which of the following statements will compile without error?

    A. `Horse h = new WorkHorse(2, 1000);`

    B. `Horse h = new RaceHorse(2, 1000);`

    C. `WorkHorse h = new RaceHorse(2, 1000);`

    D. `RaceHorse h = new WorkHorse(2, 1000);`

    E. `RaceHorse h = new Horse(2, 1000);`

27. Assume that variable h has been declared to be of type `Horse`, and has been initialized to represent a horse whose price is 100.

    Which of the following statements about the call `h.haveBirthday()` is true?

    A. Whatever kind of horse variable h actually points to, the price of that horse after the call will be 90.

    B. Whatever kind of horse variable h actually points to, the price of that horse after the call will be 80.

    C. If variable h actually points to a `RaceHorse` object, then the price of that horse after the call will be 80.

    D. If variable h actually points to a `WorkHorse` object, there will be a runtime error, since class `WorkHorse` has no `haveBirthday` method.

    E. If variable h actually points to a `WorkHorse` object, the price of that horse after the call will still be 100, since class `WorkHorse` has no `haveBirthday` method.

28. Assume that variable A is a *sorted* array of `ints`. Consider the following code segment:

    ```
    boolean flag = false;
    for (int k=1; k<A.length; k++) {
        if (A[k-1] == A[k]) flag = true;
    }
    ```

    Which of the following best describes when variable `flag` is true after this code segment executes?

    A. Always

    B. Never

    C. If and only if array A contains duplicate values

    D. If and only if the last two values in array A are the same

    E. If and only if all values in array A are the same

Questions 29 and 30 refer to the following Shape class:

```
public class Shape {
   private int numSides;
   private String color;

   // constructor
   public Shape(int n) {
      numSides = n;
      color = "Black";
   }

   public void setColor(String newColor) {
      color = newColor;
   }

   public String getColor() {
      return color;
   }
}
```

29. Consider the following code segment, with line numbers included for reference:

```
1  Shape[] myShapes;
2  myShapes = new Shape[3];
3  myShapes[0].setColor("Red");
4  myShapes[0].setColor(myShapes[0].getColor() + "Blue");
5  myShapes[0].setColor(myShapes[0].getColor() + "Green");
6  System.out.print(myShapes[0].getColor());
```

What happens when this code executes?

A. Line 2 causes an `IndexOutOfBoundsException` because `myShapes` has length 0 and it cannot be changed to have length 3.

B. Line 3 causes a `NullPointerException` because `myShapes[0]` has not been initialized.

C. There is no exception; `RedBlueGreen` is printed.

D. There is no exception; `BlackRedBlueGreen` is printed.

E. There is no exception; `GreenBlueRedBlack` is printed.

30. Consider the following data field and (incorrect) method:

```
private Shape[] myShapes;

public boolean sameColor(int k) {
// precondition: 0 <= k <  myShapes.length
//                myShapes contains no nulls
// postcondition: returns true iff some other shape in myShapes
//                has the same color as the shape at position k
    String col = myShapes[k].getColor();
    for (int j=0; j<myShapes.length; j++) {
        if (myShapes[j].getColor().equals(col)) return true;
    }
    return false;
}
```

As specified by its pre- and postconditions, method `sameColor` was intended to return `true` iff some other shape in the `myShapes` array has the same color as the shape at position k. However, when the method is tested it is discovered that it *always* returns `true`. Which of the following changes would fix `sameColor`?

A. Change the condition of the *if* statement to
   `j!=k && myShapes[j].getColor().equals(col)`

B. Change the condition of the *if* statement to
   `myShapes[j].getColor() == col`

C. Change the condition of the *if* statement to
   `!myShapes[j].getColor().equals(col)`

D. Replace the *if* statement with
   `return (myShapes[j].getColor().equals(col));`

E. Replace the *if* statement with
   `return (myShapes[j].getColor() == col);`

31. Consider the following two ways to determine whether the values in array A are in sorted order (from smallest to largest). Assume that A contains N values.

Idea 1: For each index k between 0 and $N - 1$, check whether all elements with indexes larger than k have values greater than or equal to the value in A[k]; if so, the array is sorted.

Idea 2: For each index k between 0 and $N - 2$, check whether the value in A[k+1] is greater than or equal to the value in A[k]; if so, the array is sorted.

Which of the following statements about the two ideas is true?

A. Only Idea 1 will work.

B. Only Idea 2 will work.

C. Both ideas will work; the two ideas will be equally efficient.

D. Both ideas will work; Idea 1 will be more efficient than Idea 2.

E. Both ideas will work; Idea 2 will be more efficient than Idea 1.

32. Method isEven below was intended to return true iff its parameter num is an even number; however, it does not always work as intended.

```
public static boolean isEven(int num) {
    if (num == 0) return true;
    else if (num > 0) return isEven(num-2);
    else return isEven(num+2);
}
```

Which of the following best describes what method isEven actually does?

A. Always returns true.

B. Returns true if num is a positive even number, and otherwise returns false.

C. Returns true if num is a negative even number, and otherwise returns false.

D. Returns true if num is an even number, and otherwise causes an infinite recursion.

E. Returns true if num is a positive even number, and otherwise causes an infinite recursion.

Questions 33 and 34 refer to the following recursive method:

```
public static int compute(int low, int high) {
    if ( low == high ) return 0;
    return 1 + compute(low+1, high);
}
```

33. When does a call compute(low, high) cause an infinite recursion?

A. Only when low > high.

B. Only when high − low is divisible by two.

C. Only when high − low is *not* divisible by two.

D. Only when low < high.

E. When low != high.

34. Which of the following best describes the value returned by a call compute(low, high) that does not cause an infinite recursion?

    A. low + high

    B. low – high

    C. high * low

    D. high – low

    E. The sum of the numbers from low to high.

35. Consider the following data field and method:

    ```
    private ArrayList myList;

    public String processList(int k) {
        if (k == myList.size()) return "";
        else return processList(k+1) + myList.get(k);
    }
    ```

    If myList is the list of strings shown below (with "A" in position 0 and "D" in position 3)

    ```
    [ "A", "B", "C", "D" ]
    ```

    what is returned by the call processList(0)?

    A. "ABC"

    B. "ABCD"

    C. "DCBA"

    D. "AAAA"

    E. "DDDD"

36. Assume that classes `Person` and `Animal` have been defined, and that they each include a public `getName` method that returns a `String`. Also assume that a `Game` class includes the following data fields and methods:

```
private Person[] personList;
private Animal[] animalList;

public boolean search(String personName) {
// search version 1: search for a person with the given name
   for (int k=0; k<personList.length; k++) {
      if (personName.equals(personList[k].getName())) return true;
   }
   return false;
}

public boolean search(String animalName) {
// search version 2: search for an animal with the given name
   for (int k=0; k<animalList.length; k++) {
      if (animalName.equals(animalList[k].getName())) return true;
   }
   return false;
}
```

Which of the following statements about this code is true?

A. It will not compile because the `Game` class includes two methods with the same names that have the same numbers and types of parameters.

B. It will not compile because the `Game` class includes an array of people and an array of animals.

C. It will compile. If a call to method `search` is made, the version that will execute will depend on whether `personList` or `animalList` is null.

D. It will compile. If a call to method `search` is made, the first version will be called first; if that version returns `false`, the second version will be called.

E. It will compile as long as every call to method `search` specifies which version should be called.

37. Consider the following data field and method:

```
String word;

public boolean findWord( String bigWord ) {
    int index = bigWord.indexOf( word );
    return ( (index > 0) &&
                (index + word.length() < bigWord.length()) );
}
```

For which of the following values of bigWord and word will method findWord return true?

	bigWord	word
A.	hello	he
B.	spicey	ice
C.	apple	ape
D.	palid	aid
E.	palid	lid

38. Consider the following code segment:

```
String s1 = "ab";
String s2 = s1;

s1 = s1 + "c";
System.out.println(s1 + " " + s2);
```

What is printed when this code executes?

A. abc ab

B. abc abc

C. ac ab

D. ac ac

E. ae ab

Questions 39 and 40 concern the following incomplete definition of class `HorizontalLine`.

```
public class HorizontalLine implements Comparable {
    private int startPoint;
    private int endPoint;

    // constructor
    // precondition: end > start
    public HorizontalLine(int start, int end) {
        startPoint = start;
        endPoint = end;
    }

    public int CompareTo(Object other) {
        HorizontalLine line = (HorizontalLine)other;
        .
        :   missing code
        .
    }
}
```

A `HorizontalLine` object represents a horizontal line on the x-axis of a graph. For example:

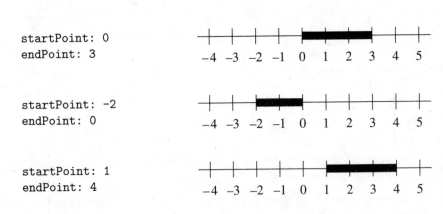

HorizontalLine object's data fields   Corresponding line on the x-axis

39. Which of the following could be used to replace *missing code* in the CompareTo method so that lines are compared according to their *length* (i.e., line1 is considered to be less than line2 if line1 is shorter than line2; equal if their lengths are the same; and greater if line1 is longer than line2)?

    A. ```
       if (startPoint < line.startPoint && endPoint < line.endPoint) return -1;
       if (startPoint == line.startPoint && endPoint == line.endPoint) return 0;
       return 1;
       ```

    B. ```
       if (startPoint < line.startPoint || endPoint < line.endPoint) return -1;
       if (startPoint == line.startPoint && endPoint == line.endPoint) return 0;
       return 1
       ```

    C. ```
       if (startPoint < line.startPoint || endPoint < line.endPoint) return -1;
       if (startPoint == line.startPoint || endPoint == line.endPoint) return 0;
       return 1;
       ```

    D. ```
       if (endPoint+startPoint < line.endPoint+line.startPoint) return -1;
       if (endPoint+startPoint == line.endPoint+line.startPoint) return 0;
       return 1;
       ```

    E. ```
       if (endPoint-startPoint < line.endPoint-line.startPoint) return -1;
       if (endPoint-startPoint == line.endPoint-line.startPoint) return 0;
       return 1;
       ```

40. Which of the following could be used to replace *missing code* in the CompareTo method so that lines are compared according to their *starting position* (i.e., line1 is considered to be less than line2 if line1 starts to the left of line2; equal if they start at the same place; and greater if line1 starts to the right of line2)?

    A. ```
       if (startPoint < line.startPoint) return -1;
       if (startPoint == line.startPoint) return 0;
       return 1;
       ```

    B. ```
       if (endPoint+startPoint < line.endPoint+line.startPoint) return -1;
       if (endPoint+startPoint == line.endPoint+line.startPoint) return 0;
       return 1;
       ```

    C. ```
       if (startPoint < line.startPoint && endPoint < line.endPoint) return -1;
       if (startPoint == line.startPoint && endPoint == line.endPoint) return 0;
       return 1;
       ```

    D. ```
       if (startPoint < line.startPoint || endPoint < line.endPoint) return -1;
       if (startPoint == line.startPoint && endPoint == line.endPoint) return 0;
       return 1;
       ```

    E. ```
       if (startPoint < line.endPoint) return -1;
       if (startPoint == line.endPoint) return 0;
       return 1;
       ```

Section II

Time: 1 hour and 45 minutes
Number of questions: 4
Percent of total grade: 50

Question 1

This question involves reasoning about the code from the Marine Biology case study.

Consider a new type of fish called OceanFish, whose environment may include currents. Partial definitions of the OceanEnvironment and OceanFish classes are given below.

```
public class OceanEnvironment extends BoundedEnvironment {


    // precondition: isValid(loc) == true
    // postcondition: returns true if the specified location is in an
    //                ocean current.
    public boolean isInCurrent(Location loc) { /* not shown */ }


    // precondition: isValid(loc) == true and isInCurrent(loc) == true
    // postcondition: returns the direction of the ocean current that
    //                loc is in
    public Direction currentDirection(Location loc) { /* not shown */ }


    // other methods not shown
}


public class OceanFish extends Fish {

    protected Location nextLocation() { /* part (a) */ }

    public void act() { /* part (b) */ }

    // returns the OceanEnvironment that contains this fish
    public Environment environment() { /* not shown */ }
}
```

Part (a)

The `nextLocation` method of an `OceanFish` returns the next location that the fish will move to using the following rules:

- If the `OceanFish` is in an ocean current and the neighboring location in the direction of the ocean current is empty, the `nextLocation` method will return that neighboring location. If that neighboring location is not empty, the `nextLocation` method will return the fish's location unchanged (i.e., the fish will not move).

- If the `OceanFish` is not in an ocean current the `nextLocation` method will return the location determined by the `nextLocation` method of the `Fish` class.

Complete the `nextLocation` method below.

```
protected Location nextLocation() {
```

Part (b)

`OceanFish` act according to the following rules:

- If the fish is not in the environment, it does nothing; otherwise:
  - The fish attempts to move.
  - If the fish is not in an ocean current, it attempts to breed.
  - The fish determines whether or not it will die in this timestep: If it is not in an ocean current it uses its stored probability of dying. If it is in an ocean current it uses two times the stored probability of dying.

Complete method `act` below.

```
public void act() {
```

Question 2

A laundry uses a Java program to keep track of its customers and their orders. One class, Laundry-Order, will be used to keep track of an individual order. Each LaundryOrder object will need to include the following information:

- The name of the customer
- The number of items to be cleaned
- Whether the order is ready

The LaundryOrder class must provide the following operations:

- Create a LaundryOrder object given a customer name and number of items.
- Access the customer name, the number of items, and whether the order is ready.
- Change the object to show that the order is ready.

Part (a)

Write a complete declaration for the LaundryOrder class.

Part (b)

The laundry also does alterations on items brought in for cleaning, and an AlterationOrder class will be used to keep track of alteration orders. An AlterationOrder is a LaundryOrder with the following additional properties:

- An AlterationOrder includes a string that specifies what is to be done (the alteration instructions).
- Alterations are performed on only one item, therefore the number of items is always 1.
- The alteration instructions can be accessed but not modified.

Write a complete declaration for the AlterationOrder class.

Part (c)

To keep track of all current orders, the laundry uses the Laundry class partially declared below.

```
public class Laundry {

    private ArrayList allOrders;  // list of LaundryOrders

    // constructor not shown

    // precondition: allOrders is a list of LaundryOrders
    // postcondition: returns an ArrayList containing the
    //                LaundryOrders in allOrders that are not ready
    public ArrayList unfinishedOrders() { /* part (c) */ }

    // other methods not shown
}
```

The unfinishedOrders method returns an ArrayList containing all of the LaundryOrders in the allOrders ArrayList that are not yet ready.

Complete method unfinishedOrders below.

```
    // precondition: allOrders is a list of LaundryOrders
    // postcondition: returns an ArrayList containing the LaundryOrders in
    //                allOrders that are not ready
    public ArrayList unfinishedOrders() {
```

Question 3

This question involves the following two (incomplete) class definitions, which define classes to be used for storing information about the students in an AP CS class.

```
public class StudentInfo {
    private String name;
    private int[] grades;
    private double averageGrade;

    // constructor
    // precondition: theGrades is not null
    public StudentInfo( String theName, int[] theGrades ) {
        /* part (a) */
    }

    public String getName() { return name; }
    public double getAverageGrade() { return averageGrade; }
}

public class APCS {
    private StudentInfo[] students;
    private String highestAverage;

    // constructor
    public APCS() { /* part (b) */ }
}
```

Part (a)

Write the constructor for the StudentInfo class. The constructor should initialize the name and grades fields using the given values, and then it should compute the average grade and use that value to initialize the averageGrade field. (If the number of grades is zero, the averageGrade field should be set to zero.)

Complete the constructor below.

```
// precondition: theGrades is not null
public StudentInfo( String theName, int[] theGrades ) {
```

Part (b)

Assume that the following methods can be used to read input values from a file:

```
public static int readInt()        // reads and returns the next
                                   // integer value
public static String readString()  // reads and returns the next
                                   // string value
```

Write the constructor for the APCS class. Assume that when the constructor is called, there is an input file ready for reading. The first piece of data in the file is a positive integer N, the number of students in the class. Then there is information for each of the N students, organized as follows:

- The student's name
- The number of grades recorded for that student
- The actual grades (integers in the range 0 to 100)

The APCS constructor should initialize its students field by creating an array of StudentInfo, using the data in the input file. It should then determine which student has the highest average and use that student's name to initialize its highestAverage field. (If two students share the same highest average, either name can be used to initialize the highestAverage field.)

For example, if the input data are as follows:

```
2
Jones
5
100 95 80 100 100
Smith
2
86 87
```

the students field should be initialized to contain two StudentInfo elements (one for Jones and one for Smith), and the highestAverage field should be initialized to "Jones", because Jones has an average grade of 95.0, whereas Smith has a (lower) average grade of 86.5.

In writing the APCS constructor, you may include calls to the StudentInfo constructor. Assume that the StudentInfo constructor works as specified, regardless of what you wrote for part (a).

Complete the APCS constructor below.

```
public APCS() {
```

Question 4
Part (a)

Write method `findZero`, as started below. Method `findZero` should return the index of the first element of array `A` that contains the value zero, starting from position pos. If no element of `A` from position pos to the end of the array contains the value zero, then `findZero` should return −1.

For example:

Array A	Position pos	Value returned by findZero(A, pos)
1 0 2 5 6	0	1
1 0 2 5 6	1	1
1 0 2 5 6	2	−1
1 0 2 0 6	0	1
1 0 2 0 6	1	1
1 0 2 0 6	2	3
1 2 3 4 5	0	−1

Complete method `findZero` below.

```
// precondition: 0 <= pos < A.length
// postcondition: returns the smallest index k such that
//                (pos <= k < A.length) and (A[k] == 0),
//                or -1 if there is no such index
public static int findZero(int[] A, int pos) {
```

Part (b)

Write method `setZeros`, as started below. Method `setZeros` should find the positions of the first two zeros in its array parameter `A`, and it should set all of the intervening values (if any) to zero. If `A` only contains one zero, if it contains no zeros, or if the first two zeros are right next to each other, `setZeros` should not modify `A`.

For example:

Array A before calling setZeros	Array A after the call setZeros(A)
0 1 2 0 4 0	0 0 0 0 4 0
1 0 2 3 4 0	1 0 0 0 0 0
1 2 0 0 4 5	1 2 0 0 4 5
1 0 2 3	1 0 2 3
1 2 3 4	1 2 3 4

In writing method `setZeros`, you may include calls to method `findZero`. Assume that method `findZero` works as specified, regardless of what you wrote for part (a).

Complete method `setZeros` below.

```
public static void setZeros( int[] A ) {
```

Answers to Section I

1.	A		21.	C
2.	C		22.	D
3.	B		23.	C
4.	C		24.	B
5.	C		25.	B
6.	A		26.	B
7.	D		27.	C
8.	A		28.	C
9.	E		29.	B
10.	B		30.	A
11.	E		31.	E
12.	D		32.	D
13.	E		33.	A
14.	A		34.	D
15.	A		35.	C
16.	A		36.	A
17.	B		37.	B
18.	A		38.	A
19.	E		39.	E
20.	A		40.	A

Answers to Section II

Question 1
Part (a)

```
protected Location nextLocation() {

    if (!environment().isInCurrent(location()))
        return super.nextLocation();

    Direction dir = environment().currentDirection(location());
    Location nextLoc = environment().getNeighbor(location(), dir);
    if (environment().isEmpty(nextLoc)) return nextLoc;
    else return location();
}
```

Part (b)

```
public void act() {
    if (!isInEnv()) return;
    move();
    Random r = RandNumGenerator.getInstance();
    if (!environment().isInCurrent(location())) {
        breed();
        if (r.nextDouble() < probOfDying) die();
    } else {
        if (r.nextDouble() < probOfDying * 2) die();
    }
}
```

Grading Guide

Part (a) `nextLocation`   5 Points

+1½ Not in an ocean current
   + ½ attempt to determine whether the fish is in an ocean current
   + ½ correct condition
   + ½ call to `super.nextLocation`

+ ½ Retrieve direction of ocean current

+1 Retrieve neighboring location based on direction
   + ½ attempt(must call `getNeighbor`)
   + ½ correct

+1 Check to see if neighboring location is empty

+ ½ Return neighboring location (must be from attempt at retrieval)

+ ½ Return unchanged location (next space not empty)

Part (b) `act`   4 Points

+ ½ Check for `isInEnv`

+ ½ Call `move`

+1 Check for `isInCurrent`
   + ½ attempt
   + ½ correct

+ ½ Breed (must occur where appropriate)

+ ½ Check probability and die for not in an ocean current

+1 Check probability and die for in an ocean current
   + ½ attempt
   + ½ correct

Question 2
Part (a)

```
public class LaundryOrder {
    private String name;
    private int numItems;
    private boolean isReady;

    public LaundryOrder(String n, int num) {
        name = n;
        numItems = num;
        isReady = false;
    }

    public String getName() { return name; }
    public int getNumItems() { return numItems; }
    public boolean orderIsReady() { return isReady; }

    public void setIsReady() { isReady = true; }
}
```

Part (b)

```
public class AlterationOrder extends LaundryOrder {
    private String instructions;

    public AlterationOrder(String n, String inst) {
        super(n, 1);
        instructions = inst;
    }

    public String getInstructions() { return instructions; }
}
```

Part (c)

```
public ArrayList unfinishedOrders() {

    ArrayList answer = new ArrayList();
    for (int i=0; i<allOrders.size(); i++) {
        LaundryOrder temp = (LaundryOrder)allOrders.get(i);
        if (!temp.orderIsReady()) answer.add(temp);
    }
    return answer;
}
```

Grading Guide

Part (a) The LaundryOrder class   3 Points

    + 1/2 Declare class LaundryOrder

    + 1/2 Private instance variable declarations

    + 1/2 Constructor

    +1 Accessor methods

        + 1/2 attempt

        + 1/2 correct

    + 1/2 Method to change state of boolean field

Part (b) The AlterationOrder class   3 Points

    +1 Declare class AlterationOrder

        + 1/2 attempt (can receive without extends)

        + 1/2 correct

    +1 1/2 Constructor

        + 1/2 attempt (can receive without super)

        + 1/2 call to super

        + 1/2 correct (including passing 1 for number of items)

    + 1/2 getInstructions

Part (c) unfinishedOrders   3 Points

    + 1/2 Create ArrayList to return

    +1 Loop over allOrders

        + 1/2 attempt

        + 1/2 correct

    +1 Check for orderIsReady and add to created ArrayList

        + 1/2 attempt at check

        + 1/2 correct with add

    + 1/2 Return created ArrayList

Question 3
Part (a)

```java
public StudentInfo( String theName, int[] theGrades ) {
   int sum = 0;

   name = theName;
   grades = theGrades;
   for (int k=0; k<grades.length; k++) {
      sum += grades[k];
   }
   if (grades.length > 0) {
      averageGrade = ((double)sum)/grades.length;
   }
   else averageGrade = 0;
}
```

Part (b)

```java
public APCS() {

   // initialize students array
   int numStudents = readInt();
   students = new StudentInfo[numStudents];
   for (int k=0; k<numStudents; k++) {
      String name = readString();
      int numGrades = readInt();
      int[] grades = new int[numGrades];
      for (int j=0; j<numGrades; j++) {
         grades[j] = readInt();
      }
      students[k] = new StudentInfo(name, grades);
   }

   // initialize highestAverage field
   double max = students[0].getAverageGrade();
   highestAverage = students[0].getName();
   for (int k=1; k<numStudents; k++) {
      double oneAv = students[k].getAverageGrade();
      if (oneAv > max) highestAverage = students[k].getName();
   }
}
```

Grading Guide

Part (a) The `StudentInfo` constructor   3 Points

> + ½ Initialization of `name`, `grades`
>
> +2 Calculating the average grade
>> + ½ loop attempt
>> + ½ loop correct
>> + ½ accumulate
>> + ½ divide by length, including cast to `double`
>
> + ½ Set average grade to 0 if no grades

Part (b) The `APCS` constructor   6 Points

> +1 Initialize array
>> + ½ `readInt`
>> + ½ array size
>
> +1 Loop over `numStudents`
>> + ½ attempt (must use value read in)
>> + ½ correct
>
> + ½ Read values (name, number of grades, grades)
>
> +1 Loop over grades
>> + ½ loop
>> + ½ `readInt`
>
> + ½ Initialize new `StudentInfo`
>
> +2 Initialize highest average
>> + ½ initialize
>> + ½ loop
>> + ½ comparison
>> + ½ assign highest average

Question 4
Part (a)

Version 1: Use a *for-loop*, exiting the loop using a return statement as soon as possible.

```
public static int findZero(int[] A, int pos) {
    for (int k=pos; k<A.length; k++) {
        if (A[k] == 0) return k;
    }
    return -1;
}
```

Version 2: Use a *while-loop* whose condition checks both for having reached the end of the array and having found a zero.

```
public static int findZero(int[] A, int pos) {
    int k=pos;
    while (k<A.length && A[k]!=0) k++;
    if (k < A.length) return k;
    else return -1;
}
```

Note that the order of the expressions in the *while-loop* condition is very important; if it were written like this:

```
(A[k]!=0 && k<A.length)
```

there would be an out-of-bounds array access whenever there was no zero to be found in array A.

Part (b)

```
public static void setZeros(int[] A) {
    int first, second;

    // find the first zero in A
    first = findZero(A, 0);

    // if no zeros or only one zero, quit; otherwise find next zero
    if (first == -1 || first == A.length) return;
    second = findZero(A, first+1);

    // set all elements in the range first+1 - second-1 to zero
    for (int k=first+1; k<second; k++) {
        A[k] = 0;
    }
}
```

Grading Guide

Part (a) `findZero`   4 Points

> + 2 Loop over items in the array
>> + 1/2 attempt
>> + 1/2 correct starting value for search
>> +1 correct loop
>
> +1 Compare the current location to 0
>
> +1 Return appropriate values
>> + 1/2 return the index
>> + 1/2 return −1

Part (b) `setZeros`   5 Points

> +1 Find the first 0
>> + 1/2 attempt (could include a reimplementation of part (a))
>> + 1/2 correct (no reimplementation—must call `findZero`)
>
> +1 Check for no zeroes or only one zero in array
>
> +1 Find the second 0
>
> +1 Loop through indices between the first and second 0
>> + 1/2 attempt
>> + 1/2 correct
>
> +1 Assign all values within range to 0

Practice Examination AB-1

Section I

Time: 1 hour and 15 minutes
Number of questions: 40
Percent of total grade: 50

1. Assume that variable L points to the first node of a nonempty, singly linked list of integers. Which of the following operations can be performed in constant (O(1)) time?

    A. Add a node at the front of the list.

    B. Add a node at the end of the list.

    C. Add a node in the middle of the list.

    D. Determine how many nodes are in the list.

    E. Compute the sum of all values in the list.

2. For which of the following trees do a preorder and an inorder traversal produce the same sequence of letters?

    A.

    B.

    C.

    D.

    E.

Questions 3 and 4 concern the following data field and method:

```
private List myList;

public void addList( List L ) {
// add the items in L to myList
   for (Iterator it = L.iterator(); it.hasNext();) {
      myList.add(0, it.next());
   }
}
```

3. Assume that `myList` and L represent the lists shown below before method `addList` is called.

    ```
    myList: [ A,  B,  C ]
    L: [ X,  Y,  Z ]
    ```

    Which of the following lists does `myList` represent when method `addList` returns?

    A. [A, B, C, X, Y, Z]
    B. [A, B, C, Z, Y, X]
    C. [X, Y, Z, A, B, C]
    D. [Z, Y, X, A, B, C]
    E. [A, X, B, Y, C, Z]

4. If `myList` is a `LinkedList` containing N items, and L contains M items, what is the running time of method `addList`?

    A. O(N)
    B. O(M)
    C. O($N * M$)
    D. O($N + M$)
    E. O(max(N, M))

5. Which of the following is a valid reason for using a doubly linked list rather than a singly linked list?

    A. Less storage is required for a doubly linked list than for a singly linked list.
    B. A doubly linked list can be used to implement a stack, whereas a singly linked list cannot.
    C. The number of items in the list can be determined more efficiently using a doubly linked list than using a singly linked list.
    D. Given a pointer to a node n in the middle of the list, the node before n can be removed more efficiently using a doubly linked list than using a singly linked list.
    E. Given a pointer to a node n in the middle of the list, a new node can be inserted immediately after n more efficiently using a doubly linked list than using a singly linked list.

6. Consider the following code segment:

    ```
    x = (x || y);
    y = (x && y);
    ```

    Assume that x and y are initialized boolean variables. Which of the following statements is true?

    A. The final value of x is the same as the initial value of x.

    B. The final value of x is the same as the initial value of y.

    C. The final value of y is the same as the initial value of y.

    D. The final value of y is the same as the initial value of x.

    E. It is not possible to say anything about the final values of x and y without knowing their initial values.

7. Consider writing a program to be used by a company that sells cars. Four kinds of cars are sold: compact cars, station wagons, convertibles, and sedans. Assume that a Car class has been defined. Which of the following is the best way to represent the four different kinds of cars?

    A. The four kinds of cars should be represented using one field of the Car class: an array of four strings.

    B. The four kinds of cars should be represented as four int fields of the Car class, with one field for each kind of car.

    C. The four kinds of cars should be represented as four subclasses of the Car class.

    D. The four kinds of cars should be represented as four new classes, unrelated to the Car class.

    E. The four kinds of cars should be represented as four new classes. The CompactCar class should be a subclass of the Car class; the StationWagon class should be a subclass of the CompactCar class; the Convertible class should be a subclass of the StationWagon class; and the Sedan class should be a subclass of the Convertible class.

8. The code segment shown below was intended to set all of the elements on the diagonals of array A (a square array of ints) to 0 and to set the element in the middle of the array to 1. However, the code segment does not work as intended. (Line numbers are included for reference.)

```
1 // precondition: A is a nonempty, square array with
2 //                an odd number of rows and columns
3    int size = A.length;
4    A[size/2][size/2] = 1;
5    for (int j=0; j<size; j++) A[j][j] = 0;
6    for (int j=0; j<size; j++) A[j][size-j-1] = 0;
```

When the code segment is tested, it is discovered that although the diagonal elements are set to 0, the middle element is also set to 0 instead of to 1. Which of the following changes fixes the code segment?

A. Change line 3 to int size = A.length-1;.

B. Change line 4 to A[size/2+1][size/2+1] = 1;.

C. Swap lines 4 and 5.

D. Swap lines 4 and 6.

E. Swap lines 5 and 6.

9. Assume that L is a ListNode that represents a linked list of Integers as shown below.

$$L \rightarrow 0 \rightarrow 5 \rightarrow 2 \rightarrow 9 \rightarrow 1$$

Consider the following code segment:

```
ListNode tmp;
ListNode newList = null;

while (L != null) {
    tmp = L.getNext();
    if (((Integer)L.getValue()).intValue() < 3) {
        L.setNext(newList);
        newList = L;
    }
    L = tmp;
}
```

Which of the following correctly shows the value of newList after the code segment executes?

A. newList → 2

B. newList → 0 → 2 → 1

C. newList → 1 → 2 → 0

D. newList → 0 → 1 → 2

E. newList → 2 → 1 → 0

10. Under which of the following conditions would it be better to use a `LinkedList` rather than an `ArrayList`?

    A. The list iterator will be used frequently.

    B. The `get` operation will be used frequently, getting items from various places in the list.

    C. The `set` operation will be used frequently, setting values at various places in the list.

    D. Items will frequently be added to the end of the list.

    E. Items will frequently be added to the front of the list.

11. A card game is played by two people as follows:

    - Initially, each person has half of the cards, placed face-down in a pile.
    - Repeat until at least one person has no more cards:

        Each person turns over the top card of his or her pile.

        If the cards are the same, they are both discarded.

        Otherwise, the person with the higher card takes both cards and puts them face-down on the bottom of his or her pile.

    Which of the following would be the most appropriate data structure(s) to use in a program that simulates this card game?

    A. A single stack

    B. A single queue

    C. Two stacks, one for each person

    D. Two queues, one for each person

    E. A stack for one person and a queue for the other person

Questions 12 and 13 concern the following definition of class newList, intended to be used to represent a list of objects (note that the newList class uses the standard ListNode class).

```
public class newList {
    private ListNode first;  // pointer to the first node in the list
    private ListNode last;   // pointer to the last node in the list

    // constructor
    public newList( ) {
        first = null;
        last = null;
    }

    public void addToEnd(Object ob) {
        ListNode tmp = new ListNode(ob, null);
        if (last != null) last.setNext(tmp);
        last = tmp;
    }
}
```

An empty list is intended to be represented by a newList in which first and last are both null. A nonempty list is intended to be represented by a newList in which:

- The items in the list are stored in a linked list.
- first points to the first node in the linked list.
- last points to the last node in the linked list.

However, the newList class has not been implemented correctly.

12. What is the problem with the implementation of the newList class?

   A. The constructor is not implemented correctly.
   B. The types of the first and last fields are wrong.
   C. The addToEnd method will not work correctly when the first value is added to the list.
   D. The addToEnd method will not work correctly when a value other than the first is added to the list.
   E. The addToEnd method will not work correctly when a duplicate value is added to the list.

13. Which of the following best characterizes the running time of the version of addToEnd given above for a list that contains n values?

   A. $O(1)$
   B. $O(\log n)$
   C. $O(n)$
   D. $O(n \log n)$
   E. $O(n^2)$

14. Consider adding the following recursive method to the standard `TreeNode` class:

```
public int mystery( ) {
    if (left == null && right == null) return 1;
    if (left == null) return (1 + right.mystery());
    if (right == null) return (1 + left.mystery());
    return(1 + left.mystery() + right.mystery());
}
```

Which of the following best describes what method `mystery` does?

A. Always returns 0

B. Returns the number of nodes in the tree

C. Returns the number of leaves in the tree

D. Returns the number of non-leaves in the tree

E. Returns the height of the tree

15. Under which of the following conditions will an `ArrayList` iterator return items in the order in which they were added to the list?

A. All items were added to the *front* of the list.

B. All items were added to the *end* of the list.

C. No items were ever *removed* from the list.

D. Items were added either to the *front* or the *end* of the list, but never to the middle.

E. The `ArrayList`'s get method was never called.

16. Assume that `A` is an `ArrayList` and that `val` is a non-null `Object`. Consider the following code segment:

```
boolean tmp = false;
for (int k=0; k<A.size(); k++) {
    if (!tmp) tmp = (val.equals(A.get(k)));
}
return tmp;
```

Which of the following best characterizes the conditions under which this code segment returns `true`?

A. Whenever `A` contains value `val`

B. Whenever the first item in `A` has value `val`

C. Whenever the last item in `A` has value `val`

D. Whenever more than one item in `A` has value `val`

E. Whenever exactly one item in `A` has value `val`

For questions 17 and 18, assume that binary trees are implemented using the standard `TreeNode` class. Consider adding the following (incomplete) method to that class:

```
public void traverseTree(some-type X) {
    X.add-op( value );
    if (left != null) left.traverseTree(X);
    X.remove-op();
    X.add-op( value );
    if (right != null) right.traverseTree(X);
}
```

Assume that variable T is a `TreeNode`, initialized as shown below.

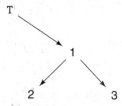

17. Assume that *some-type* is a stack of `Integers` and that *add-op* and *remove-op* are push and pop, respectively. Also assume that parameter X is an empty stack of `Integers`. Which of the following correctly describes what happens as the result of the call `T.traverseTree(X)`?

    A. A runtime error occurs when processing the root node of the tree due to an attempt to pop an empty stack.

    B. A runtime error occurs when processing a leaf node of the tree due to an attempt to pop an empty stack.

    C. The program executes without error; the final value of stack X is 1 2 3 (with 1 at the top).

    D. The program executes without error; the final value of stack X is 1 3 3 (with 1 at the top).

    E. The program executes without error; the final value of stack X is 3 1 1 (with 3 at the top).

18. Assume that *some-type* is a queue of `Integers` and that *add-op* and *remove-op* are enqueue and dequeue, respectively. Also assume that parameter X is an empty queue of `Integers`. Which of the following correctly describes what happens as the result of the call `T.traverseTree(X)`?

    A. A runtime error occurs when processing the root node of the tree due to an attempt to dequeue from an empty queue.

    B. A runtime error occurs when processing a leaf node of the tree due to an attempt to dequeue from an empty queue.

    C. The program executes without error; the final value of queue X is 1 2 3 (with 1 at the front of the queue).

    D. The program executes without error; the final value of queue X is 1 3 3 (with 1 at the front of the queue).

    E. The program executes without error; the final value of queue X is 3 1 1 (with 3 at the front of the queue).

19. Assume that A is a nonempty, rectangular, two-dimensional array of non-null objects. Consider the following method:

```
for (int j=0; j<A[0].length; j++) {
    if (! A[0][j].equals(A[A.length-1][j])) return false;
}
return true;
}
```

Which of the following best characterizes the conditions under which this code segment returns true?

A. Whenever the first and second rows of array A contain the same values

B. Whenever the first and last rows of array A contain the same values

C. Whenever the first and last columns of array A contain the same values

D. Whenever the first row and the first column of array A contain the same values

E. Whenever the first row and the last column of array A contain the same values

20. Which of the following best defines what it means to have a *collision* in a hashtable?

A. The hashtable becomes full.

B. The hash function returns a negative value.

C. Two different values that hash to the same location are inserted into the hashtable.

D. The hash function returns a value that is greater than the size of the hashtable.

E. The hash function is called more than once with the same value, so it returns the same result multiple times.

21. Consider adding a new version of the add method to the ap.java.util.LinkedList class. The header for the new method is shown below.

```
public void add(Object x, boolean toFront)
```

If parameter toFront is true, the new method would add x to the front of the list; otherwise, it would add x to the end of the list.

Which of the following statements about this proposal is true?

A. The new method cannot be added to the LinkedList class because that class already has a method with the same name.

B. The new method cannot be added to the LinkedList class because that class already has an add method with a parameter of type Object.

C. The new method as defined above cannot be added to the LinkedList class; however, if both parameters were Objects, the new method could be added to the LinkedList class.

D. The new method as defined above cannot be added to the LinkedList class; however, if the parameters were specified in the opposite order, public void add(boolean toFront, Object x), the new method could be added to the LinkedList class.

E. The new method can be added to the LinkedList class because the existing add method only has one parameter whereas the new method has two.

Questions 22–24 involve reasoning about the Marine Biology case study.

22. Consider changing the `UnboundedEnvironment` class to use a `Set` instead of an `ArrayList` to store the objects in the environment. Which of the following methods would *not* need to be modified?

    A. `ObjectAt`
    B. `allObjects`
    C. `isEmpty`
    D. `remove`
    E. `recordMove`

23. Consider changing the `UnboundedEnvironment` class to use a `LinkedList` instead of an `ArrayList` to store the objects in the environment. For which of the following methods would the Big-O worst-case runtime change?

    I.   `numObjects`
    II. `allObjects`
    III. `objectAt`

    A. I only
    B. II only
    C. III only
    D. I and II
    E. II and III

24. Consider a new implementation of the Environment interface in which the allObjects method returns a Map of the objects in the environment. In the returned Map, the objects' locations are the keys, and the associated values are the objects themselves. Which of the following could be used to replace the assignment statement and the *for-loop* in the step method of the Simulation class?

I.
```
public void step() {
    Map theFishes = theEnv.allObjects();
    for (int i=0; i<theFishes.size(); i++){
        ((Fish)theFishes.get(i)).act();
    }
}
```

II.
```
public void step() {
    Map theFishes = theEnv.allObjects();
    Iterator it = theFishes.iterator();
    while (it.hasNext()){
        ((Fish)it.next()).act();
    }
}
```

III.
```
public void step() {
    Map theFishes = theEnv.allObjects();
    Set theKeys = theFishes.keySet();
    Iterator it = theKeys.iterator();
    while (it.hasNext() {
        ((Fish)theFishes.get(it.next())).act();
    }
}
```

A. I only

B. II only

C. III only

D. I and II

E. I and III

Questions 25 and 26 concern the SortedList class, a class for storing a list of Comparable objects in ascending order. A partial class definition is given below.

```
public class SortedList {
    private int numVals;          // the number of values in the list
    private type vals;            // the values in the list,
                                  // stored in ascending order

    public SortedList() ...            // constructor
    public void add(Comparable x) ... // adds x to the sorted list
    public Comparable get(int k) ...  // returns the kth value in the
                                      // list (counting from 0)
    public int size() ...             // returns the number of values
                                      // in the list
}
```

25. Consider two ways to implement the SortedList class:

Implementation I: The values are stored *in ascending order* in an array (i.e., *type* is Comparable[]). The array is initially of size 10. Whenever the array becomes full, a new array of twice the size is created, and the values are copied from the old array to the new array.

Implementation II: The values are stored *in ascending order* in a linked list using the standard ListNode class to represent each node in the list (i.e., *type* is ListNode, and vals is a pointer to the first node in the linked list).

Which of the SortedList methods can be implemented more efficiently (in terms of Big-O notation) using an array rather than a linked list?

A. Method add only

B. Method get only

C. Methods add and get only

D. Methods add and size only

E. Methods add, get, and size

26. Consider writing a private `SortedList` method to help test whether the `SortedList` class has been implemented correctly. An incomplete version of the method is given below.

```
private void test( ) {
    for (int k=0; k<size()-1; k++) {
        if (condition) {
            System.out.println (
                "error: list not sorted in ascending order");
        }
    }
}
```

Which of the following would be the best replacement for the placeholder *condition*?

A. `length() != k`

B. `length() > k`

C. `add(k)`

D. `get(k).compareTo(get(k+1)) > 0`

E. `!get(k).equals(get(k+1))`

27. Assume that priority queues of `Integers` are implemented using the following (incomplete) class definition:

```
public class IntPriorityQueue implements PriorityQueue {
    .
    .    missing implementation
    .
}
```

Also assume that `A` is an array of `Integers`. Consider the following code segment:

```
PriorityQueue PQ = new IntPriorityQueue();
for (int k=0; k<A.length; k++) {
    PQ.add(A[k]);
}
while (!PQ.isEmpty()) {
    Integer oneInt = (Integer)PQ.removeMin();
    System.out.println(oneInt.intValue());
}
```

Assume that array `A` contains N values. What is printed when this code segment executes?

A. The values 0 to $N - 1$

B. `A`'s N values in the order in which they occur in `A`

C. `A`'s N values in the *reverse* of the order in which they occur in `A`

D. `A`'s N values in sorted order from smallest to largest

E. `A`'s N values in sorted order from largest to smallest

Questions 28 and 29 concern the following information:

Assume that binary trees are implemented using the standard `TreeNode` class. Consider adding the following methods to the `TreeNode` class:

```
private static int max(Comparable x, Comparable y) {
   if (x.compareTo(y) > 0) return x;
   else return y;
}


public Comparable treeComp() {
   if (left == null && right == null) {
      return((Comparable)value);
   }
   if (left == null) {
      return(max((Comparable)value, right.treeComp()));
   }
   if (right == null) {
      return(max((Comparable)value, left.treeComp()));
   }
   return(max((Comparable)value,
           max(left.treeComp(), right.treeComp())));
}
```

28. Assume that T is a non-null `TreeNode`. Which of the following best describes the value returned by the call `T.treeComp()`?

    A. The largest value in the tree rooted at T

    B. The largest value in a leaf of the tree rooted at T

    C. The value in the root of the tree rooted at T

    D. The value in the leftmost leaf of the tree rooted at T

    E. The value in the rightmost leaf of the tree rooted at T

29. Assume that variable T is the root of a tree, every node of which contains the same kind of value. Consider the call `T.treeComp()`. The call will *not* cause a runtime error if the values in T have which of the following types?

    I.   `Object`
    II. `Integer`
    III. `String`

    A. I only

    B. II only

    C. III only

    D. II and III only

    E. I, II, and III

30. Which of the following is a binary search tree?

A.

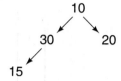

B.

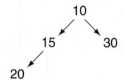

C.

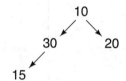

D.

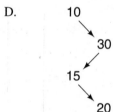

E.

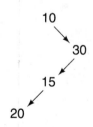

31. Assume that doubly linked lists are implemented using the following (incomplete) class:

```
public class DblListNode {
    private Object value;
    private DblListNode previous;
    private DblListNode next;

    public void removeFromList() { method body }
}
```

Also assume that variables L and `tmp` are `DblListNodes`, with values as illustrated below.

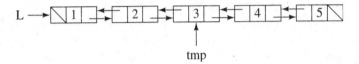

Which of the following code segments could be used to replace *method body* so that the call `tmp.removeFromList()` removes the node pointed to by `tmp` from the list pointed to by L?

A. `next = previous = null;`

B. `next = previous;`

C. `next = previous;`
`previous = next;`

D. `next.previous = previous;`
`previous.next = next;`
`next = previous = null;`

E. `next.previous = previous.next;`
`previous.next = next.previous;`
`next = previous = null;`

Questions 32–34 concern the following algorithm, which copies values from an array into a binary search tree and then prints the values, using an inorder traversal of the tree.

Step 1: Initialize the tree to be empty.

Step 2: For each value in the array from left to right, insert the value into the tree.

Step 3: Print the values in the tree using an inorder traversal.

32. Which of the following best describes the sequence of values printed by step 3 of the algorithm?

A. The values are printed in sorted order.

B. The values are printed in random order.

C. The values are printed in the same order in which they occur in the array.

D. The values are printed in the reverse of the order in which they occur in the array.

E. The smallest value is printed first, then the largest value, then the second smallest, then the second largest, and so on.

33. Assume that the array contains N values. Which of the following best characterizes the worst-case running time of the algorithm?

    A. O(1)

    B. O(log N)

    C. O(N)

    D. O(N log N)

    E. O(N^2)

34. The algorithm is guaranteed to exhibit its worst-case running time under which of the following conditions?

    A. The array contains only positive values.

    B. The array contains only negative values.

    C. Half of the values in the array are positive and half are negative.

    D. The values are stored in the array in sorted order.

    E. The values are stored in the array in nonsorted order.

35. Which of the following is *not* a min-heap?

    A.

    B.

    C.

    D.

    E.

36. Consider the following data field and method:

```
private List myList; // a list of Comparable values
public boolean checkList() {
// precondition: myList.size() > 0 and myList contains no nulls
   Iterator it = myList.iterator();
   Object ob = it.next();
   while (it.hasNext()) {
      Object nextOb = it.next();
      if (ob.compareTo(nextOb) > 0) return false;
      ob = nextOb;
   }
   return true;
}
```

Which of the following best characterizes the lists for which method `checkList` returns `true`?

A. Lists that contain duplicate values
B. Lists that are sorted in ascending order
C. Lists that are sorted in descending order
D. Lists that contain at least one positive value
E. Lists that contain at least one negative value

37. Consider the following three code segments, each of which is intended to remove from Set S1 all objects that are also in Set S2.

<table>
<tr><td align="center">**Segment I**</td><td align="center">**Segment II**</td></tr>
<tr><td>

```
Iterator it = S1.iterator();
while (it.hasNext()) {
  if (S2.contains(it.next()) {
    it.remove();
  }
}
```

</td><td>

```
Iterator it = S2.iterator();
while (it.hasNext()) {
  S1.remove( it.next() );
}
```

</td></tr>
</table>

Segment III

```
Iterator it = S2.iterator();
while (it.hasNext()) {
  if (S1.contains( it.next() ) {
    S1.remove( it.next() );
  }
}
```

Which of the code segments works as intended?

A. I only
B. II only
C. III only
D. I and II
E. II and III

38. Assume that variable `classInfo` is a `Map` with the names of teachers as the keys, and sets of their students' names as the associated objects.

Consider the following code segment:

```
Set S = (Set)classInfo.get("Anita Smith");
if (S == null) return false;
for (Iterator it = S.iterator(); it.hasNext();) {
    if (classInfo.containsKey(it.next())) return true;
}
return false;
```

Which of the following best describes the circumstances under which this code returns `true`?

A. When Anita Smith and at least one of her students are teachers.

B. When Anita Smith is both a teacher and a student.

C. When Anita Smith is a teacher but not a student.

D. When Anita Smith is a student.

E. When Anita Smith and all of her students are teachers.

39. Consider the following data field and method:

```
Set mySet; // a set of Comparable values

public boolean testSet(Comparable val) {
    for (Iterator it=mySet.iterator(); it.hasNext();) {
        Comparable oneVal = (Comparable)it.next();
        if (oneVal.compareTo(val) <= 0) return false;
    }
    return true;
}
```

Which of the following best describes the circumstances under which method `testSet` returns `true`?

A. When all items in `myList` are greater than `val`.

B. When all items in `myList` are less than `val`.

C. When no item in `myList` is greater than `val`.

D. When no item in `myList` is less than `val`.

E. When no item in `myList` is equal to `val`.

40. Consider the following recursive method:

```
public static void printArray(String[] A, int k) {
    if (k < A.length) {
        printArray(A, k+1);
        System.out.print(A[k]);
    }
}
```

Assume that array A has been initialized to be of length 4 and to contain the values "a", "b", "c", and "d" (with "a" in A[0], "b" in A[1], and so on). What is output as a result of the call printArray(A,0)?

A. bcd

B. dcb

C. abcd

D. dcba

E. dddd

Section II

Time: 1 hour and 45 minutes
Number of questions: 4
Percent of total grade: 50

Question 1

This question involves reasoning about the code from the Marine Biology case study.

Consider defining a new type of environment, FoodEnvironment, that includes a list of locations containing food, and a new type of fish, EatingFish, that tries to move to the closest such location. Partial declarations for the two classes are given below.

```
public class FoodEnvironment extends BoundedEnvironment {

    private List foodLocations;        // a list of Locations

    // precondition: foodLocations.size() > 0
    // postcondition: returns the location containing food that is
    //                closest to startLoc as determined by the
    //                distance method.
    public Location nearestFood(Location startLoc) { /* part (a) */ }

    // returns the distance from startLoc to endLoc
    public static int distance(startLoc, endLoc) { /* body not shown */ }
}

public class EatingFish extends Fish {
    protected Location nextLocation() { /* part (b) */ }
}
```

Part (a)

Write the FoodEnvironment method nearestFood. The nearestFood method should return the location in the foodLocations list that is closest to startLoc. In writing nearestFood you may include calls to the distance method; assume that the value returned by the distance method is never negative.

Complete method nearestFood below.

```
// precondition: foodLocations.size() > 0
// postcondition: returns the location containing food that is
//                closest to startLoc as determined by the
//                distance method.
public Location nearestFood(Location startLoc) {
```

Part (b)

Write the EatingFish method nextLocation. The nextLocation method should return the next location that the fish will move to based on the following rules:

- The fish finds the location containing food that is closest to its own current location.
- If the fish's neighboring location in the direction of the food is empty, the fish moves into that neighboring location; if that location is not empty, the fish moves according to the normal movements of a fish.

In writing the nextLocation method you may make the following assumptions:

- The fish's current location does *not* contain food.
- The fish's environment method returns a FoodEnvironment.
- The nearestFood method works as specified regardless of what you wrote in part (a).

Complete method nextLocation below.

```
protected Location nextLocation() {
```

Part (c)

The foodLocations instance variable in the FoodEnvironment class can be an ArrayList or a LinkedList. Fill in the chart below giving the Big-O running times for your implementation of the nearestFood method for each kind of list assuming that there are *n* items in the list.

List Type	Expected Running Time for nearestFood
ArrayList	
LinkedList	

Question 2

A client wants a data structure to store a list of tasks that need to be done, each of which has an integer priority of zero or more—the higher the priority, the more urgent the task. The operations to be performed using the data structure are as follows:

1.   Add a new task (with its priority) to the data structure.
2.   Get the set of all of the tasks in the data structure that have a given priority.

One way to implement the data structure is to use a binary search tree in which each node stores two values: the priority and the task. The tree is organized so that for every node n, the priorities in n's left subtree are less than or equal to the priority in n, and the priorities in n's right subtree are strictly greater than the priority in n.

An incomplete declaration of the `TreeNode` class used to represent the nodes of the binary search tree is given below, followed by a declaration of the `BinarySearchTree` class.

```
public class TreeNode {
   private int priority;
   private Object task;
   private TreeNode left;
   private TreeNode right;

   // constructor
   public TreeNode(int pri, Object tsk) {
      priority = pri;
      task = tsk;
      left = null;
      right = null;
   }

   // adds the given priority and task in a new leaf of the tree rooted
   // at this node
   public void addTask( int pri, Object task ) { /* part (a) */ }

   // returns a Set containing all of the tasks in the tree rooted
   // at this node that have the given priority
   public Set getTasksWithPriority( int pri ) { /* part (b) */ }
}

public class BinarySearchTree {
   private TreeNode root;

   // constructor
   public BinarySearchTree() {
      root = null;
   }
```

```
      public void addTask(int priority, Object task) {
         if (root == null) {
            root = new TreeNode(priority, task);
         } else {
            root.addTask(priority, task);
         }
      }


      public Set getTasksWithPriority( int priority ) {
         if (root == null) return new HashSet();
         else return root.getTasksWithPriority(priority);
      }
   }
```

Part (a)

Write the addTask method for the TreeNode class. Remember that tasks with equal or lower priorities should be added to the left subtree of a TreeNode, and tasks with higher priorities should be added to the right subtree of a TreeNode.

Complete method addTask below

```
   // adds the given priority and task in a new leaf of the tree rooted
   // at this node
   public void addTask( int pri, Object task ) {
```

Part (b)

Write the getTasksWithPriority method for the TreeNode class. If there are no tasks with the given priority in the tree, the method should return an empty Set; otherwise, it should return a Set that contains the tasks with the given priority.

Complete method getTasksWithPriority below.

```
   // returns a Set containing all of the tasks in the tree rooted
   // at this node that have the given priority
   public Set getTasksWithPriority( int pri ) {
```

Question 3

Consider designing and implementing some classes and interfaces to represent circus performers, including both people and animals.

Part (a)

A circus animal contains two pieces of information: what kind of food it eats (a String), and whether it is dangerous (a boolean). Both values are set when the animal is created, and can be accessed but not modified. Write the CircusAnimal interface that abstracts this functionality.

Part (b)

A circus person contains two pieces of information: the current salary (a double), and whether the person works with dangerous animals (a boolean). Both values are set when the person is created, and can be both accessed and modified. Write the CircusPerson interface that abstracts this functionality.

Part (c)

A circus performer contains a name and an age. The CircusPerformer class is declared as follows:

```
public class CircusPerformer {
    private String name;
    private int age;

    // constructor
    public CircusPerformer( String n, int a ) {
        name = n;
        age = a;
    }

    public String getName() { return name; }
    public int getAge() { return age; }
    public void incrementAge() { age++; }
}
```

A lion tamer is a circus performer and also a circus person who works with dangerous animals. Write the complete LionTamer class declaration, including appropriate instance variables, a constructor, and the required methods.

Question 4

The `Orchard` class partially defined below is used to represent a kiwi orchard in which the kiwi vines are planted in a rectangular grid. Grid coordinates are represented using the `Position` class, also defined below.

```
public class Position {
    private int row;
    private int column;

    // constructor
    public Position(int initX, int initY) {
        row = initRow;
        column = initColumn;
    }

    public int getRow() { return x; }
    public int getColumn() { return y; }
}

public class Orchard {
    private String[][] plants; // each array element is either
                               // "male" or "female"

    public boolean willFruit( Position p ) { /* part (a) */ }
    public ArrayList willNotFruit() { /* part (b) */ }
}
```

Each kiwi plant is either male or female. The `plants` array (which is a private field of the `Orchard` class) keeps track of the genders of the plants in the orchard: each element of the array contains a string, either `"male"` or `"female"`, depending on the gender of the plant in that position.

In order to produce fruit, a female plant must have a male plant no more than two positions away horizontally or vertically, or no more than one position away diagonally. For example, consider the orchard represented using the following array:

	0	1	2	3	4
0	male	female	female	female	female
1	female	female	female	female	male
2	female	**female**	**female**	female	female

In this orchard, the plants shown in bold (in positions (2,1) and (2,2)) will not produce fruit because no male plant is close enough to them.

Part (a)

Write the Orchard class's willFruit method. The method should return true if and only if the female plant at the given position will produce fruit.

Complete method willFruit below.

```
// precondition: Position p is inside the plants array and
//                the plant at position p is female
public boolean willFruit( Position p ) {
```

Part (b)

Write the Orchard class's willNotFruit method. The method should return an ArrayList containing the Positions of all of the female plants in the orchard that will not fruit. For example, for the orchard shown above, the method would return a list containing two Positions: (2,1) and (2,2).

In writing method willNotFruit, you may include calls to method willFruit. Assume that method willFruit works as specified, regardless of what you wrote for part (a).

Complete method willNotFruit below.

```
// postcondition: returns an ArrayList containing the Positions
//                 of all of the female plants in the orchard
//                 that will not fruit
public ArrayList willNotFruit() {
```

Answers to Section I

1.	A	21.	E
2.	E	22.	C
3.	D	23.	E
4.	B	24.	C
5.	D	25.	B
6.	C	26.	D
7.	C	27.	D
8.	D	28.	A
9.	C	29.	D
10.	E	30.	D
11.	D	31.	D
12.	C	32.	A
13.	A	33.	E
14.	B	34.	D
15.	B	35.	B
16.	A	36.	B
17.	E	37.	D
18.	D	38.	A
19.	B	39.	A
20.	C	40.	D

Answers to Section II

Question 1
Part (a)

```java
public Location nearestFood(Location startLoc) {
    Location minLoc = (Location)foodLocations.get(0);
    int minDist = distance(startLoc, minLoc);
    for (int i=1; i<foodLocations.size(); i++) {
        Location loc = (Location)foodLocations.get(i);
        int tempDist = distance(startLoc, loc);
        if (tempDist < minDist) {
            minDist = tempDist;
            minLoc = loc;
        }
    }
    return minLoc;
}
```

Part (b)

```java
protected Location nextLocation() {
    FoodEnvironment env = (FoodEnvironment)environment();
    Location minLoc = env.nearestFood(location());
    Direction dir = env.getDirection(location(), minLoc);
    Location possible = env.getNeighbor(location(), dir);
    if (env.isEmpty(possible)) return possible;
    else return super.nextLocation();
}
```

Part (c)

List Implementation	Expected Running Time for nearestFood
ArrayList	$O(n)$
LinkedList	If iterated: $O(n)$ If indexed: $O(n^2)$

Grading Guide

Part (a) nearestFood   4 Points

+1 Correct initialization of closest location or index of that location

+1 Traverse foodLocations (either indexed or iterated)
   + ½ attempt (must attempt to reference a part of foodLocations within loop)
   + ½ correct

+1 Compare distances
   + ½ call to distance with appropriate parameters
   + ½ compare distance with minimum stored

+ ½ Update minimum location

+ ½ Return a location based on search

Part (b) nextLocation   3 Points

+ ½ Retrieve location of nearest food

+ ½ Retrieve direction of nearest food

+ ½ Retrieve nearest neighbor in direction of food

+ ½ Check to see if nearest neighbor is empty

+1 Return the next location based on check
   + ½ if neighbor is empty
   + ½ if neighbor is not empty

Part (c) Big-O   2 Points

+1 ArrayList correct

+1 LinkedList correct

Question 2
Part (a)

```java
public void addTask( int pri, Object task ) {
    if (pri<=priority) {
        if (left != null) left.addTask(pri, task);
        else left = new TreeNode(pri, task);
    } else {
        if (right != null) right.addTask(pri, task);
        else right = new TreeNode(pri, task);
    }
}
```

Part (b)

```java
public Set getTasksWithPriority( int pri ) {
    Set tmp = new HashSet();
    if ((pri <= priority) && (left != null)) {
        tmp = left.getTasksWithPriority(pri);
    }
    if ((pri > priority) && (right != null)) {
        tmp = right.getTasksWithPriority(pri);
    }
    if (pri == priority) {
        tmp.add(task);
    }
    return tmp;
```

Grading Guide

Part (a) addTask   4 Points

> +1 Check the current priority against the parameter
>
> +1½ Left actions
> > + ½ check if left is null
> > + ½ if yes, create new node
> > + ½ if no, recursive call
>
> +1½ Right actions
> > + ½ check if right is null
> > + ½ if yes, create new node
> > + ½ if no, recursive call

Part (b) getTasksWithPriority   5 Points

> + ½ Create a new Set to return (HashSet or TreeSet)
>
> +3 Recursive call
> > + ½ compare current priority with parameter pri
> > + ½ check for null child
> > +1 only process one child
> > +1 recursive call
> > > + ½ attempt
> > > + ½ correct
>
> +1 Include current task if appropriate
>
> + ½ Return result

Question 3
Part (a)

```
public interface CircusAnimal {
   public String getFood();
   public boolean getIsDangerous();
}
```

Part (b)

```
public interface CircusPerson {
   public double getSalary();
   public void setSalary(double amt);
   public boolean handlesDangerousAnimals();
   public void setHandlesDangerousAnimals(boolean handles);
}
```

Part (c)

```
public class LionTamer extends CircusPerformer implements CircusPerson {
   private double salary;
   private boolean handlesDanger;

   public LionTamer(String name, int age, double sal, boolean danger) {
      super(name, age);
      salary = sal;
      handlesDanger = danger;
   }

   public double getSalary() {
      return salary;
   }
   public void setSalary(double amt){
      salary = amt;
   }
   public boolean getHandlesDangerousAnimals(){
      return handlesDanger;
   }
   public void setHandlesDangerousAnimals(boolean handles){
      handlesDanger = handles;
   }
}
```

Grading Guide

Part (a) The `CircusAnimal` interface   2 Points

> +1 Interface declaration
>
> +1 Methods
>> + 1/2 attempt to declare methods
>> + 1/2 correctly declare both methods (no method bodies)

Part (b) The `CircusPerson` interface   3 Points

> + 1/2 Interface declaration
>
> +1 Methods `getSalary` and `getHandlesDangerousAnimals`
>
> +1 Attempt `setSalary` and `setHandlesDangerousAnimals` methods (must have both methods, could have wrong parameters or return types)
>
> + 1/2 Correct `setSalary` and `setHandlesDangerousAnimals` methods

Part (c) The `LionTamer` class   4 Points

> +1 Class declaration
>> + 1/2 attempt (must reference either `CircusPerformer` or `CircusPerson` in some way)
>> + 1/2 correct
>
> + 1/2 Field declarations
>
> +1 1/2 Constructor
>> + 1/2 attempt (some constructor declared)
>> + 1/2 correct call to super
>> + 1/2 correct parameters and field initialization
>
> +1 Methods from `CircusPerson`
>> + 1/2 attempt (must declare some methods written in part (b))
>> + 1/2 correct (this depends on what was written in part (b); needs to satisfy requirements of interface written, not of interface specified by problem)

Question 4

Part (a)

Note that method `willFruit` is much easier to write if you first write an auxiliary method that tests one position of the array to see whether that position is inside the `plants` array and, if so, contains a male plant:

```
private boolean isMale(int row, int col) {
    if (row < 0 || row >= plants.length ||
        col < 0 || col >= plants[0].length) return false;
    return( plants[row][col].equals("male"));
}
```

This auxiliary method is used by both versions of the `willFruit` method given below.

Version 1: Check each position explicitly.

```
public boolean willFruit( Position p ) {
    return(isMale(p.getRow(), p.getColumn()-1) ||
           isMale(p.getRow(), p.getColumn()+1) ||
           isMale(p.getRow()-1, p.getColumn()) ||
           isMale(p.getRow()-1, p.getColumn()-1) ||
           isMale(p.getRow()-1, p.getColumn()+1) ||
           isMale(p.getRow()+1, p.getColumn()) ||
           isMale(p.getRow()+1, p.getColumn()-1) ||
           isMale(p.getRow()+1, p.getColumn()+1) ||
           isMale(p.getRow()+2, p.getColumn()) ||
           isMale(p.getRow()-2, p.getColumn()) ||
           isMale(p.getRow(), p.getColumn()+2) ||
           isMale(p.getRow(), p.getColumn()-2));
}
```

Version 2: Use a loop to check all positions one step away (horizontally, vertically, or diagonally), then check all positions two steps away horizontally or vertically.

```
public boolean willFruit( Position p ) {
    int r = p.getRow();
    int c = p.getColumn();

    // check one step away
    for (int row=r-1; row<=r+1; row++) {
        for (int col=c-1; col<=c+1; col++) {
            if (isMale(row, col)) return true;
        }
    }
```

```
                // check two steps away horizontally or vertically
                return(isMale(p.getRow()+2, p.getColumn()) ||
                       isMale(p.getRow()-2, p.getColumn()) ||
                       isMale(p.getRow(), p.getColumn()+2) ||
                       isMale(p.getRow(), p.getColumn()-2));
    }
```

Part (b)

```
    public ArrayList willNotFruit() {
        ArrayList L = new ArrayList();

        for (int j=0; j<plants.length; j++) {
            for (int k=0; k<plants[0].length; k++) {
                if (plants[j][k].equals("female")) {
                    Position p = new Position(j,k);
                    if (!willFruit(p)) {
                        L.add(p);
                    }
                }
            }
        }
        return L;
    }
```

Grading Guide

Part (a) `willFruit`   4 Points

    + ½ Correctly access row and col values of position P somewhere in method

    +2 Check one step away

        + ½ attempt to traverse all locations one step away

        + ½ attempt to check for `isMale` of all locations one step away

        + ½ correct

        + ½ return appropriate value for checked positions

    +1 Check two steps away

        + ½ attempt to traverse all locations two steps away

        + ½ correct

    + ½ Return `true`/`false` correctly based on all searches

Part (b) `willNotFruit`   5 Points

    + ½ Create `ArrayList` to return

    +1 ½ Traverse matrix

        + ½ attempt to traverse rows

        + ½ attempt to traverse columns

        + ½ correct

    +1 Comparison for female

        + ½ attempt (must compare with value from matrix)

        + ½ correct

    + ½ Create new position

    + ½ Call to `willFruit`

    + ½ Add to `ArrayList` if appropriate

    + ½ Return created `ArrayList`

Practice Examination AB-2

Section I

Time: 1 hour and 15 minutes
Number of questions: 40
Percent of total grade: 50

1. Which node of a binary tree is the first node visited by a preorder traversal?

   A. The root node

   B. The leftmost leaf

   C. The rightmost leaf

   D. The node that contains the largest value

   E. The node that contains the smallest value

2. Which of the following is a valid reason for using a singly linked list rather than a doubly linked list?

   A. Less storage is required for a singly linked list than for a doubly linked list.

   B. A singly linked list can be used to implement a queue, whereas a doubly linked list cannot.

   C. The number of items in the list can be determined more efficiently using a singly linked list than using a doubly linked list.

   D. The average of the values in the list can be computed more efficiently using a singly linked list than using a doubly linked list.

   E. Given a pointer to one of the nodes in the list, it is possible to determine whether it is the last node if the list is singly linked, but not if it is doubly linked.

3. Assume that the following recursive method has been added to the standard `ListNode` class:

```
public int listCompute( ) {
    if (next == null) return 1;
    return(1 + next.listCompute( ));
}
```

Which of the following best describes what method `listCompute` does?

A. Returns the sum of the values in the list

B. Returns the average of the values in the list

C. Returns the largest value in the list

D. Returns the smallest value in the list

E. Returns the number of nodes in the list

4. Assume that `A` is a nonempty array of `Comparable` values. Consider the following code segment:

```
int x = 0;
for (int k=1; k<A.length; k++) {
    if (A[k].compareTo(A[x]) < 0) x = k;
}
return A[x];
```

Which of the following best describes what this code segment does?

A. It returns the index of the smallest element of `A`.

B. It returns the index of the largest element of `A`.

C. It returns the value of the smallest element of `A`.

D. It returns the value of the largest element of `A`.

E. It is not possible to determine what the code segment does without knowing how `A` is initialized.

5. Consider the following recursive method (assume that method `readInt` reads the next integer value from a file):

```
public static void printVals(int n) {
    if (n > 0) {
        int x = readInt();
        printVals(n-1);
        if (x > 0) System.out.print(x + " ");
    }
}
```

Assume that the input file contains the values:

```
10   -10   20   -20   30   -30
```

What is printed as a result of the call `printVals(3)`?

A. 10 20

B. 20 10

C. 10 20 30

D. 10 -10 20

E. 20 -10 10

6. Assume that the following method has been added to the standard `TreeNode` class:

```
public int treeCount() {
    if ((left == null) && (right == null)) return 0;
    if (left == null) return(1 + right.treeCount());
    if (right == null) return(1 + left.treeCount());
    return(1 + left.treeCount() + right.treeCount());
}
```

Which of the following best describes what method `treeCount` does?

A. Always returns 0

B. Returns the number of nodes in the tree

C. Returns the number of leaves in the tree

D. Returns the number of non-leaves in the tree

E. Returns the height of the tree

7. Consider the following code segment:

```
x = !y;
y = x || y;
```

Assume that x and y are boolean variables that have been initialized before this code executes. What is true about the values of x and y after the code executes?

A. Variable x is true.

B. Variable y is true.

C. Variable x has the same value as it did before the code executed.

D. Variable y has the same value as it did before the code executed.

E. Variable y has the same value as variable x had before the code executed.

8. Assume that two classes, Plant and Animal, and two interfaces, Tropical and Spotted, have been defined. Consider defining a new class named Mold. Which of the following statements is true?

A. The Mold class can extend at most one of the Plant and Animal classes, and it can implement at most one of the Tropical and Spotted interfaces.

B. The Mold class can extend at most one of the Plant and Animal classes, but it can implement both the Tropical and Spotted interfaces.

C. The Mold class can extend both the Plant and Animal classes, but it can implement at most one of the Tropical and Spotted interfaces.

D. The Mold class can extend both the Plant and Animal classes, and it can implement both the Tropical and Spotted interfaces.

E. If the Mold class implements both the Tropical and Spotted interfaces, it can extend at most one of the Plant and Animal classes. If it implements just one of the Tropical and Spotted interfaces, it can extend both the Plant and Animal classes.

9.   Consider the following data field and method:

```
private List myList;

public boolean testList() {
    Set mySet = new Set();
    Iterator it = myList.iterator();
    while (it.hasNext()) {
        mySet.add(it.next());
    }
    return (mySet.size() == myList.size());
}
```

Which of the following best describes the circumstances under which method testList returns true?

A. Always.

B. When myList is in sorted order.

C. When myList is not in sorted order.

D. When myList contains duplicates.

E. When myList contains no duplicates.

10. Assume that variable S is a stack of `Integers` and that Q is a queue of `Integers`, initialized as shown below.

	Top	**Bottom**			**Front**	**Rear**
S:	2 4 6 8			Q:	1 3 5 7	

Consider the following code segment:

```
Object ob;
while (!S.empty()) {
    ob = S.pop();
    Q.enqueue(ob);
}
while (!Q.empty()) {
    ob = Q.dequeue();
    S.push(ob);
}
```

Which of the following best illustrates the values of S and Q after the code segment executes?

	S		Q	
	Top	**Bottom**	**Front**	**Rear**
A.	2 4 6 8		1 3 5 7	
B.	1 3 5 7		2 4 6 8	
C.	2 4 6 8 1 3 5 7		(empty)	
D.	1 3 5 7 2 4 6 8		(empty)	
E.	8 6 4 2 7 5 3 1		(empty)	

11. Assume that variable S is a stack of Integers and that Q is a queue of Integers, initialized as shown below.

	Top			Bottom			Front			Rear
S:	2	4	6	8		Q:	1	3	5	7

Consider the following code segment:

```
Object ob;
while (!Q.empty()) {
    ob = Q.dequeue();
    S.push(ob);
}
while (!S.empty()) {
    ob = S.pop();
    Q.enqueue(ob);
}
```

Which of the following best illustrates the values of S and Q after the code segment executes?

	S Top ... Bottom	Q Front ... Rear
A.	2 4 6 8	1 3 5 7
B.	1 3 5 7	2 4 6 8
C.	(empty)	7 5 3 1 2 4 6 8
D.	(empty)	1 3 5 7 2 4 6 8
E.	(empty)	8 6 4 2 1 3 5 7

12. Consider writing a method to move N values from the front of an array to the end of the array. For example, the figure below illustrates moving three values in an array; the values that are moved are shown in bold italic font for emphasis.

Original array	After moving three values
10 14 12 17 13 19 20	17 13 19 20 *10 14 12*

Assume that the method works as follows:

Repeat N times:

> Save the value at the front of the array in a temporary variable.
> Move all values in the array one place to the left.
> Put the saved value into the last position in the array.

If the array contains M values, which of the following best characterizes the running time of the method?

A. $O(M)$

B. $O(N)$

C. $O(M+N)$

D. $O(M*N)$

E. $O(M^N)$

13. Which of the following is a valid reason for choosing to store a sequence of values in an array rather than in a linked list?

A. It is possible to store values of any type in an array, but only scalar values can be stored in a linked list.

B. An array can be returned as the result of a method call, but a linked list cannot.

C. The value in the kth position in the array can be accessed in $O(1)$ time, whereas accessing the value in the kth node of a linked list requires $O(k)$ time.

D. A new value can be added to the beginning of an array of size N in $O(1)$ time, whereas adding a new value to the front of a linked list with N nodes requires $O(N)$ time in the worst case.

E. The value at the beginning of an array of size N can be removed in $O(1)$ time, whereas removing the first node from a linked list with N nodes requires $O(N)$ time in the worst case.

14. Consider the following data field and method.

```
private Set S;  // a set of strings

public String[][] makeArray() {
    // precondition: S.size() > 0
    int num = S.size();
    int n = (int)Math.sqrt(num);
    String[][] result = new String[n][n];
    Iterator it = S.iterator();
    for (int j=0; j<n; j++) {
        for (int k=0; k<n; k++) {
            result[j][k] = (String)it.next();
        }
    }
    return result;
}
```

If S represents the set

```
{ "a", "b", "c", "d" }
```

which of the following might be the value returned by a call to `makeArray`?

I.	II.	III.
"a" "b" "c" "d"	"a" "a" "a" "a"	"b" "a" "d" "c"

A. I only

B. II only

C. III only

D. I and II

E. I and III

Questions 15–17 rely on the following information:

Assume that the two methods partially specified below have been added to the TreeNode class.

```
public boolean lookup(Object ob) {
// postcondition: returns true if value ob is in the tree rooted at
//                this node; otherwise, returns false
    .
    .
    .

}


public boolean subset(TreeNode T) {
// precondition: T is not null
// postcondition: returns true if every value in the tree rooted
//                at this node is also in the tree rooted at T;
//                otherwise, returns false
    if (! T.lookup(value)) return false;
    if (left == null && right == null) return true;
    if (left == null) return right.subset(T);
    else if (right == null) return left.subset(T);
    else missing code
}
```

15. Assume that method `lookup` has been implemented correctly. Which of the following could be used to replace *missing code* in method `subset` so that it works as specified by its pre- and postcondition?

    A. `return true;`
    B. `return (left.subset(T) && right.subset(T));`
    C. `return (left.subset(T) || right.subset(T));`
    D. `return (left.subset(T.getLeft()) && right.subset(T.getRight()));`
    E. `return (left.subset(T.getLeft()) || right.subset(T.getRight()));`

16. Assume that the subset method has been implemented correctly. Consider adding an equals method to the TreeNode class to be used to determine when two binary trees are the same. Two trees are considered to be the same when they contain exactly the same values (even if the values are stored in different places in the two trees). Which of the following versions of the equals method work(s) correctly?

Version I:

```
public boolean equals(TreeNode T) {
    if (!subset(T)) return false;
    return (T.subset(this));
}
```

Version II:

```
public boolean equals(TreeNode T) {
    return (subset(T) && T.subset(this) );
}
```

Version III:

```
public boolean equals(TreeNode T) {
    return (subset(T) || T.subset(this) );
}
```

A. I only

B. II only

C. III only

D. I and II

E. I and III

17. Assume that the equals method defined in the previous question has been implemented correctly and that T1 and T2 are both non-null TreeNodes. Which of the following correctly characterizes the conditions under which the two expressions T1 == T2 and T1.equals(T2) both evaluate to true?

A. Always

B. Never

C. Whenever the two variables both point to the same chunk of storage

D. Whenever the trees rooted at T1 and T2 are both binary search trees containing the same values

E. Whenever the trees rooted at T1 and T2 have the same shape and contain the same values

Questions 18 and 19 refer to the following recursive method:

```
public static int compute(int x, int y) {
   if (x > y) return x;
   else return( compute(x+2, y-2) );
}
```

18. What is returned by the call compute(1, 5)?

    A. 1

    B. 3

    C. 5

    D. 7

    E. No value is returned because an infinite recursion occurs.

19. Which of the following best characterizes the circumstances under which the call compute(x, y) leads to an infinite recursion?

    A. Never

    B. Whenever x = y

    C. Whenever x < y

    D. Whenever x > y

    E. Whenever both x and y are odd

Questions 20–22 involve reasoning about the Marine Biology case study.

20. Consider changing the UnboundedEnvironment class to use a LinkedList instead of an ArrayList to store the objects in the environment. Which of the following methods would need to be modified?

    A. ObjectAt

    B. allObjects

    C. isEmpty

    D. add

    E. None of the UnboundedEnvironment methods would need to be modified

For questions 21 and 22, consider defining a new class, NewEnvironment, that extends the Bounded-Environment class. A partial declaration of the NewEnvironment class is given below.

```
public class NewEnvironment extends BoundedEnvironment {
    private int numRows, numCols;  // numbers of rows and columns
                                   // in the environment
    private Set objectSet;         // the objects in the environment

    // other fields and methods not shown
}
```

21. Which of the following is a correct implementation of the isEmpty method for the New-Environment class?

A.
```
public boolean isEmpty(Location loc){
    for (int i=0; i<objectSet.size(); i++) {
        Location nextLoc = (Location)objectSet.get(i);
        if (nextLoc.equals(loc)) return false;
    }
    return true;
}
```

B.
```
public boolean isEmpty(Location loc){
    Iterator it = objectSet.iterator();
    while (it.hasNext()) {
        Location nextLoc = (Location)it.next();
        if (nextLoc.equals(loc)) return false;
    }
    return true;
}
```

C.
```
public boolean isEmpty(Location loc){
    Iterator it = objectSet.iterator();
    while (it.hasNext()) {
        Location nextLoc = ((Locatable)it.next()).location();
        if (nextLoc.equals(loc)) return false;
    }
    return true;
}
```

D.
```
public boolean isEmpty(Location loc){
    for (int i=0; i<objectSet.size(); i++) {
        Location nextLoc = ((Locatable)objectSet.get(i);
        if (nextLoc.equals(loc)) return false;
    }
    return true;
}
```

E.
```
public boolean isEmpty(Location loc){
    Iterator it = objectSet.iterator();
    while (it.hasNext()) {
        Object nextLoc = it.next();
        if (nextLoc.equals(loc)) return false;
    }
    return true;
}
```

22. Which of the following is a correct implementation of the isValid method for the New-Environment class?

    A.
    ```
    public boolean isValid(Location loc) {
            if (loc == null) return false;
            return (! isEmpty(loc));
        }
    ```

    B.
    ```
    public boolean isValid(Location loc) {
            if (loc == null) return false;
            return (isEmpty(loc));
        }
    ```

    C.
    ```
    public boolean isValid(Location loc) {
            if (loc == null) return false;
            return (loc.row() >= 0 && loc.col() >= 0) &&
                    loc.row() < rows && loc.col() < cols);
        }
    ```

    D.
    ```
    public boolean isValid(Location loc) {
            Iterator it = objectSet.iterator();
            while (it.hasNext()) {
               Object nextLoc = it.next();
               if (nextLoc.equals(loc)) return false;
            }
            return true;
        }
    ```

    E.
    ```
    public boolean isValid(Location loc) {
            Iterator it = objectSet.iterator();
            while (it.hasNext()) {
               Object nextLoc = it.next();
               if (nextLoc.equals(loc)) return true;
            }
            return false;
        }
    ```

23. Consider the following two ways to store a set of N integer values.

    Method 1: Store the values in sorted order in an array of length N.
    Method 2: Store the values in a binary search tree.

    Which of the following describes a valid reason to prefer Method 1 over Method 2?

    A. Computing the sum of the values can be done in O(log N) time using Method 1, but it will require O(N) time in the worst case using Method 2.

    B. Determining whether a given value is in the set can be done in O(1) time using Method 1, but it will require O(N^2) time in the worst case using Method 2.

    C. Printing the smallest value in the set can be done in O(1) time using Method 1, but it will require O(N) time in the worst case using Method 2.

    D. Printing all values in sorted order can be done in O(N) time using Method 1, but it will require O(N log N) time in the worst case using Method 2.

    E. Method 1 requires O(N) space, whereas Method 2 requires O(N log N) space in the worst case.

24. Assume that linked lists of Integers are implemented using the standard ListNode class, and that the following method has been added to the ListNode class. (Line numbers are included for reference.)

    ```
    1 public int ListNode search(){
    2     int k = ((Integer)value).intValue();
    3     if (k <= 0) return k;
    4     if (next == null) return 1;
    5     return next.search();
    6 }
    ```

    Which of the following best describes what method search does?

    A. Always returns 1

    B. Returns the first positive value in the list, or 1 if there is no such value

    C. Returns the last positive value in the list, or 1 if there is no such value

    D. Returns the first nonpositive value in the list, or 1 if there is no such value

    E. Returns the last nonpositive value in the list, or 1 if there is no such value

25. Which of the following operations can be implemented more efficiently (in terms of worst-case time) on a sorted array of integers than on an unsorted array of integers?

    A. Searching for a given value in the array

    B. Adding a new value to the array

    C. Removing a value from the array

    D. Printing all values in the array

    E. Computing the sum of all values in the array

26. Assume that variable `A` is a nonempty `ArrayList`. Consider the following statement:

```
String s = (String)A.get(0);
```

Which of the following statements about this use of a class cast is true?

A. The statement would compile and execute without error whether or not the cast is used.

B. The statement would compile without error whether or not the cast is used, but the use of the cast prevents a runtime error when the first item in `A` is not a `String`.

C. The statement would compile without error whether or not the cast is used, but there will be a runtime error if the first item in `A` is not a `String` whether or not the cast is used.

D. The statement would cause a compile-time error if the cast were not used, and the use of the cast also prevents a runtime error if the first item in `A` is not a `String`.

E. The statement would cause a compile-time error if the cast were not used, and there will be a runtime error if the first item in `A` is not a `String` even though the cast is used.

Questions 27 and 28 concern the following information:

A company has locations in 1,000 cities. The company has 100 managers, each in charge of some set of cities. The following two data structures are being considered to store information about the cities handled by each manager:

Data Structure 1: A two-dimensional array `A` of booleans. The rows of `A` correspond to the managers, and the columns of `A` correspond to the cities. Entry `A[j][k]` is `true` if and only if manager `j` handles city `k`.

Data Structure 2: A one-dimensional array `A` of linked lists. The list in `A[j]` contains the numbers of the cities handled by manager `j`.

27. Which of the following operations can be implemented more efficiently using Data Structure 1 than using Data Structure 2?

A. Determine whether a given manager handles a given city.

B. Determine how many cities are handled by a given manager.

C. Determine whether any manager handles no cities.

D. Determine which manager handles the most cities.

E. Print the list of cities handled by a given manager.

28. Which of the following operations can be implemented more efficiently using Data Structure 2 than using Data Structure 1?

A. Determine which manager handles a given city.

B. Determine whether a given manager handles more than one city.

C. Remove a given city from the set handled by a given manager.

D. Add a given city to the set handled by a given manager.

E. Change the manager of a given city.

29. Consider implementing a hashtable to be used to store strings. Which of the following statements about the hash function is (are) true?

I.   If the hash function is called with strings A and B such that A is the same as B, then hash(A) must be the same as hash(B).

II. If the hash function is called with strings A and B such that A is not the same as B, then hash(A) must not be the same as hash(B).

III. If the hash function is called with strings A and B such that A comes before B in alphabetical order, then hash(A) must be less than hash(B).

A. I only

B. II only

C. I and II only

D. I and III only

E. I, II, and III

30. A min-heap is a good data structure to use to implement which of the following?

A. A stack

B. A queue

C. A priority queue

D. A singly linked list

E. A doubly linked list

31. Assume that a subclass of the `LinkedList` class, called `NewList`, has been defined, including the method specified below.

    ```
    public void add(Object x) {
        // postcondition: adds x to the list
           .
           .
           .
    }
    ```

    Note that the `LinkedList` class has an add method with the same signature. Consider the following code segment:

    ```
    LinkedList L1 = new LinkedList();
    LinkedList L2 = new NewList();
    L1.add(new LinkedList());
    L2.add(new Integer(5));
    ```

    Which of the following statements about the two calls to add is true?

    A. Both calls will call the add method of the `LinkedList` class, because both L1 and L2 are declared to be `LinkedLists`.

    B. Both calls will call the add method of the `NewList` class, because that method has overridden the add method of the `LinkedList` class.

    C. Both calls will call the add method of the `LinkedList` class, because that is a standard java class, whereas `NewList` is a user-defined class.

    D. The first call will call the add method of the `LinkedList` class because L1 points to a `LinkedList`, and the second call will call the add method of the `NewList` class because L2 points to a `NewList`.

    E. The first call will call the add method of the `LinkedList` class because its argument is a `LinkedList`, and the second call will call the add method of the `NewList` class because its argument is not a `LinkedList`.

32. Consider designing classes to represent different kinds of animals: mammals, reptiles, birds, and insects. Which of the following is the best design?

    A. Use five unrelated classes: `Animal`, `Mammal`, `Reptile`, `Bird`, and `Insect`.

    B. Use one class, `Animal`, with four fields: `Mammal`, `Reptile`, `Bird`, and `Insect`.

    C. Use one class, `Animal`, with four subclasses: `Mammal`, `Reptile`, `Bird`, and `Insect`.

    D. Use five classes, `Animal`, `Mammal`, `Reptile`, `Bird`, and `Insect`, with `Mammal` as a subclass of `Animal`, `Reptile` as a subclass of `Mammal`, and so on.

    E. Use four classes, `Mammal`, `Reptile`, `Bird`, and `Insect`, each with an `Animal` subclass.

Questions 33 and 34 rely on the following information:

Assume that circular linked lists are implemented using the standard ListNode class and that the numNodes method shown below has been added to the ListNode class. Method numNodes was intended to return the number of nodes in the circular linked list containing the node whose numNodes method was called. However, the method does not always work correctly. (Line numbers are included for reference.)

```
1  public int numNodes( ) {
2  // precondition: this node is part of a circular linked list.
3     Object tmp = value;
4     int count = 1;
5     ListNode L = next;
6     while (!L.value.equals(tmp)) {
7         count++;
8         L = L.next;
9     }
10    return count;
11 }
```

33. Which of the following best characterizes the circular linked lists for which method numNodes does *not* work correctly?

    A. Circular linked lists with just one node
    B. Circular linked lists with more than one node
    C. Circular linked lists in which every node contains a different value
    D. Circular linked lists in which two nodes contain the same value
    E. Circular linked lists in which some node contains the same value as the node whose numNodes method was called

34. Which of the following changes fixes method numNodes so that it works correctly for every list that satisfies its precondition?

    A. Change line 3 to ListNode tmp = this;, remove line 5, change line 6 to while (tmp != null), and replace line 8 with: tmp = tmp.next;.
    B. Change line 3 to ListNode tmp = this;, and change line 6 to while (L != tmp).
    C. Change line 4 to int count=0;.
    D. Remove line 3, and change line 6 to while (L != null).
    E. Change line 5 to ListNode L = this;.

35. Assume that variable L is a ListNode and has been initialized to point to the first node of a nonempty singly linked list. Which of the following code segments sets variable isOdd to true if there are an odd number of nodes in the list pointed to by L, and to false otherwise?

A.
```
isOdd = true;
while (L != null) {
    L = L.getNext();
    isOdd = !isOdd;
}
```

B.
```
isOdd = false;
while (L != null) {
    L = L.getNext();
    isOdd = !isOdd;
}
```

C.
```
isOdd = true;
while (L != null) {
    L = L.getNext();
    isOdd = isOdd || isOdd;
}
```

D.
```
isOdd = false;
while (L != null) {
    L = L.getNext();
    isOdd = isOdd || isOdd;
}
```

E.
```
isOdd = true;
while (L != null) {
    L = L.getNext();
    isOdd = isOdd && isOdd;
}
```

36. Assume that p and q are String variables and that the expression

     (p != q)

evaluates to true. Which of the following must also evaluate to true?

I.   !p.equals(q)
II. p.length() != q.length()
III. (p!=null) || (q!=null)

A. I only

B. II only

C. III only

D. I and II

E. None of the expressions necessarily evaluates to true.

37. Assume that T is a binary tree with N nodes (but is *not* a binary search tree). Which of the following operations cannot always be performed in $O(N)$ time?

    A. Convert T to a binary search tree.
    B. Count the number of leaves in T.
    C. Find the smallest value in T.
    D. Add 1 to every value in T.
    E. Copy the values in T into an array of length N.

38. Under which of the following conditions would it be better to use a LinkedList rather than an ArrayList?

    I.   Items will be added only at the front of the list.
    II. Items will be added only at the end of the list.
    III. Items will be added only in the middle of the list.

    A. I only
    B. II only
    C. III only
    D. I and II only
    E. I, II, and III

39. An array of size N can be sorted by using a priority queue (implemented using a min-heap) as follows.

    Step 1: Start with an empty priority queue.
    Step 2: Make one pass over the array, inserting each value into the priority queue.
    Step 3: Use N calls to removeMin, putting each value back into the array from left to right.

    Which of the following best characterizes the worst-case running times for steps 2 and 3?

	Step 2	*Step 3*
A.	$O(N \log N)$	$O(N^2)$
B.	$O(N)$	$O(N)$
C.	$O(N \log N)$	$O(N \log N)$
D.	$O(N^2)$	$O(N^2)$
E.	$O(\log N)$	$O(N)$

40. Assume that variable `authorInfo` is a `Map` with authors' names as the keys, and sets of book titles (the books they've written) as the associated objects. Also assume that variable `bookInfo` is a `Map` with book titles as the keys, and sets of reviewers' names as the associated objects.

Consider the following code segment:

```
Set S1 = authorInfo.get("John Brown");
if (S1 == null) return false;
for (Iterator it = S1.iterator(); it.hasNext();) {
   Set S2 = bookInfo.get(it.next());
   if (S2 != null && S2.contains("Ann Green")) return true;
}
return false;
```

Which of the following best describes the circumstances under which this code returns `true`?

A. When both John Brown and Ann Green have written at least one book each.

B. When both John Brown and Ann Green have reviewed at least one book each.

C. When there is at least one book that has been reviewed by both John Brown and Ann Green.

D. When John Brown and Ann Green have both written a book with the same title.

E. When at least one book written by John Brown was reviewed by Ann Green.

Section II

Time: 1 hour and 45 minutes
Number of questions: 4
Percent of total grade: 50

Question 1

Consider a new type of Fish named TravelerFish. TravelerFish prefer to move to locations in the environment that they have not visited as often as other locations. A partial declaration for the TravelerFish class is given below.

```java
public class TravelerFish extends Fish {

    private Map visited;        // maps Locations to Integers (for each
                                // location that has been visited at
                                // least once, maps that location to the
                                // number of times it has been visited)

    // returns the next location the fish will move to
    protected Location nextLocation() { /* part (a) */ }

    // acts for one step in the simulation
    public void act() { /* part (b) */ }

    // postcondition: returns true if the fish can move (if it has
    //                at least one empty neighboring location)
    protected boolean canMove() { /* not shown */ }
}
```

Part (a)

Write method nextLocation. If this fish has no empty neighboring location, method nextLocation should return the fish's current location. Otherwise, it should return the empty neighboring location that has been visited the fewest times (using the visited map to determine how many times each empty neighboring location has been visited). If there are two or more locations with the same minimum number of visits, method nextLocation can return any of those locations.

Complete method nextLocation below.

```java
// returns the next location the fish will move to
protected Location nextLocation() {
```

Part (b)

Write method act. A TravelerFish acts according to the following rules:

- The fish checks whether it is in the environment; if not, it does nothing.
- If the fish is in the environment, it checks whether it can move using method canMove; if not, it does nothing.
- If the fish can move, it calls its move method and then updates the visited map to reflect the fact that it has visited its current location one more time. Note that a location is in the map only if it has been visited at least once.

Complete method act below.

```
// acts for one step in the simulation
public void act() {
```

Question 2

An online shopping Web site uses a `Customer` class to represent its customers. Each `Customer` object includes a username and password, plus other information about the customer. No two customers have the same username. The `Customer` class includes the following public methods:

```
public String getUsername()  // returns this customer's username
public String getPassword()  // returns this customer's password
```

The incomplete `CustomerDatabase` class shown below is used to store information about all current customers. It includes methods to add a set of new customers, to remove a customer, and to check whether there is a customer with a given username and password.

```
public class CustomerDatabase {

    private some type allCustomers;

    public void addCustomers(Set newCustomers) { /* part (c) */ }
    public void removeCustomer(String userName) { /* not shown */ }
    public boolean verifyLogin(String userName, String pass) { /* part (b) */}
    // other methods not shown
}
```

Part (a)

Choose a type from the choices below for `allCustomers` that allows the `addCustomers`, `remove-Customer`, and `verifyLogin` methods to be implemented efficiently. Also specify how the data are to be organized using the representation that you choose. Then give the expected running times for the `removeCustomer` and `verifyLogin` methods using Big-O notation, and assuming that the type that you chose is used for `allCustomers`. The running times should be in terms of n, where n is the number of customers in the database.

Your Representation (circle one)	How Data Is Organized
ArrayList	
LinkedList	
TreeSet	
TreeMap	
HashSet	
HashMap	

Method	Expected Running Time
removeCustomer	
verifyLogin	

Part (b)

Write the `verifyLogin` method. The `verifyLogin` method has two parameters: a username and a password; it should return `true` if the user is in the database and the password is correct. If the user is not in the database or the password is incorrect the method should return `false`. Assume that your choice of type for `allCustomers` has been used.

Complete method `verifyLogin` below.

```
// precondition: allCustomers is not null
public boolean verifyLogin(String userName, String pass) {
```

Part (c)

Write method `addCustomers`, which adds each customer in `newCustomers` to the database. Assume that your choice of type for `allCustomers` has been used.

Complete method `addCustomers` below.

```
// precondition: newCustomers is a non-null set of Customers
//               allCustomers is not null
// postcondition: all customers in newCustomers have been added
//                appropriately to the database.
public void addCustomers(Set newCustomers) {
```

Question 3

This question involves binary trees and doubly linked lists, both implemented using the following
Node class:

```
public class Node {
   private Object data;
   private Node left;        // for a tree, root of left subtree;
                             // for a doubly linked list, previous node
   private Node right;       // for a tree, root of right subtree;
                             // for a doubly linked list, next node


   // constructor
   public Node(Object dataVal, Node leftVal, Node rightVal) {
      data = dataVal;
      left = leftVal;
      right = rightVal;
   }
   public Object getData() { return data; }
   public Node getLeft() { return left; }
   public Node getRight() { return right; }
   public void setLeft(Node newLeft) { left = newLeft; }
   public void setRight(Node newRight) { right = newRight; }

   // precondition: this Node is the first node in a doubly
   //               linked list
   // postcondition: returns the last node in the list
   public Node lastNode( ) {
      /* part (a) */
   }

   // precondition: this Node is the root of a binary tree
   // postcondition: converts the tree to a doubly linked list,
   //                and returns the first node in the list
   public Node treeToList( ) {
      /* part (b) */
   }
}
```

Part (a)

Write the `lastNode` method of the `Node` class. Method `lastNode` should return the last node in the doubly linked list.

Complete method `lastNode` below.

```
// precondition: this Node is the first node in a doubly linked list
// postcondition: returns the last node in the list
public Node lastNode( ) {
```

Part (b)

Write the `treeToList` method of the `Node` class. Method `treeToList` should convert the binary tree rooted at the `Node` whose method was called to a doubly linked list as explained below, and it should return the first node in the list.

The following algorithm should be used to convert a binary tree rooted at node T to a doubly linked list:

1. Recursively convert T's left and right subtrees to doubly linked lists L1 and L2, respectively (a null subtree should be converted to a `null` list).

2. If L1 is not `null`, set the `right` field of the last node in list L1 to be node T, and set the `left` field of node T to be the last node in list L1.

3. If L2 is not `null`, set the `left` field of the first node in list L2 to be node T, and set the `right` field of node T to be the first node in list L2.

4. If L1 is not `null`, return the first node in list L1; otherwise, return node T.

For example:

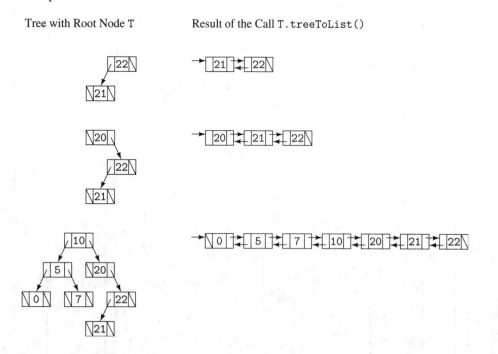

To receive full credit for this question, the linked list created by your code must occupy the same storage as the binary tree. You must only modify the `left` and `right` fields of the nodes; you must not allocate new storage for the list nodes.

In writing method `treeToList`, you may include calls to method `lastNode`. Assume that `lastNode` works as specified, regardless of what you wrote for part (a).

Complete method `treeToList` below.

```
// precondition: T is the root of a binary tree
// postcondition: converts the tree to a doubly linked list, and
//                   returns the first node in the list
public Node treeToList( ) {
```

Question 4

For many board games (e.g., chess, checkers, and go), the board can be represented using a two-dimensional array of integers, where the value in position [j][k] tells which piece (if any) is currently at that position. When deciding what move to make next, it is often useful to look for certain important patterns on the board.

These ideas lead to the following (partially specified) classes:

```java
public class Position {
    private int row;
    private int column;

    // constructor
    public Position(int theRow, int theCol) {
        row = theRow;
        col = theCol;
    }
}


public class BoardGame {
    private int[][] board;

    public BoardGame() { ... }  // constructor
    public Position patternPos( int[][] pattern ) { /* part (a) */ }
    public Position rotatedPatternPos(int[][] pattern ) { /* part (c) */ }

    /*** private method ***/
    private static int[][] rotate( int[][] A ) { /* part (b) */ }
}
```

Part (a)

Write the `patternPos` method of the `BoardGame` class, as started below. The `patternPos` method looks for the given pattern in the `board` array, and it returns the position in the `board` array where the upper-left corner of the pattern was found (if the pattern occurs more than once in the `board` array, the position corresponding to any of those occurrences can be returned). If the pattern does not occur in the `board` array, method `patternPos` returns `null`.

For example, assume that the `board` array is as follows:

1	2	3	4
5	6	7	8
9	10	11	12

Below are the results of some calls to `patternPos`.

pattern Array	Value Returned by the Call `patternPos( pattern )`
1 2 3 / 5 6 7	(0,0)
6 7 / 10 11	(1,1)
12	(2,3)
6 2 / 7 3	null
1 3 / 5 7	null

Complete method `patternPos` below.

```
// precondition: both board and pattern are nonempty, rectangular
//                   arrays
// postcondition: if pattern occurs in the board array, returns
//                   the position in the array where the upper-
//                   left-hand corner of the pattern was found;
//                   otherwise, returns null
public Position patternPos( int[][] pattern ) {
```

Part (b)

Write the private `rotate` method of the `BoardGame` class. The `rotate` method should return a rectangular, two-dimensional array that contains the same values as its parameter `A`, but rotated 90 degrees clockwise. (The `BoardGame`'s `rotate` method can be used to rotate a given pattern so that it can be found in different orientations on the board.)

Below are some examples of calls to `rotate`.

Array A						**Value Returned by the Call** `rotate( A )`	
1	2	3				6	1
6	7	8				7	2
						8	3

1	2	3	4	5		6	1
6	7	8	9	10		7	2
						8	3
						9	4
						10	5

1	2	3	4	5		11	6	1
6	7	8	9	10		12	7	2
11	12	13	14	15		13	8	3
						14	9	4
						15	10	5

Note that when array `A` is rotated, row 0 becomes the last column; row 1 becomes the second-to-last column, and so on.

Complete method `rotate` below.

```
// precondition: A is a nonempty, rectangular array
private static int[][] rotate( int[][] A ) {
```

Part (c)

Write the `rotatedPatternPos` method of the `BoardGame` class. The `rotatedPatternPos` method should look in the `board` array for the given pattern rotated 90, 180, or 270 degrees clockwise. It should return the position in the `board` array where the upper-left corner of the rotated pattern was found. If the rotated pattern occurs more than once in the `board` array, the position corresponding to any of those occurrences can be returned. If the rotated pattern does not occur in the `board` array, method `rotatedPatternPos` should return `null`.

For example, assume that the board array is as follows:

1	2	3	4
5	6	7	8
9	10	11	12

Below are the results of some calls to `rotatedPatternPos`.

pattern **Array**	Value Returned by the Call `rotatedPatternPos( pattern )`	Degrees of Rotation
3 7 / 2 6	(0,1)	90
7 6 / 3 2	(0,1)	180
6 2 / 7 3	(0,1)	270
4 8 12 / 3 7 11	(0,2)	90

In writing `rotatedPatternPos`, you may include calls to methods `patternPos` and `rotate`. Assume that those methods work as specified, regardless of what you wrote for parts (a) and (b).

Complete method `rotatedPatternPos` below.

```
// precondition: both board and pattern are nonempty, rectangular
//                 arrays
// postcondition: if pattern occurs in the board array rotated 90,
//                 180, or 270 degrees clockwise, then returns the
//                 position in the array where the upper-left-hand
//                 corner of the pattern was found;
//                 otherwise, returns null
public Position rotatedPatternPos( int[][] pattern ) {
```

Answers to Section I

1.	A	21.	C
2.	A	22.	C
3.	E	23.	C
4.	C	24.	D
5.	B	25.	A
6.	D	26.	E
7.	B	27.	A
8.	B	28.	B
9.	E	29.	A
10.	E	30.	C
11.	C	31.	D
12.	D	32.	C
13.	C	33.	E
14.	E	34.	B
15.	B	35.	B
16.	D	36.	C
17.	C	37.	A
18.	C	38.	A
19.	A	39.	C
20.	E	40.	E

Answers to Section II

Question 1
Part (a)

```
protected Location nextLocation(){
   ArrayList empty = emptyNeighbors();
   if (empty.size() == 0) return location();

   Location minLoc = null;
   int minTimes = 0;
   for (int k=0; k<empty.size(); k++){
      Location tempLoc = (Location)empty.get(k);
      Integer times = (Integer)visited.get(tempLoc);
      if (times == null) return tempLoc;
      if (minLoc == null) {
         minLoc = tempLoc;
         minTimes = times.intValue();
      } else {
         int tempTimes = times.intValue();
         if (tempTimes < minTimes){
            minTimes = tempTimes;
            minLoc = tempLoc;
         }
      }
   }
   return minLoc;
}
```

Part (b)

```
public void act() {
   if (! isInEnv() ) return;
   if (canMove()) {
      move();
      Integer k = (Integer)visited.get(location());
      if (k == null) {
         visited.put(location(), new Integer(1));
      } else {
         int newK = k.intValue()+1;
         visited.put(location(), new Integer(newK));
      }
   }
}
```

Grading Guide

Part (a) nextLocation   6 Points

+ ½ Retrieve empty neighbors

+ ½ Return current location if there are no empty neighbors

+1 Loop over empty neighbors

    + ½ attempt (must access ArrayList in loop)

    + ½ correct

+1 Return a location that is not in the visited map (that location has been visited 0 times)

+2½ Otherwise, update current min value(s)

    + ½ attempt

    +2 correct

+ ½ Return min found

Part (b) act   3 Points

+ ½ Check if in environment

+ ½ Check if can move and call move

+1 Handle current location not in Map

    + ½ attempt

    + ½ correct

+1 Handle current location is in Map

    + ½ retrieve old value

    + ½ update

Question 2
Part (a)

Full credit will be given for either of the following choices of datatype:

HashMap: The key will be the username, and the `Customer` object itself will be the associated information.

TreeMap: The key will be the username, and the `Customer` object itself will be the associated information.

The answers given for parts (b) and (c) assume that a `HashMap` is used.

The correct running times for the different choices of datatype are shown below. For `HashMap` and `TreeMap` we assume the implementations described above. For `HashSet`, we assume that the hash function uses the username; that is, two `Customer` objects will be considered equal if they have the same username (this allows the `removeCustomer` operation to have constant running time). Similarly, for `TreeSet`, we assume that the `compareTo` and `equals` methods use only the username; that is, `customer1` will be considered less than `customer2` if `customer1.getUsername()` comes before `customer2.getUsername()` in alphabetical order, they will be considered equal if their usernames are the same, and `customer1` will be considered greater than `customer2` if `customer1.getUsername()` comes after `customer2.getUsername()` in alphabetical order. Again, this allows the `removeCustomer` method to have an efficient running time.

Data Structure	removeCustomer	verifyLogin
ArrayList (unsorted)	$O(n)$	$O(n)$
LinkedList (unsorted)	$O(n)$	$O(n)$
ArrayList (sorted by username)	$O(\log n)$	$O(\log n)$
LinkedList (sorted by username)	$O(n)$	$O(n)$
HashSet	$O(1)$	$O(n)$
TreeSet	$O(\log n)$	$O(n)$
HashMap	$O(1)$	$O(1)$
TreeMap	$O(\log n)$	$O(\log n)$

Part (b)

```
public boolean verifyLogin(String userName, String pass) {
    if (allCustomers.containsKey(username)) {
        Customer cust = (Customer)allCustomers.get(userName);
        return cust.getPassword().equals(pass);
    }
    return false;
}
```

Part (c)

```
public void addCustomers(Set newCustomers) {
    Iterator it = newCustomers.iterator();
    while(it.hasNext()) {
        Customer c = (Customer)it.next();
        allCustomers.add(c.getUsername(), c);
    }
}
```

Grading Guide

Part (a) Data structure and running times   3½ Points

    +1½ Data structure

        +1 choose HashMap or TreeMap

        +½ correct description of how data are organized

    +2 Complexity (can earn no matter what implementation chosen)

        +1 verifyLogin

        +1 removeCustomer

Part (b) verifyLogin   2½ Points

    +1 Retrieve correct Customer from allCustomers based on implementation in part (a)

    +1½ Return correct value

        +1 when there is a customer with the given name

        +½ when there is no such customer

Part (c) addCustomers   3 Points

    +1 Traverse newCustomers

    +1 Attempt to place all elements from newCustomers into allCustomers

    +1 Correctly place all elements from newCustomers into allCustomers based on
        implementation chosen in part (a)

Question 3
Part (a)
Version 1: Use recursion.

```java
public Node lastNode( ) {
   if (right == null) return this;
   return right.lastNode();
}
```

Version 2: Use iteration.

```java
public Node lastNode( ) {
   Node tmp = this;
   while (tmp.right != null) tmp = tmp.right;
   return tmp;
}
```

Part (b)

```java
public Node treeToList( ) {
   Node L1, L2;

   // convert left and right subtrees to lists
   if (left==null) L1 = null;
   else L1 = left.treeToList();
   if (right==null) L2 = null;
   else L2 = right.treeToList();

   // set the fields
   if (L1 != null) {
      Node last = L1.lastNode();
      last.setRight(this);
      left = last;
   }
   if (L2 != null) {
      L2.setLeft(this);
      right = L2;
   }

   // return the list
   if (L1 != null) return L1;
   else return this;
}
```

Grading Guide

Part (a) `lastNode`   3 Points

+1 Handle base case correctly (check for `right == null` and return the current node)

+2 Correct recursion or iteration

Part (b) `treeToList`   6 Points

+1 Convert left subtree to list
  + 1/2 attempt (may not have null check)
  + 1/2 correct with null check

+1 Convert right subtree to list
  + 1/2 attempt (may not have null check)
  + 1/2 correct with null check

+1 Check for left and right lists != null

+1 Locate the last node in the left list
  + 1/2 attempt (can reimplement `lastNode`)
  + 1/2 correct (must use `lastNode` for correct point)

+ 1/2 Assign the current node to the end of the left list

+1 Assign right list to end of list
  + 1/2 attempt
  + 1/2 correct

+ 1/2 Return appropriate created list

Question 4

Part (a)

Note that method `patternPos` is much easier to write if you first write an auxiliary method that tests one position of the array to see whether there is a match using that position as the upper-left corner.

```
private boolean patternPosAux( int[][] pattern, int row, int col ) {
// precondition: pattern is a rectangular array;
//                row < pattern.length;
//                col < pattern[0].length
//                row + pattern.length-1 < board.length
// postcondition: returns true if pattern occurs in board with its
//                 upper-left corner at board[row][col];
//                 otherwise, returns false
    int patRow = 0, patCol;
    int boardRow = row, boardCol = col;
    while (patRow < pattern.length && boardRow < board.length) {
        patCol = 0;
        boardCol = col;
        while (patCol < pattern[0].length && boardCol < board[0].length) {
            if (board[boardRow][boardCol] != pattern[patRow][patCol]) {
                return false;
            }
            patCol++;
            boardCol++;
        }
        patRow++;
        boardRow++;
    }
    return true;
}


public Position patternPos( int[][] pattern ) {
    for (int j=0; j<=board.length-pattern.length; j++) {
        for (int k=0; k<=board[0].length-pattern[0].length; k++) {
            if (patternPosAux(pattern, j, k)) {
                return new Position(j, k);
            }
        }
    }
    return null;
}
```

Part (b)

```
private static int[][] rotate( int[][] A ) {
   int[][] newA = new int[A[0].length][A.length];
   int newrow, newcol = A.length-1;
   for (int j=0; j<A.length; j++) {
      newrow = 0;
      for (int k=0; k<A[0].length; k++) {
         newA[newrow][newcol] = A[j][k];
         newrow++;
      }
      newcol--;
   }
   return newA;
}
```

Part (c)

Version 1: Use a loop to try each rotation in turn.

```
public Position rotatedPatternPos( int[][] pattern ) {
   int[][] tmp = rotate(pattern);
   int rotation = 90;
   while (rotation <= 270) {
      Position p = patternPos(tmp);
      if (p != null) return p;
      rotation +=90;
      tmp = rotate(tmp);
   }
   return null;
}
```

Version 2: Try each rotation explicitly.

```
public Position rotatedPatternPos1( int[][] pattern ) {
   int[][] tmp = rotate(pattern);
   Position p = patternPos(tmp);
   if (p != null) return p;
   tmp = rotate(tmp);
   p = patternPos(tmp);
   if (p != null) return p;
   tmp = rotate(tmp);
   p = patternPos(tmp);
   if (p != null) return p;
   return null;
}
```

Grading Guide

Part (a) `PatternPos`   4 Points

+1 Test all positions in board array as possible upper-left corner of pattern

+2 Test for pattern

    +1 attempt

    +1 correct

+ $\frac{1}{2}$ Return position if pattern is found

+ $\frac{1}{2}$ Return null otherwise

Part (b) `rotate`   3 Points

+1 Create new array of appropriate size

    + $\frac{1}{2}$ declare array

    + $\frac{1}{2}$ instantiate to correct size

+$1\frac{1}{2}$ Traverse `A` copying to new array

    + $\frac{1}{2}$ attempt row/col traversal

    + $\frac{1}{2}$ copy some value from array based on traversal

    + $\frac{1}{2}$ correct

+ $\frac{1}{2}$ Return new array

Part (c) `rotatedPatternPos`   2 Points

+1 Check each rotation

    + $\frac{1}{2}$ attempt

    + $\frac{1}{2}$ correct

+1 Return appropriate values for each

Practice Examination AB-3

Section I

Time: 1 hour and 15 minutes
Number of questions: 40
Percent of total grade: 50

1. Assume that `val` is an `int` variable initialized to be greater than zero and that `A` is an array of `ints`. Consider the following code segment:

```
for (int k=0; k<A.length; k++) {
    while (A[k] < val) {
        A[k] *= 2;
    }
}
```

Which of the following best describes when this code segment will go into an infinite loop?

A. Always

B. Whenever `A` includes a value greater than `val`

C. Whenever `A` includes a value less than `val`

D. Whenever `A` includes a value equal to `val`

E. Whenever `A` includes a value less than or equal to zero

2. Which of the following is a property of all binary search trees?

A. For all nodes n, the number of nodes in n's left subtree is the same as the number of nodes in n's right subtree.

B. The number of leaves is the same as the number of non-leaves.

C. The time required to search for a given value is proportional to the height of the tree (the longest path from the root to a leaf) in the worst case.

D. Every node has either 0 or 2 children.

E. The time required to insert a new value into a tree with N nodes is $O(N^2)$ in the worst case.

Questions 3 and 4 concern the design of a data structure to store information about which seats in a theater are reserved. The theater has 10 rows; each row has 50 seats. Two data structures are being considered:

Data Structure 1: A two-dimensional array of booleans. The rows of the array correspond to the rows in the theater, and the columns of the array correspond to the seats in each row. An array element is true if and only if the corresponding seat is reserved.

Data Structure 2: A linked list of Reservations. Each Reservation has two integer fields: a row number and a seat number. The list is initially empty. Each time a seat is reserved, a new node is added to the front of the list, containing the row and seat numbers of the newly reserved seat.

3. Assume that the same amount of storage is required for an integer and a boolean. Under which of the following conditions does Data Structure 1 require less storage than Data Structure 2?

    A. No seats are reserved.

    B. All seats are reserved.

    C. Only a single seat in the first row is reserved.

    D. Only a single seat in the last row is reserved.

    E. Data Structure 1 never requires less storage than Data Structure 2.

4. Which of the following operations can be implemented more efficiently using Data Structure 1 than using Data Structure 2?

    Operation I: Determine how many seats are reserved.
    Operation II: Determine whether a particular seat (given its row and seat number) is reserved.
    Operation III: Determine whether the seats on either side of a particular seat (given its row and seat number) are both reserved.

    A. I only

    B. II only

    C. III only

    D. I and II

    E. II and III

5. Consider writing a program to be used to manage information about the animals on a farm. The farm has three kinds of animals: cows, pigs, and goats. The cows are used to produce both milk and meat. The goats are used only to produce milk, and the pigs are used only to produce meat.

   Assume that an `Animal` class has been defined. Which of the following is the best way to represent the remaining data?

   A. Define two subclasses of the `Animal` class: `MilkProducer` and `MeatProducer`. Define two subclasses of the `MilkProducer` class: `Cow` and `Goat`; and define two subclasses of the `MeatProducer` class: `Cow` and `Pig`.

   B. Define three subclasses of the `Animal` class: `Cow`, `Goat`, and `Pig`. Also define two interfaces: `MilkProducer` and `MeatProducer`. Define the `Cow` and `Goat` classes to implement the `MilkProducer` interface, and define the `Cow` and `Pig` classes to implement the `Meat-Producer` interface.

   C. Define five new classes, not related to the `Animal` class: `Cow`, `Goat`, `Pig`, `MilkProducer`, and `MeatProducer`.

   D. Define five subclasses of the `Animal` class: `Cow`, `Goat`, `Pig`, `MilkProducer`, and `Meat-Producer`.

   E. Define two subclasses of the `Animal` class: `MilkProducer` and `MeatProducer`. Also define three interfaces: `Cow`, `Goat`, and `Pig`. Define the `MilkProducer` class to implement the `Cow` and `Goat` interfaces, and define the `MeatProducer` class to implement the `Cow` and `Pig` interfaces.

6. Consider three different kinds of linked lists:

   - A singly linked list with a pointer to the first node
   - A doubly linked list with pointers to the first and last nodes
   - A circular, doubly linked list with a pointer to the first node

   Assume that each list has N nodes. Which of the following best characterizes the times required, for each kind of list, to access the second-to-last node in the list?

Singly linked, pointer to first node	Doubly linked, pointers to first and last nodes	Circular, doubly linked, pointer to first node
A. $O(1)$	$O(1)$	$O(1)$
B. $O(1)$	$O(N)$	$O(N)$
C. $O(N)$	$O(1)$	$O(1)$
D. $O(N)$	$O(N)$	$O(1)$
E. $O(N)$	$O(N)$	$O(N)$

7. Consider the following code segment:

```
String S = "happy";
ListNode L = null;
ListNode tmp = null;

for (int k=0; k<S.length(); k++) {
    tmp = new ListNode(S.substring(k, k+1), L);
    L = tmp;
}
while (L != null) {
    System.out.print(L.getValue());
    L = L.getNext();
}
System.out.println();
```

What will be printed when this code segment executes?

A. happy
B. happ
C. yppah
D. yppa
E. Nothing will be printed.

Questions 8 and 9 assume that the following method has been added to the ListNode class:

```
public boolean checkList(Comparable v) {
// precondition: The values in this list are comparable to v
//               and are in sorted order (low to high).
   if (v.compareTo(value) == 0) return true;
   if (v.compareTo(value) < 0) return false;
   return next.checkList(v);
}
```

8. When does method checkList cause a runtime error due to an attempt to dereference a null pointer?

A. Never
B. Whenever the value v is somewhere in the list
C. Whenever the value v is *not* in the list
D. Whenever v is greater than all values in the list
E. Whenever v is less than all values in the list

9. When does method checkList return true?

A. When the value v is somewhere in the list
B. Only when the value v is the first value in the list
C. Only when the value v is the last value in the list
D. When a value greater than v is somewhere in the list
E. Only when a value greater than v is the first value in the list

Questions 10 and 11 rely on the following information:

Assume that binary trees are implemented using the standard `TreeNode` class. Two binary trees are considered to be equal if they are both empty or if the following three conditions all hold:

1. The values at the roots of the two trees are the same.

2. The left subtrees of the roots of the two trees are equal.

3. The right subtrees of the roots of the two trees are equal.

The method shown below was intended to determine whether its two binary tree parameters are equal. However, the method does not always work correctly. (Line numbers are included for reference.)

```
 1  public static boolean treeEq(TreeNode T1, TreeNode T2) {
 2      if (T1 == null && T2 != null) || (T1 !=null && T2 == null)) {
 3          return false;
 4      }
 5      if (!T1.getValue().equals(T2.getValue())) {
 6          return false;
 7      }
 8      return(treeEq(T1.getLeft(), T2.getLeft()) &&
 9          treeEq(T1.getRight(), T2.getRight());
10  }
```

10. For which of the following values of T1 and T2 will method `treeEq` *fail* to work correctly?

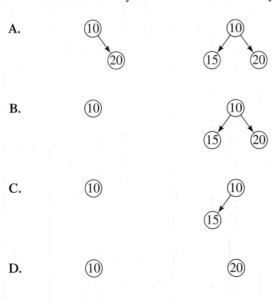

Tree Pointed to by T1   Tree Pointed to by T2

A.

B.

C.

D.

E.

11. Which of the following changes fixes method `treeEq` so that it always works correctly?

   A. Before line 2, add `if (T1==null && T2==null) return true;`.

   B. Before line 2, add `if (T1==null || T2==null) return true;`.

   C. In line 2, change the `||` operator to the `&&` operator.

   D. Change line 3 to `return true;`.

   E. In line 8, change the `&&` operator to the `||` operator.

12. Assume that the following method has been added to the `TreeNode` class:

```
public void mystery( Stack S ) {
    if (right != null) right.mystery(S);
    S.push(value);
    if (left != null) left.mystery(S);
}
```

Assume that `T` is a `TreeNode` that is the root of a binary search tree, and that `T`'s `mystery` method is initially called with an empty stack `S`. Which of the following best describes `S` after the call?

   A. `S` is empty.

   B. `S` contains only the value at the root of the tree.

   C. `S` contains all of the values in the tree in unsorted order.

   D. `S` contains all of the values in the tree in sorted order; the smallest value is at the top of the stack.

   E. `S` contains all of the values in the tree in sorted order; the largest value is at the top of the stack.

13. Assume that variables `L`, `tmp`, and `previous` are `ListNodes` with values as illustrated below.

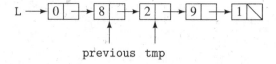

Which of the following code segments removes the node pointed to by `tmp` from the list pointed to by `L`?

   A. `tmp = null;`

   B. `previous.setNext(tmp.getNext());`
      `tmp.setNext(null);`

   C. `tmp.setValue(previous.getValue());`

   D. `previous = tmp.getNext();`
      `tmp.setNext(null);`

   E. `tmp.setNext(previous);`

14. Consider the following class definition:

```
public class Node {
    private Object data;
    private Node left;
    private Node right;

    public void change() {
        left = right;
        right = left;
    }
}
```

Assume that variable x is a Node, initialized as shown below.

Which of the following best illustrates the result of the call X.change()?

A.   x ⟶ 10
           ↙   ↘
         30   20

B.   x ⟶ 10
           ↙   ↘
         30   30

C.   x ⟶ 10
           ↙   ↘
         20   30

D.   x ⟶ 10
           ↙   ↘
         20   20

E.   x ⟶ 10
            ( )
             30

15. Consider the following three partial class definitions:

    Class I:

    ```
    public class Person implements Comparable {
        public int compareTo(Person p) { ... }
    }
    ```

    Class II:

    ```
    public class Animal implements Comparable {
        public boolean compareTo(Object ob) { ... }
    }
    ```

    Class III:

    ```
    public class Mineral implements Comparable {
        public int compareTo(Object ob) { ... }
    }
    ```

    Which of the three classes does (do) *not* correctly implement the `Comparable` interface?

    A. I only

    B. II only

    C. III only

    D. I and II

    E. II and III

16. Consider the following code segment:

    ```
    ArrayList first = new ArrayList();
    ArrayList second;
    first.add(new Integer(1));
    second = first;
    first.add(new Integer(2));
    second.add(new Integer(100);
    ```

    What are the values of `first` and `second` after this code executes?

first	second
A. [1, 2]	[100]
B. [1, 2, 100]	[1, 2, 100]
C. [1, 2]	[1, 100]
D. [1, 2]	[1, 2, 100]
E. [1, 2, 100]	[100]

Questions 17 and 18 concern the following two possibilities for a data structure to be used to store students' grades on an exam. There are N students, and each grade is an integer in the range 0 to 100.

Data Structure 1: Use an array A of length 101 (each element of the array corresponds to one possible grade). For each value of k from 0 to 100, A[k] contains a linked list of strings: the names of the students who got grade k on the exam.

Data Structure 2: Use an array A of length N (each element of the array corresponds to one student). For each value of k from 0 to $N - 1$, A[k] contains a Student object that has two fields: the name of the kth student and that student's grade. The Students are stored in the array in sorted order according to the students' names.

The data structure will be used to support three operations:

I.   Given a student's name, look up that student's exam grade.

II.   Given the names of two students, determine whether they got the same grade.

III. Print the names of all the students who got 100 on the exam.

17. Which of the three operations could be performed more efficiently using Data Structure 1 than using Data Structure 2?

   A. I only

   B. II only

   C. III only

   D. I and II

   E. II and III

18. Which of the three operations could be performed more efficiently using Data Structure 2 than using Data Structure 1?

   A. I only

   B. II only

   C. III only

   D. I and II

   E. II and III

19. Assume that neither stack S nor queue Q contains null. Which of the following code segments correctly determines whether S and Q contain the same sequence of items, from top to bottom in the stack, and from front to rear in the queue?

A.
```
while (!S.empty() && !Q.empty() ) {
    if (!S.pop().equals( Q.dequeue() )) return false;
}
return (S.empty() && Q.empty());
```

B.
```
while (!S.empty() ) {
    if (Q.empty() || !(S.pop().equals( Q.dequeue()) )) return false;
}
return true;
```

C.
```
while (!S.empty() && !Q.empty() ) {
    if (!S.pop().equals( Q.dequeue() ) return false;
}
return true;
```

D.
```
while (!S.empty() ) {
    if (!(S.pop().equals( Q.dequeue() ) || Q.empty() )) return false;
}
return Q.empty();
```

E.
```
while (!S.empty() || !Q.empty() ) {
    if (!S.pop().equals( Q.dequeue() ) return false;
}
return (S.empty() || Q.empty());
```

Questions 20 and 21 concern the following data fields and method:

```
Set mySet;
HashSet HS;
TreeSet TS;

public boolean compareSets(Set s) {
    Iterator it = mySet.iterator();
    while (it.hasNext()) {
        Object ob = it.next();
        if (!s.contains(ob)) return false;
    }
    return true;
}
```

20. Which of the following best describes what method `compareSets` does?

    A. Returns true iff `mySet` is a subset of `s`.

    B. Returns true iff `s` is a subset of `mySet`.

    C. Returns true iff `mySet` and `s` contain exactly the same items.

    D. Returns true iff `mySet` contains no duplicates.

    E. Returns true iff `s` does not contain any item that is in `mySet`.

21. Assume that `mySet`, `HS`, and `TS` have been initialized as follows:

    ```
    mySet = new TreeSet();
    HashSet HS = new HashSet();
    TreeSet TS = new TreeSet();
    ```

    and that the following (incomplete) statement is in a method in the same class as method `compareSets`:

    ```
    boolean b = missing code;
    ```

    Which of the following replacements for *missing code* would compile without error?

    I.   `compareSets(mySet);`
    II. `compareSets(TS);`
    III. `compareSets(HS);`

    A. I only

    B. II only

    C. III only

    D. I and III only

    E. I, II, and III

Questions 22–24 involve reasoning about the Marine Biology case study.

22. Consider changing the UnboundedEnvironment class to use a LinkedList instead of an ArrayList to store the objects in the environment. For which of the following methods would the Big-O worst-case runtime change?

   I.   numObjects
   II. allObjects
   III. objectAt

   A. I only

   B. II only

   C. III only

   D. I and II

   E. II and III

23. Which of the following best explains the circumstances under which the add method of the UnboundedEnvironment class throws an IllegalArgumentException?

   A. When an attempt is made to add an object in a nonempty location.

   B. When an attempt is made to add an object that is not a Fish.

   C. When an attempt is made to add an object that is not a Locatable.

   D. When an attempt is made to add an object that is null.

   E. When an attempt is made to add an object that would cause the number of occupied locations to be greater than the number of empty locations.

24. Which of the following best describes what the recordMove method of the Unbounded-Environment class does?

   A. Moves obj to a new location in the environment.

   B. Verifies that obj moved correctly.

   C. Verifies that obj's new location is a valid location in the environment.

   D. Verifies that obj's old location was a valid location in the environment.

   E. Checks whether any other object is at obj's new location, and if so, removes that object from the environment.

Questions 25 and 26 concern using a data structure to store a "to-do" list: a list of tasks, including the number of minutes needed for each. For example, a to-do list might include the following:

shop, 10

take bath, 10

eat lunch, 15

walk dog, 5

clean garage, 5

25. Assume that the operations to be performed on a to-do list are the following:

    Operation 1: determine whether the list is empty
    Operation 2: add a new task to the list
    Operation 3: remove and return one task from the list

    and that an `ArrayList` is used to store the to-do list. Which of the following is the most efficient way to implement the add and remove operations?

    A. Add and remove tasks at the beginning of the list.

    B. Add and remove tasks at the end of the list.

    C. Add tasks at the beginning of the list, and remove them from the end of the list.

    D. Add tasks at the end of the list, and remove them from the beginning of the list.

    E. Add tasks at the beginning of the list, and remove them from randomly selected positions in the list.

26. Now assume that Operation 3 (removing and returning one task from the list) needs to be implemented so that the task with the `shortest` time is returned. Which of the following is the best way to implement the to-do list?

    A. Use an `ArrayList`. Keep the tasks sorted by the time required, and implement the remove operation by removing and returning the first item in the list.

    B. Use a `LinkedList`. Keep the tasks sorted by the time required, and implement the remove operation by removing and returning the first item in the list.

    C. Use a `PriorityQueue` implemented using a min-heap and ordered by the time required for each task. Implement the remove operation using the `PriorityQueue`'s `removeMin` method.

    D. Use a `Set`. Implement the remove operation by iterating through the set to find the task with the shortest time.

    E. Use a `Map`, where the times are the key values. Implement the remove operation by calling the `Map`'s `remove` method with the values 1, 2, 3, . . . until a non-null value is returned.

27. Consider the following code segment:

```
y = x || y;
y = !x;
```

Assume that x and y are initialized boolean variables. Which of the following statements is true?

A. The final value of y is the same as the initial value of x.

B. The final value of y is different from the initial value of x.

C. The final value of x is the same as the initial value of y.

D. The final value of x is different from the initial value of y.

E. The final value of x is different from the final value of y.

28. Under which of the following conditions would it be better to use an `ArrayList` rather than a `LinkedList`?

A. The `get` operation will be used frequently, getting items from various places in the list.

B. The `get` operation will be used infrequently.

C. Items will only be added to the front of the list.

D. Items will only be removed from the front of the list.

E. Items will only be added to the end of the list.

29. Assume that variable `letterMap` is a Map that maps lowercase letters to their position in the alphabet; for example, "a" is mapped to 1, "b" is mapped to 2, and so on. Consider the following code segment.

```
letterMap.put("A", new Integer(1));
letterMap.put("B", new Integer(28));
letterMap.put("B", new Integer(2));
```

Which of the following best describes what happens when this code segment executes?

A. There is a runtime exception because the first call to put tries to map "A" to 1, and "a" is already mapped to 1.

B. There is a runtime exception because the third call to put tries to map "B" to 2, and "B" is already mapped to 28.

C. There is no exception. After the code executes, all lowercase letters are mapped to their positions in the alphabet; "A" is mapped to 1, and "B" is mapped to the pair (28, 2).

D. There is no exception. After the code executes, all lowercase letters are mapped to their positions in the alphabet; "A" is mapped to 1, and "B" is mapped to 2.

E. There is no exception. After the code executes, all lowercase letters are mapped to their positions in the alphabet; "A" is mapped to 1, and "B" is mapped to 28.

30. Recall that a `LinkedList` is implemented using a doubly linked list, and that iterating through a list of size N takes $O(N)$ time. Which of the following is most likely to be the way the iterator is implemented?

   A. When the iterator is created, it stores a pointer to the first node in the list. The `next` method returns the data stored in the current node, and sets the pointer to point to the next node.

   B. When the iterator is created, it stores a pointer to the last node in the list. The `next` method returns the data stored in the current node, and sets the pointer to point to the previous node.

   C. When the iterator is created, it stores the index 0. The `next` method returns the result of the list's `get` method called with the current index, and increments that index.

   D. When the iterator is created, it stores the index 0. The `next` method starts at the beginning of the list and uses the index to determine how many pointers it should follow forward; it returns the data stored in the node it reaches, and increments the stored index.

   E. When the iterator is created, it stores the index 0. The `next` method starts at the end of the list and uses the index to determine how many pointers it should follow backward; it returns the data stored in the node it reaches, and increments the stored index.

Questions 31 and 32 concern the following information:

For the purposes of these questions, assume that a binary search tree (BST) contains no duplicate values. Also assume that two BSTs are considered equal if they contain exactly the same set of values *even if they are stored in different places in the two trees.*

Below are three proposed algorithms for determining whether BSTs T1 and T2, both of which contain N values, are equal:

Algorithm I

1. Traverse T1 using a *preorder* traversal. Each time a node is visited, look up that node's value in T2; if it is not there, return false.
2. Return true.

Algorithm II

1. Start with two empty `ArrayLists`, L1 and L2.
2. Traverse T1 using a *preorder* traversal. Each time a node is visited, add its value to the end of L1.
3. Traverse T2 using a *preorder* traversal. Each time a node is visited, add its value to the end of L2.
4. Iterate through the two lists; for each position k, compare the value in position k of L1 with the value in position k of L2. If they differ, return false.
5. Return true.

Algorithm III

- Same as Algorithm II, but use an *inorder* traversal in steps 2 and 3.

31. Which algorithms work?

    A. I only
    B. II only
    C. III only
    D. I and III
    E. II and III

32. Recall that T1 and T2 each contain N values. Assume that both T1 and T2 are *balanced*. What are the worst-case times for each algorithm (whether they work or not)?

	Algorithm I	Algorithm II	Algorithm III
A.	$O(N)$	$O(N)$	$O(N)$
B.	$O(N \log N)$	$O(N)$	$O(N)$
C.	$O(\log N)$	$O(N^2)$	$O(N^2)$
D.	$O(N \log N)$	$O(N \log N)$	$O(N \log N)$
E.	$O(N^2)$	$O(N^2)$	$O(N^2)$

33. A binary tree can be used to store the names in a family tree using the format shown below:

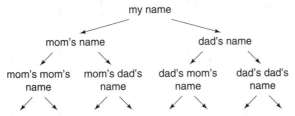

Note that for each node in the tree, the left child represents a woman and the right child represents a man.

Assume that binary trees are implemented using the standard `TreeNode` class. Consider the incomplete method `printFemaleAncestors` shown below. The method is intended to print the names of all of the female ancestors of node `N` (in any order).

```java
public static void printFemaleAncestors( TreeNode N ) {
    if (N == null) return;
        missing code
}
```

Which of the following replacements for *missing code* correctly completes method `print-FemaleAncestors`?

A.
```java
TreeNode left = N.getLeft();
if (left != null) {
    System.out.println(left.getValue());
    printFemaleAncestors(left);
}
```

B.
```java
TreeNode left = N.getLeft();
while (left != null) {
    System.out.println(left.getValue());
    left = left.getLeft();
}
printFemaleAncestors(N.getRight());
```

C.
```java
TreeNode left = N.getLeft();
if (left != null) {
    System.out.println(left.getValue());
    printFemaleAncestors(left);
}
printFemaleAncestors(N.getRight());
```

D.
```java
TreeNode left = N.getLeft();
System.out.println(left.getValue());
printFemaleAncestors(left);
printFemaleAncestors(N.getRight());
```

E.
```java
TreeNode left = N.getLeft();
TreeNode right = N.getRight();
System.out.println(left.getValue());
printFemaleAncestors(left);
System.out.println(right.getValue());
printFemaleAncestors(right);
```

34. Consider the following data field and method:

```
private List myList;

public void printList( ) {
    for (Iterator it = myList.iterator(); it.hasNext();) {
        Object ob = it.next();
        System.out.print(it.next() + " ");
    }
}
```

Assume that `myList` represents the list shown below before method `printList` is called.

```
myList: [ 1,  2,  3, 4 ]
```

What happens when method `printList` executes?

A. The *for-loop* causes an `IndexOutOfBoundsException`.

B. The *for-loop* causes a `NoSuchElementException`.

C. There is no exception. 1 2 is printed.

D. There is no exception. 2 4 is printed.

E. There is no exception. 1 2 3 4 is printed.

35. Consider the following two code segments:

```
Segment 1
for (Iterator it = myList.iterator(); it.hasNext();) {
    System.out.println(it.next());
}
```

```
Segment 2
for (Iterator it = myList.listIterator(); it.hasNext();) {
    System.out.println(it.next());
}
```

Assume that `myList` is an `ArrayList` containing N items. Note that Segment 1 uses an `Iterator` while Segment 2 uses a `ListIterator`. Which of the following statements about these two code segments is true?

A. The two code segments will produce the same output and will both be $O(N)$.

B. The two code segments will produce different output and will both be $O(N)$.

C. The two code segments will produce the same output; Segment 1 will be $O(N)$ and Segment 2 will be $O(N^2)$.

D. The two code segments will produce different output; Segment 1 will be $O(N^2)$ and Segment 2 will be $O(N)$.

E. The two code segments will produce the same output and will both be $O(N^2)$.

36. Consider the following data field and method:

```
private Comparable[][] grid;

public boolean testGrid() {
    for (int j=0; j<grid[0].length; j++) {
        Comparable val = grid[0][j];
        for (int k=1; k<grid.length; k++) {
            if (! val.compareTo(grid[k][j]) < 0) return false;
        }
    }
    return true;
}
```

Which of the following best describes the circumstances under which method `testGrid` returns true?

A. When for every column of the grid, the largest value for that column is in the last row.

B. When for every column of the grid, the smallest value for that column is in the last row.

C. When for every column of the grid, the largest value for that column is in the first row.

D. When for every column of the grid, the smallest value for that column is in the first row.

E. When for every column of the grid, all values for that column are the same.

37. Which of the following best explains what is meant by `overloading` a method?

A. Defining another method that does the same thing

B. Defining another method with the same number of parameters

C. Defining another method with the same parameter names

D. Defining another method with the same precondition

E. Defining another method with the same name but different numbers or types of parameters

38. Which of the following statements about a binary search tree is true?

A. If the values in the nodes are printed using a *preorder* traversal, they will be printed in the order in which they were added to the binary search tree.

B. If the values in the nodes are printed using an *inorder* traversal, they will be printed in the order in which they were added to the binary search tree.

C. If the values in the nodes are printed using a *postorder* traversal, they will be printed in the order in which they were added to the binary search tree.

D. If the values in the nodes are printed using a *preorder* traversal, they will be printed in sorted order.

E. If the values in the nodes are printed using an *inorder* traversal, they will be printed in sorted order.

Questions 39 and 40 concern the following two class definitions:

```java
public class Liquid {
   private int amount;

   // constructor
   public Liquid() {
      System.out.print("liquid ");
      amount = 0;
   }

   public int getAmount() { return amount; }
   public void setAmount(int am) { amount = am; }
}

public class Milk extends Liquid {
   private int percentFat;

   // constructor
   public Milk(int percent) {
      System.out.print("milk ");
      percentFat = percent;
   }
}
```

39. Consider the following code segment:

```java
Liquid liq = new Milk(2);
Milk mil = new Milk(4);
```

What is printed when this code executes?

A. `milk milk`

B. `liquid milk`

C. `liquid liquid`

D. `liquid milk liquid milk`

E. `milk liquid milk liquid`

40. Consider the following code segment:

```
Liquid water = new Liquid();
Liquid rain = water;
rain.setAmount(10);
water.setAmount(20);
Liquid water = new Liquid();
System.out.println(water.getAmount() + " " + rain.getAmount());
```

What is printed when this code executes?

A. 0 0

B. 0 10

C. 0 20

D. 20 10

E. 20 20

Section II

Time: 1 hour and 45 minutes
Number of questions: 4
Percent of total grade: 50

Question 1

This question involves reasoning about the code from the Marine Biology case study.

Consider a new implementation of the Environment interface called UnboundedSetEnv. An UnboundedSetEnv will be similar to an UnboundedEnvironment, except that the Locatable objects in the environment will be stored in a HashSet instead of an ArrayList.

A partial declaration of the UnboundedSetEnvironment class is given below.

```
public class UnboundedSetEnvironment implements Environment {

    private HashSet objectSet; // set of Locatable objects in this
                               // environment


    // precondition: objectSet contains the Locatable objects in this
    //                 environment
    // postcondition: returns an array of all Locatable objects in this
    //                 environment
    public Locatable[] allObjects() { /* part (a) */ }


    // precondition: objectSet contains the Locatable objects in this
    //                 environment
    // postcondition: returns the object at location loc
    //                 or null if loc is empty
    public Locatable objectAt(Location loc) { /* part (b) */ }


    // precondition: objectSet contains the Locatable objects in this
    //                 environment and obj is in this environment
    // postcondition: obj has been removed from this environment
    public void remove(Locatable obj) { /* body not shown */ }


    // other methods not shown
}
```

Part (a)

Write the `allObjects` method for the `UnboundedSetEnvironment` class. The method should return an array of all of the `Locatable` objects in the environment.

Write method `allObjects` below.

```
// precondition: objectSet contains the Locatable objects in this
//               environment
// postcondition: returns an array of all Locatable objects in this
//               environment
public Locatable [] allObjects() {
```

Part (b)

Write the `objectAt` method for the `UnboundedSetEnvironment` class. The method should return the object at location `loc` if that location is occupied; otherwise, it should return null.

Write method `objectAt` below.

```
// precondition: objectSet contains the Locatable objects in this
//               environment
// postcondition: returns the object at location loc
//                 or null if loc is empty
public Locatable objectAt(Location loc) {
```

Part (c)

Give the expected Big-O running times for each of the methods listed below, assuming that the `UnboundedSetEnvironment` implementation given above is used and that the environment contains *n* objects.

Method	Expected Runtime
allObjects	
objectAt	
remove	

Question 2

Assume that binary trees are implemented using the standard `TreeNode` class. For this question, you will augment the `TreeNode` class by adding the following three methods:

```
// postcondition: returns the value stored in the rightmost leaf of
//                the tree rooted at this node
public Object rightmostLeafVal( )


// precondition: the leaves of the tree rooted at this node contain
//               values v₁, v₂, ..., vₙ
// postcondition: the leaves of the tree rooted at this node contain
//                values inval, v₁, v₂, ..., vₙ₋₁;
//                returns value vₙ
public Object pushLeavesRight( Object inval )


// precondition: the leaves of the tree rooted at this node contain
//               values v₁, v₂, ..., vₙ
// postcondition: the leaves of the tree rooted at this node contain
//                values vₙ, v₁, v₂, ..., vₙ₋₁;
public void rotateLeaves( )
```

Part (a)

Write the `rightmostLeafVal` method of the `TreeNode` class. Method `rightmostLeafVal` should return the value stored in the rightmost leaf of the tree rooted at the node whose `rightmostLeafVal` method is called.

For example:

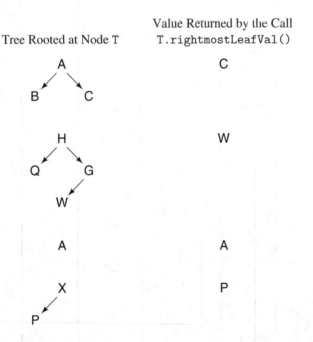

| | Value Returned by the Call |
| Tree Rooted at Node T | T.rightmostLeafVal() |

Complete method `rightmostLeafVal` below.

```
// postcondition: returns the value stored in the rightmost leaf
//                of the tree rooted at this node
public Object rightmostLeafVal( ) {
```

Part (b)

Write the `pushLeavesRight` method of the `TreeNode` class. Method `pushLeavesRight` should change the values in all of the leaves of the tree rooted at the node whose `pushLeavesRight` method is called, inserting the value `inval` into the leftmost leaf, inserting the value that was originally in the leftmost leaf into the second-to-leftmost leaf, and so on, finally returning the value that was in the rightmost leaf. For example:

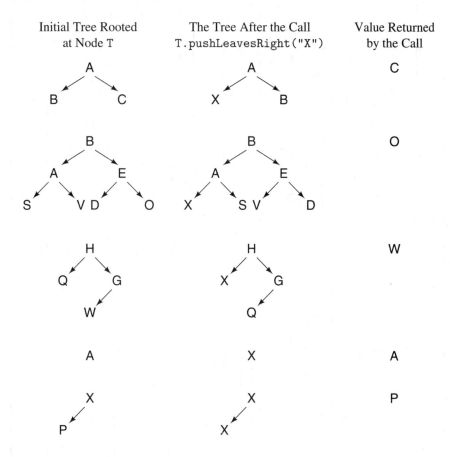

Complete method pushLeavesRight below.

```
// precondition: the leaves of the tree rooted at this node contain
//               values v1, v2, ..., vn
// postcondition: the leaves of the tree rooted at this node contain
//                values inval, v1, v2, ..., vn-1;
//                returns value vn
public Object pushLeavesRight( Object inval ) {
```

Part (c)

Write the `rotateLeaves` method of the `TreeNode` class. Method `rotateLeaves` should change the values in all of the leaves of the tree rooted at the node whose `rotateLeaves` method was called, inserting `Object` v_n from the rightmost leaf of the tree into the leftmost leaf, inserting the value that was originally in the leftmost leaf into the second-to-leftmost leaf, and so on.

For example:

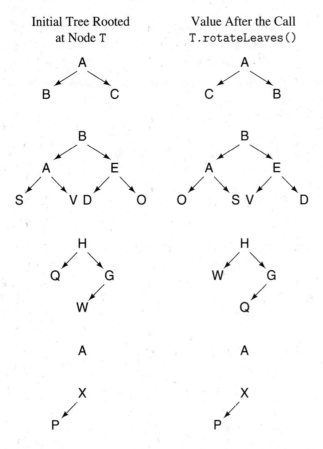

In writing method `rotateLeaves`, you may include calls to methods `rightmostLeafVal` and `pushLeavesRight`. Assume that both methods work as specified, regardless of what you wrote for parts (a) and (b).

Complete method `rotateLeaves` below.

```
// precondition: the leaves of the tree rooted at this node contain
//                values v1, v2, ..., vn
// postcondition: the leaves of the tree rooted at this node contain
//                values vn, v1, v2, ..., vn-1
public void rotateLeaves( ) {
```

Question 3

This question involves the two classes partially defined below. The Person class is used to store information about one person; the Family class is used to store information about a family (containing zero or more people). The Family class contains a ListNode field that either is null or points to the first node of a linked list of the people in the family, sorted by age (from youngest to oldest).

```
public class Person {
    private String name;
    private int age;

    // constructor
    public Person(String theName, int theAge) {
        name = theName;
        age = theAge;
    }
    public String getName() { return name; }
    public int getAge() { return age; }
}

public class Family {
    private ListNode peopleList;    // pointer to linked list of
                                    // people in this family,
                                    // sorted by age (from youngest
                                    // to oldest)

    // constructor
    public Family() {
        peopleList = null;
    }

    // adds person p to this family
    public void addPerson(Person p) { /* part (b) */ }

    /*** private method ***/
    private ListNode personBefore(int age) { /* part (a) */ }
}
```

Part (a)

Write the `personBefore` method of the `Family` class. Method `personBefore` should search through the linked list pointed to by `peopleList`, looking for the person whose age is closest to the value of parameter age without being larger. It should return a pointer to that node of the linked list. If there is no such person (i.e., if the linked list is empty or all ages are greater than the value of parameter age), method `personBefore` should return `null`.

Complete method `personBefore` below.

```
// precondition: the peopleList field is null, or it points to the
//               first node of a linked list;
//               the list is sorted according to the ages of the
//               people in the list (from youngest to oldest)
//
// postcondition:  returns a pointer to the node in the linked list
//                 for the person in this family whose age is closest
//                 to the given age without being larger;
//                 returns null if there are no people in this family
//                 at all, or none whose age is less than or equal to
//                 the given age
private ListNode personBefore(int age) {
```

Part (b)

Write the `addPerson` method of the `Family` class. Method `addPerson` should add person p to the family, so that the family's list of people is still sorted by age (from youngest to oldest).

In writing method `addPerson`, you may include calls to method `personBefore`. Assume that `personBefore` works as specified, regardless of what you wrote in part (a).

Complete method `addPerson` below.

```
// precondition: the peopleList field is null, or it points to the
//               first node of a linked list;
//               the list is sorted according to the ages of the
//               people in the list (from youngest to oldest)
// postcondition: p has been added to the linked list in sorted
//                 order (by age)
public void addPerson(Person p) {
```

Question 4

A SongCollection class will be used to keep track of songs for an MP3 player. A partial declaration of the SongCollection class is given below.

```
public class SongCollection {

    private Queue songQueue;

    // constructor
    // postcondition: all of the songs originally in songList are now in
    //                songQueue in random order; songList is empty
    public SongCollection( ArrayList songList ) { /* part (a) */ }

    // precondition: newSongs.length <= songQueue.size()
    // postcondition: all of the songs in the newSongs list have been added
    //                to songQueue, evenly spaced
    public void addNewSongs( ArrayList newSongs ) { /* part (b) */ }
}
```

Assume that a ListQueue class implementing the Queue interface has been provided.

Part (a)

Write the SongCollection constructor. The constructor should move all of the songs from songList to songQueue in random order. One way to do this is as follows: While songList is not empty, randomly choose a valid position in songList; remove the song at that position from songList and add it to songQueue.

Complete the SongCollection constructor below.

```
// constructor
// postcondition: all of the songs originally in songList are now in
//                songQueue in random order; songList is empty
public SongCollection( ArrayList songList ) {
```

Part (b)

Write the method addNewSongs. Method addNewSongs should add all of the songs in the newSongs list to songQueue, evenly spaced. If songQueue initially contains *n* songs and songList contains *m* songs, then when method addNewSongs finishes, songQueue should start with the first *n/m* songs that were initially in the queue, followed by one song from songList, then the next *n/m* songs that were initially in the queue, then the next song from songList, etc.

For example, if songQueue initially contains 5 songs: (song1, song2, song3, song4, song5), with song1 at the front of the queue, and songList contains 2 songs: [new1, new2], then when addNew-Songs finishes, songQueue should contain 5/2 = 2 songs from the original queue, followed by 1 song from the list of new songs, followed by 2 songs from the original queue, etc.; that is, it should contain: (song1, song2, new1, song3, song4, new2, song5), with song1 at the front of the queue.

Complete method addNewSongs below.

```
// precondition: songList.length <= songQueue.size()
// postcondition: all of the songs in the newSongs list have been added
//                to songQueue, evenly spaced
public void addNewSongs( ArrayList newSongs ) {
```

Answers to Section I

1.	E	21.	E
2.	C	22.	E
3.	B	23.	A
4.	E	24.	B
5.	B	25.	B
6.	C	26.	C
7.	C	27.	E
8.	D	28.	A
9.	A	29.	D
10.	E	30.	A
11.	A	31.	D
12.	D	32.	B
13.	B	33.	C
14.	E	34.	D
15.	D	35.	A
16.	B	36.	D
17.	C	37.	E
18.	D	38.	E
19.	A	39.	D
20.	A	40.	B

Answers to Section II

Question 1
Part (a)

```
public Locatable[] allObjects() {
    Locatable[] ans = new Locatable[objectSet.size()];
    Iterator it = objectSet.iterator();
    int k = 0;
    while (it.hasNext()) {
        ans[k] = (Locatable)it.next();
        k++;
    }
    return ans;
}
```

Part (b)

```
public Locatable objectAt(Location loc) {
    Iterator it = objectSet.iterator();
    while (it.hasNext()) {
        Locatable obj = (Locatable)it.next();
        if (obj.location().equals(loc)) {
            return obj;
        }
    }
    return null;
}
```

Part (c)

Method	Expected Runtime
allObjects	$O(n)$
objectAt	$O(n)$
remove	$O(1)$

Grading Guide

Part (a) `AllObjects`   4 Points

> +1 Initialize/return array
>> + ½ initialization to `objectSet.size()`
>> + ½ return at end of method
>
> +1 Loop over set
>> + ½ attempt
>> + ½ correct
>
> +2 Place objects into the array
>> +1 retrieve next item in set (lose this point for double `next` call)
>> +1 put the item in appropriate place in array
>>> + ½ attempt
>>> + ½ correct (lose this point for not updating subscript of array)

Part (b) `objectAt`   3½ Points

> +1 Loop over set
>> + ½ attempt
>> + ½ correct
>
> +1½ Retrieve/compare next object
>> + ½ attempt
>> +1 correct
>
> +1 Appropriate locations of returns
>> + ½ return `obj`
>> + ½ return `null`

Part (c) `Efficiency`   1½ Points

> + ½ `allObjects`
> + ½ `objectAt`
> + ½ `remove`

Question 2
Part (a)

Version 1: Use recursion.

```
public Object rightmostLeafVal( ) {
    if (left == null && right == null) {
        // this node is a leaf--return its value
        return value;
    }
    else if (right == null) return left.rightmostLeafVal();
    else return right.rightmostLeafVal();
}
```

Version 2: Use iteration.

```
public Object rightmostLeafVal1( ) {
    TreeNode n = this;
    while (true) {
        if (n.left == null && n.right == null) {
            // n is rightmost leaf -- return its value
            return n.value;
        }
        if (n.right != null) n = n.right;
        else n = n.left;
    }
}
```

Part (b)

```
public Object pushLeavesRight( Object inval ) {
    if (left == null && right == null) {
        // at a leaf--change its value, returning the original value
        Object tmp = value;
        value = inval;
        return tmp;
    }
    // here if not at a leaf
    if (left != null) {
        inval = left.pushLeavesRight(inval);
        if (right != null) return right.pushLeavesRight(inval);
        else return inval;
    }
    else return right.pushLeavesRight(inval);
}
```

Part (c)

```
public void rotateLeaves( ) {
    pushLeavesRight(rightmostLeafVal());
}
```

Grading Guide

Part (a) `rightmostLeafVal`   3 Points

Recursive Solution:

+1 Check to see if node is a leaf

   + 1/2 attempt

   + 1/2 correct

+1 Node only has a left subtree

   + 1/2 check for possibility

   + 1/2 return left recursive call

+1 Return right recursive call

   + 1/2 attempt

   + 1/2 correct

Iterative Solution:

+ 1/2 Create a temporary traversal node

+ 1/2 Loop through tree until a rightmost leaf is found

+1 Node is a leaf

   + 1/2 check to see if node is a leaf

   + 1/2 return

+1 Update temporary traversal node depending on status of left and right subtrees

   + 1/2 no right children, move to the left

   + 1/2 move to the right

Part (b) `pushLeavesRight`   4 Points

+1 1/2 Check to see if node is a leaf and act accordingly

   + 1/2 check for node being a leaf

   + 1/2 update value of node

   + 1/2 return `inval`

+ 1/2 Check for no left subtree

The following points should only be given if the code is in an appropriate decision structure:

+ 1/2 Recursive call to left

+ 1/2 Recursive call to right

+ 1/2 Return value from right

+ 1/2 Return value from left subtree

Part (c) `rotateLeaves`   2 Points

+1 Call `rightmostLeafVal`

+1 Call `pushLeavesRight`

   + 1/2 attempt

   + 1/2 correct (must have an `Object` parameter; not necessarily the return from
      `rightmostLeafVal`)

Question 3
Part (a)

```
private ListNode personBefore(int age) {
   ListNode tmp = peopleList;
   Person currentPerson;

   // return null if no one in the list has age <= given age
   if (tmp == null) return null;
   currentPerson = (Person)tmp.getValue();
   if (currentPerson.getAge() > age) return null;

   // there is at least one person whose age is less than or equal
   // to the given age; find the oldest such person
   while (tmp.getNext() != null) {
      // return current ListNode if next person's age > given age,
      // else go on to next node in list
      currentPerson = ((Person)tmp.getNext().getValue());
      if (currentPerson.getAge() > age) return tmp;
      tmp = tmp.getNext();
   }
   // here if all people in the list have ages <= given age;
   // return the last node in the list
   return tmp;
}
```

Part (b)

```
public void addPerson(Person p) {
   ListNode n = personBefore(p.getAge());
   if (n == null) {
      // add p at front of list
      ListNode newNode = new ListNode(p, peopleList);
      peopleList = newNode;
   }
   else {
      // add p after node n
      ListNode newNode = new ListNode(p, n.getNext());
      n.setNext(newNode);
   }
}
```

Grading Guide

Part (a) `personBefore`

> +$1/2$ Check list for `null`, return `null`
>
> +1 Check first person for age requirement
>
> > +$1/2$ attempt
> >
> > +$1/2$ correct with return `null` for appropriate value
>
> +1 Traverse list to find appropriate person
>
> > +$1/2$ attempt
> >
> > +$1/2$ correct
>
> +1 Retrieve the next person in the list
>
> +1 Check the age of the current person and return if appropriate
>
> > +$1/2$ attempt
> >
> > +$1/2$ correct
>
> +$1/2$ Return appropriate value

Part (b) `addperson`

> +1 Call to `personBefore`
>
> > +$1/2$ attempt
> >
> > +$1/2$ correct
>
> +$1 1/2$ Handle `null` case
>
> > +$1/2$ check for `null`
> >
> > +$1/2$ create new node
> >
> > +$1/2$ assign to `peopleList`
>
> +$1 1/2$ Handle not `null` case
>
> > +$1/2$ create new node
> >
> > +1 `setNext` to the new node

Question 4
Part (a)

```
public SongCollection(ArrayList songList){
    songQueue = new ListQueue();
    Random r = new Random();

    while (songList.size() > 0) {
        int k = r.nextInt(songList.size());
        Object s = songList.remove(k);
        songQueue.enqueue(s);
    }
}
```

Part (b)

```
public void addNewSongs(ArrayList newSongs) {
    ListQueue newQ = new ListQueue();
    int spacing = songQueue.size()/newSongs.size();

    for (int i=0; i<newSongs.size(); i++) {
        for (int k=0; k<spacing; k++) {
            newQ.enqueue(songQueue.dequeue());
        }
        newQ.enqueue(newSongs.get(i));
    }
    while (songQueue.size() > 0) newQ.enqueue(songQueue.dequeue());
    songQueue = newQ;
}
```

Grading Guide

Part (a) The SongCollection constructor   4 Points

> +1 Create new ListQueue (must not be new Queue)
>
> +1 Loop over values in songList
>> +½ attempt
>> +½ correct (every value in the list is added to the Queue exactly once)
>
> +1 Retrieve random value from songList
>> +½ attempt (must somehow attempt to retrieve a random element)
>> +½ correct
>
> +1 Random creation and usage
>> +½ instantiate new Random object (OK to use RandomNumGenerator from case study)
>> +½ generate random number in appropriate place

Part (b) addNewSongs   5 Points

> +½ Create temporary holder for values in songQueue (using songQueue itself instead of a holder gets this ½ point)
>
> +½ Determine spacing for elements of newSongs
>
> +1 Loop over newSongs
>> +½ attempt (must access List within the loop)
>> +½ correct
>
> +1 Retrieve the appropriate number of elements from songQueue and place in holder (or dequeue and enqueue appropriate number of elements if not using a holder)
>> +½ attempt
>> +½ correct
>
> +½ Retrieve and place the next item from newSongs
>
> +1 Add any remaining items from songQueue to holder. Note: If the original queue is used instead of a holder it must be in the appropriate order when the method finishes to get this point
>
> +½ Assign from holder to songQueue (using songQueue itself instead of a holder gets this ½ point)

Glossary

actual parameter. One of the values passed when a method is called (see also formal parameter).

add. One of the operations for many of the AP CS standard classes and interfaces, including `ArrayList` and `LinkedList`.

argument. Same as actual parameter.

arithmetic operators. + - * / % (addition, subtraction, multiplication, division, and modulus).

ArrayList. One of the AP CS standard Java classes; an `ArrayList` implements a list using an array.

assignment operators. = += -= *= /= %= (plain assignment, add-then-assign, subtract-then-assign, multiply-then-assign, divide-then-assign, and modulus-then-assign).

average case time/space. (AB only) The amount of time or space that an algorithm or data structure will require on average.

base case. Every recursive method must have a base case, which is a condition under which the method does not call itself.

Big-O. (AB only) Notation for expressing the time or space required by an algorithm.

binary search. An efficient technique for finding a value in a sorted array; a value can be found in an array of N elements in time proportional to $\log_2 N$ (see also sequential search).

binary search tree. (AB only) A data structure that supports efficient insertion and look-up of ordered values ($O(\log N)$ if the tree is balanced).

binary tree. (AB only) A tree in which every node has at most two children.

casting. Used to convert one datatype to another. For example: `int(3.5)` converts the floating-point value 3.5 to an integer (by truncating it to 3).

circular linked list. (AB only) A linked list in which the last node points back to the first node.

class. The basic mechanism provided by object-oriented languages to support abstract datatypes.

compound assignment. += -= *= /= %= (add-then-assign, subtract-then-assign, multiply-then-assign, divide-then-assign, and modulus-then-assign).

constant time/space. (AB only) The amount of time or space required by an algorithm or data structure is independent of the amount of data; if the amount of data doubles, the amount of time or space will stay the same.

constructor. A class's constructor(s) should initialize the fields of the class.

decrement operator. -- (subtracts one from its operand).

default constructor. A constructor with no arguments.

dequeue. (AB only) One of the standard queue operations; it removes and returns the item at the front of the queue.

doubly linked list. (AB only) A linked list in which each node has two pointers: one that points to the next node in the list and one that points to the previous node in the list (see also singly linked list, circular linked list).

dynamic dispatch. The technique used to determine which version of a method that has been overridden by a subclass is actually called at runtime.

efficiency. How much time and/or space is required by an algorithm or data structure.

enqueue. (AB only) One of the standard queue operations; it adds a given item to the end of the queue.

equality operators. == and != (equal to and not equal to).

exponential time/space. (AB only) If the amount of data increases by one, the amount of time or space required by the algorithm or data structure will double.

field (nonstatic). A variable associated with each instance of a class (see also instance variable).

field (static). A variable associated with a class (see also instance variable).

for-loop. A loop of the form for (*init-expression*; *test-expression*; *update-expression*) *statement*.

formal parameter. One of the identifiers listed in a method header that corresponds to the values passed when the method is called (see also actual parameter).

hash function. (AB only) A function that maps values to integers; used to determine where to store a value in a hashtable.

HashSet. (AB only) One of the AP CS standard Java classes; a HashSet implements a set using a hashtable.

hashtable. (AB only) A data structure used to support efficient insert and look-up operations (can have O(1) average-case time).

HashTree. (AB only) One of the AP CS standard Java classes; a HashTree implements a hashtable using a balanced tree.

heap. (AB only) A data structure that can be used to provide an efficient implementation of a priority queue.

if statement. A statement of the form `if` (*expression*) *statement* or `if` (*expression*) *statement* `else` *statement*.

increment operator. `++` (adds one to its operand).

inorder traversal. (AB only) Visiting all nodes of a binary tree using the following algorithm: visit the left subtree in inorder, visit the root, visit the right subtree in inorder.

Insertion Sort. A sorting algorithm that takes time proportional to N^2 to sort N items.

instance variable. Another name for a field of a class.

isEmpty. (AB only) One of the standard stack, queue, and priority queue operations; it returns `true` if the stack, queue, or priority queue is empty, and otherwise it returns `false`.

iteration. One execution of the body of a loop.

iterator. (AB only) One of the AP CS standard Java interfaces; it provides a way to iterate through the objects in some collection of objects, one at a time.

length. For a one-dimensional array A, `A.length` is the length of the array; for a rectangular two-dimensional array A, `A.length` is the number of rows in the array, and `A[0].length` is the number of columns in the array. For a `String S`, `S.length()` is the number of characters in the string.

linear time/space. (AB only) If the amount of data doubles, the amount of time or space required by the algorithm or data structure will also double.

linked list. (AB only) A common data structure used to represent an ordered collection of objects (see also circular linked list, doubly linked list, singly linked list).

LinkedList. (AB only) One of the AP CS standard Java classes; a `LinkedList` implements a list using a linked list.

ListNode. (AB only) The standard AP CS class used to implement the nodes of a linked list.

List. (AB only) One of the AP CS standard Java interfaces; a `List` represents an ordered collection of objects.

logarithmic time/space. (AB only) If the amount of data doubles, the amount of time or space required by the algorithm or data structure will increase by one.

logical operators. `!` `&&` `||` (logical NOT, logical AND, and logical OR).

Map. (AB only) One of the AP CS standard Java interfaces; a `Map` represents a set of unique keys, each with an associated object.

Merge Sort. A sorting algorithm that takes time proportional to $\log_2 N$ to sort N items.

min-heap. (AB only) See heap.

new operator. Used to create a new instance of an `Object` (it allocates memory from free storage).

null. A special value used for a pointer that does not point to any memory location.

overloading. Defining two versions of a method in the same class with the same name but with different numbers or types of parameters.

overriding. Defining a method in a subclass with the same name, the same numbers and types of parameters, and the same return type as a method in a superclass. Dynamic dispatch is used to determine which version is actually called at runtime. This is one of the *polymorphic* aspects of Java.

parameter. Same as formal parameter.

peekFront. (AB only) One of the standard queue operations; it returns the item at the front of the queue without removing it.

peekMin. (AB only) One of the standard priority queue operations; it returns the smallest item from the priority queue without removing it.

peekTop. (AB only) One of the standard stack operations; it returns the item at the top of the stack without removing it.

pointer. A location whose value is another location (a memory address). The computer memory associated with an `Object` holds a pointer to the actual object.

pointer equality. When two pointers are compared using `==` or `!=`, they are considered equal only if they point to the same address; if they point to different addresses that contain the same value, the pointers are considered not equal. Pointer equality is also the default for an object's `equals` method.

pointer parameters. Objects are really pointers, so when an object is passed as a value parameter, although the object itself cannot be changed by the method, the contents of the location that it points to can be changed.

polymorphism. Literally, "many forms." In object-oriented languages like Java, there are several kinds of *polymorphism*: a method with a parameter of type T can be called with an actual parameter of type T or any subtype of T (and that method is a *polymorphic method*), and when a method call of the form *identifier.methodname(parameters)* is executed, if *identifier* is an object, then the method called depends on the runtime type of that identifier (i.e., what kind of object it actually points to) rather than its declared type.

pop. (AB only) One of the standard stack operations; it removes and returns the top item.

postcondition. A method's postcondition specifies what will be true when the method returns, assuming that the method's preconditions are satisfied when it is called.

postorder traversal. (AB only) Visiting all nodes of a binary tree using the following algorithm: visit the left subtree in postorder, visit the right subtree in postorder, visit the root.

precondition. A method's precondition specifies what is expected to be true whenever the method is called.

preorder traversal. (AB only) Visiting all nodes of a binary tree using the following algorithm: visit the root, visit the left subtree in preorder, visit the right subtree in preorder.

priority queue. (AB only) A data structure used to store objects with an underlying ordering (i.e., objects that could be sorted). Priority queue operations include inserting an object and removing (and returning) the smallest object currently in the priority queue.

private. One of the levels of access that can be specified for a class's fields and methods; private fields and methods can only be accessed/called by an instance of the class (see also public).

public. One of the levels of access that can be specified for a class's fields and methods; public fields and methods can be accessed/called by a client of the class (see also private).

push. (AB only) One of the standard stack operations; it adds a given item to the top of the stack.

quadratic time/space. (AB only) If the amount of data doubles, the amount of time or space required by the algorithm or data structure will quadruple.

queue. (AB only) A first-in-first-out data structure.

Quick Sort. A sorting algorithm that takes time proportional to $\log_2 N$ to sort N items if good choices are made for the pivot items, and otherwise can take time proportional to N^2.

recursive method. A method that calls itself (either directly or indirectly).

relational operators. < <= > >= (less than, less than or equal to, greater than, and greater than or equal to).

removeMin. (AB only) One of the standard priority queue operations; it removes and returns the smallest item from the priority queue.

return statement. Executing a `return` statement causes control to be transferred from the currently executing method to the calling method; for a non-`void` method, a `return` statement is also used to return a value.

return type. The type returned by a non-`void` method.

Selection Sort. A sorting algorithm that takes time proportional to N^2 to sort N items.

sequential search. An algorithm that looks for a value in an array by starting with the first element and examining each element in turn; it requires time proportional to the size of the array on average (see also binary search).

Set. (AB only) One of the AP CS standard Java interfaces; a `Set` represents a collection of objects with no duplicates.

short-circuit evaluation. Expressions involving the logical AND and OR operators are guaranteed to be evaluated from left to right, and evaluation stops as soon as the final value is known.

singly linked list. (AB only) A linked list in which each node has only one pointer, which points to the next node in the list (see also doubly linked list, circular linked list).

stack. (AB only) A first-in-last-out data structure.

static. A field or method of a class associated with the class itself rather than with an instance of the class.

String. A standard Java class used to represent strings (sequences of characters).

subclass. A class that extends an existing class. (The subclass should have an "*is-a*" relationship with the class that it extends.)

superclass. A class that is extended by a new class.

traversal. (AB only) An algorithm for visiting all nodes of a binary tree (see also inorder traversal, postorder traversal, preorder traversal).

tree height. (AB only) The height of an empty tree is 0; the height of a nonempty tree is the number of nodes in the longest path from the root to a leaf.

tree leaf. (AB only) A tree node with no outgoing edges.

TreeMap. (AB only) One of the AP CS standard Java classes; a `TreeMap` implements a map using a balanced tree.

TreeNode. (AB only) The standard AP CS class used to implement the nodes of a tree.

tree parent. (AB only) If a tree includes an edge from node n to node m, then n is the parent of m.

tree root. (AB only) A tree node with no incoming edges (no parent).

TreeSet. (AB only) One of the AP CS standard Java classes; a `TreeSet` implements a set using a balanced tree.

value parameter. In Java, all parameters are passed by value: when a method is called, the actual parameters are copied into new locations (named with the names of the formal parameters); therefore, changes made to the formal parameter by the called method do not change the corresponding actual parameter.

void. The return type of a method that performs an action rather than computing (and returning) a result.

while-loop. A loop of the form `while` (*expression*) *statement*. A while-loop may execute zero times (see also for-loop).

worst-case time/space. (AB only) The amount of time or space that an algorithm or data structure will require in the worst case.

Index